FINDING BALANCE

12 Priorities For Interdependence And Joyful Living

Terry Kellogg
Marvel Harrison

Health Communications, Inc.
Deerfield Beach, Florida

This book is printed on recycled paper.

Library of Congress Cataloging-in-Publication Data
Terry Kellogg
    Finding balance: 12 priorities for interdependence and joyful living / Terry
Kellogg and Marvel Harrison.
      p.   cm.
    Includes bibliographical references.
    ISBN 1-55874-132-1
    1. Co-dependents — Rehabilitation.   2. Health.   I. Harrison, Marvel.
II. Title.
RC569.5.C63K44   1991   90-29862
158'.2—dc20   CIP

©1991 Marvel Harrison
ISBN 1-55874-132-1

Publisher: Health Communications, Inc.
              3201 S.W. 15th Street
              Deerfield Beach, FL 33442-8190

DEDICATION

We joyfully dedicate this book to our siblings

Brian
Delynn
Jim
Pat
Renee
Roberta
Ron
Shannon

And all our sisters and brothers everywhere.
May the child we see in them touch our childness.

ACKNOWLEDGMENTS

When we accept the challenge to grow something, whether a garden, a family, a book or project, we open ourselves up to the opportunity for our own growth spurt. During this project we ran with this book, we swam it, skied it, rollerbladed it, discussed it, argued it. We plodded through some parts and sailed through others. We ate our way sometimes and other times enjoyed peaceful, grateful moments at sunset. We are nurtured by what we nurture and grow. Because of this experience we are no longer the same as individuals nor as a couple.

We are grateful for this challenging project and to the people and organizations who supported us. Often when writers acknowledge people for their contribution, they simply state the acknowledgment and move on as if their debt is paid. We choose to be indebted, which connotes an ongoing appreciation and connectedness with people who have supported us. They are our life teachers.

Of utmost importance are the people who attend our lectures, workshops and classes, our clients and students whose willingness to take risks and grow is a source of new insights. Their courage is astounding and inspiring. Thank you.

We also respect and appreciate therapists, lecturers and teachers who refuse to use shaming tactics, who do not use deep emotional and regression work as lecture tools and who provide a safe and gentle place for students and clients.

We would like to acknowledge all people who are willing to take risks to make a difference, accept challenge to make changes and *push* the system without exploding it. Change is necessary. We trust that using the 12 priorities as a guide will promote growth in healthy directions. In our journey we each leave footprints on the world.

People who continue to make an impact on our lives and believe in us have been our guiding lights: Ginny Moore Philips, who models the beauty of a steadfast true friend; Bill and Rachael, who introduced us to Isch and Ischa; Tom and Ellen, who model intimacy; Barbara and Michael, for professional and personal support; Dan Barmettler of the Institute for Integral Development, who is a national leader in offering top-quality training to mental health professionals, and introduced the two of us and continues to stand by us; Chris Stevens, a leader on the BRAT team who holds it all together when everyone else is shaking;

Glenn Leach, another BRAT member whom we've adopted, hangs in there when most folks would have bolted; the Harrison entourage of Mom, Dad, sisters, brother and their partners and kids, who will go the extra mile, in almost any direction, at a moment's notice (especially Renee who endured with us through the final stages of this manuscript), lending us living evidence that families of origin truly can function; the Kellogg clan of Mom, Dad, Pat, Jim, Dave, Dan and Jessica; Peter Vegso of Health Communications, who has been challenging, supportive and playful. Thank you.

Writing this book was an intense experience. We have vague memories of struggles long into the night at Amity Place, being crouched in corners of busy airline terminals and pounding out notes during coast-to-coast flights on "red-eye" specials. Our endurance has been tested, our brains strained and sanity waned . . . and we have landed with our feet on the ground and, God willing, still running.

As we traveled with our little portable Mac we gained an appreciation for the environments that were conducive to brainstorming and trans-forming our work and ideas into words. The many places of inspiration included the refreshing splash of St. Albans Bay; the early morning calls of the Canada geese who made their home next to ours on the lake; the serenity of many sunsets as we rollerbladed through the bird refuge at Carver Park; the invigorating yet humbling lessons of the Pacific surf; the spurring sensations of long beach walks and runs; the coziness of San Clemente; the splendor of Lake Louise and the majesty of the Canadian Rockies. Thank you, God, you done a good job!

CONTENTS

INTRODUCTION

The recovery movement is building a grass-roots momentum in our society: It is a movement toward honesty, spirituality and community; it connotes a life-style of care and balance. Through the movement our society and our planet have a chance of survival. Through this movement we all have a chance for joy, serenity and balanced living.

There is no single "right" way to recover. Addiction and co-dependency recovery is contradictory, controversial and dynamic. In this spirit we challenged ourselves to write a *progressive conservative* book — one that conserves useful information, while simultaneously confronting what hasn't worked and introducing and integrating new concepts for recovery. This book contains no absolute answers or ultimate truths on how to recover. Rather, it is a book of suggestions and ideas that you may choose to integrate into your own recovery program.

Our approach is an accumulation of our individual experiences and our experiences together. This is unique because of who we are, but we know that others have shared similar thought patterns. We believe in the concept of *diffusion:* When a thought or movement is ready to be born, it will be conceived concurrently in many places, by many people. Thus the thoughts and concepts and how they are presented are our own, yet they are shared by many. These ideas about co-dependency and other aspects of recovery are a result of diffusion — their time has come.

This book is written for people who care about themselves, about others and about our planet. It is written for anyone interested in recovering their birthright, which is the affirmation, nurturing, modeling and safety to achieve our full potential of joy and intimacy. Helping professionals may find it both personally and professionally beneficial, as each of us must evaluate and maintain our own journey as the basis for what we offer others. We must model our own priorities and continue our learning process. People familiar with recovery and therapy will find new challenges for their continued quest. *Finding Balance* offers efficient guidelines and suggestions for newcomers..

We have written this book with the intention that the chapters be read in chronological order. One chapter is a building block for the next. But since few of us *always* follow the rules and seldom read a self-help book from front cover to back cover, we will understand if you want to *flip* from section to section. Following is a guide for your "flipping" adventure.

Chapter 1 is a general introduction to our basic concepts of recovery. It is an overview of our working philosophy, which we call *interdependence*. Interdependence offers a healthy posture toward life and a way to channel the priorities of recovery.

Chapter 2 includes a series of questions and answers we are commonly asked regarding recovery. The final section contains comments and notes regarding the process and suggestions for therapists to use and clients to be aware of.

Chapters 3 through 14 each cover a different priority of recovery. In the process of recovery there are several areas of living that require our attention. Each is important and some need to be addressed earlier than others. None are isolated from the others. As we work on priorities one and two, Identity and Emotional Fluency, we do so with a sense of spirituality, which is priority five. This does not mean that spirituality is not as important as priorities one and two, but quite the contrary, spirituality is actually the *essence* of recovery and is included in our identity. To focus on spirituality first often results in religiosity and prevents us from gaining recovery in a full and meaningful way.

Each priority chapter begins with a narrative on the topic. We include some real-life examples of our own and others who were willing to share. Each section concludes with related suggestions, affirmations and thoughts.

The final chapter is the epilogue, our chance to question the system, ourselves and where we are headed. It ends with a challenge to us all for the '90s.

Co-authoring this book is a living example of our belief in interdependence. It is having common beliefs and values, sharing the work load, respecting each other's strengths and flat spots, finding a balance of when to fight and when to let go and growing something together while maintaining identity. In the spirit of interdependence, we have integrated our knowledge *and concepts and presented them together,* respecting that each of us has contributed our individuality toward a *shared* uniqueness as an end product.

We have attempted to write this book with a consciousness of the ideals of interdependence. We hope to tickle your brain, nudge your heart and stir your feelings so that you might find some challenges for your personal journey of becoming who you were meant to be by your Creator.

Interdependence:
Recovery From Co-dependence

Recovery is a spiritual process. Our spirituality is the basis of our relationship with creation and the universal process of becoming, an unfolding and blossoming. Our recovery/discovery is a joint venture with creation that enables us to inhale life, the breath of the Creator. We embrace ourselves, our feelings, our reality and become connected to this universe. We find our guides, signs and pathways in and around us. The recovery journey of joy has painful stretches that lead to the meaning of our existence.

The journey of our recovery continues long after we are dust, carried on by all the descendants of the people we have touched. Just as dysfunction is intergenerational, so too is recovery. We didn't choose to be hurt, to be addicts; we didn't even choose our addictions. We *can* choose recovery, giving those around us and those who follow us the gift of choice, which is the gift of freedom.

Recovery is the process of using our resources, inner and outer, to achieve our potential. This is not a static state of achievement but a dynamic and changing process. We absorb the energy of sharing and caring to fuel our self-acceptance, guardianship, play and the heroic noticing of consequences. We discover a careful journey in which we forgive ourselves so we can give of ourselves, know ourselves so we can forget ourselves. Recovery gives us a still mind, an awareness of the oneness of creation and the acceptance of transformation and change. Recovery enhances our enjoyment and creates energy toward service and teaching.

Each of us has within us all that is necessary for a full and healthy life that includes self-love, intimacy and healthy sexuality. Victims of torture and molestation have achieved peace. People who have lived in severe isolation or deprivation discover a passion for living. Offenders develop remorse and conscience, addicts find sobriety, victims move to self-esteem and strength, and families heal intergenerational relationships.

THE RECOVERY JOURNEY: FROM CO-DEPENDENCE TO INTERDEPENDENCE

Co-dependency is not about a relationship with an addict, but it is the absence of relationship with self. Co-dependency can be an over-involvement in relationships with others, or it can be the avoidance of relationship. The avoidance may come from the fear of over-involvement, the fear of intimacy, the fear of abandonment or the fear of losing too much of oneself in a relationship. Independence is the opposite side of the coin of co-dependence. A person with co-dependency may adopt a posture of independence. A person who isolates from relationships is in as much pain as a person who becomes lost in relationships.

In reaction to co-dependence many people become counterdependent, defying or rebelling against authority, against intimacy, against law, against their own dependency needs. They reject dependency in themselves and others. Counterdependence is a more aggressive posture than independence, and involves a battle with self in a system that creates more chaos and isolation. Sometimes counterdependence is necessary to break out of the repression of being overcontrolled. Adolescents, for example, become counterdependent because their curiosity, creativity or being has been repressed or abusively controlled. It is a reactive co-dependent posture because it does not create true identity and facilitate integration and boundary development. Counterdependence can be a posture of power, but it is not self-empowering and tends to destroy the power of others. Much acting out is counterdependence.

When we were discussing a name for our philosophy of vulnerability and strength, healthy dependency and spiritual stewardship, Terry was leaning toward the term integration. As therapy heals the disintegration-events of childhood, recovery is an accumulation and blend of styles, knowledge and aspects of self. Through integration healing we find integrity, which is balance, wholeness and holiness. Marvel preferred the term interdependence, in recognition of the value of caring, nurturing and cooperation as much as individuation. Interdependence represents the balance between co-dependence and other dependencies at one end of the spectrum and independence and counterdependence at the other. Our interest in Native American spirituality and its strong focus on interdependence convinced us to adopt this concept as our therapeutic approach. Recovery from co-dependence involves discovering interdependence: accepting our healthy dependency on others, ourselves, our planet and a Higher Power, a balance of mutuality and complementarity.

Interdependence holds integration as a key therapeutic process. We will continue to work and pray for a planet whose inhabitants are moving from co-dependence to interdependence in a celebration of our strengths, needs and oneness. Writing this book exemplified our adventure into interdependence.

INTERDEPENDENCE: A NEW APPROACH

We use an eclectic approach to therapy, teaching and counseling. We maintain a Rogerian attitude of empathy, warmth and unconditional positive regard, while employing techniques from many other models and theories of psychotherapy. These include family systems, Jung, addictions theory, Gestalt, bio-energetics, psychoanalytic theories, developmental theories, Eriksonian hypnosis, imagery, reframing, mirroring, modeling, affirmations, psychodrama, reconstruction and Post-Traumatic Stress Disorder (PTSD) debriefing. We also make referrals to movement, dance, art, music and massage therapy.

Interdependence is not simply a technique or style. For us it is a posture toward life, about a different way of being, with new traditions, attitudes, values and ways of thinking. It is about living more fully in the present while challenging ourselves about working toward a world that presently doesn't exist. This future world values so-called "feminine" ways of thinking and being as much as so-called "masculine" ones without using these terms, which have been burdened by layers of constructed meaning and biases.

Interdependence values cooperation and nurturing as much as independence and assertiveness. Caring for others is as important as asserting individual needs and goals. It is based on a *nonhierarchical* model. Rather than focusing on one side as better, this model recognizes the interconnection between opposing or different sides of life, ourselves and each other.

Our concept of interdependence concerns family, community and the world at large as well as the individual. It is concerned with the "isms" resulting from social hierarchies such as class, race, disabilities, sexual orientation and body size. We believe in helping people value all sides of themselves, using different characteristics to meet different challenges and learning to value the differences in other individuals and groups.

With an interdependence perspective, we work toward transforming hierarchical relationships into more egalitarian ones, beginning with counselor-client and teacher-student relationships. The teacher or the counselor is not there to dominate, have power over or demean in any way the student or client. Egalitarian, however, does not mean sameness. The teacher and the student, counselor and client, are not the same. Each has a different and valuable role.

The counselor's role is to *empower* people so they can gain more self-confidence and experience more choices in life. The client's role is self-exploration. The teacher's role is *modeling* rather than telling, directing or dictating. The student's role is to adventure into new territory and make choices and mistakes. The counselor must also self-explore and acknowledge that the client empowers and teaches. The teacher and counselor must also be the student and learner, while the student and client must also be the teacher. No role is superior. What is true for the counselor and teacher roles is also true for our role as parents. Often counselors and teachers fulfill the sacred functions of parenting. They are called on to provide the parenting so many of us missed in childhood. Too often therapists, teachers and parents operate from a position of arrogance and ignorance, belittling their students, clients and children.

Interdependence counseling is a process, not a technique or theory. It adopts and adapts the strengths, tools and techniques from various therapeutic models. The counselor or therapist must be authentic and congruent with feelings, sharing what they are attempting to do with the client. The interdependence process includes the following:

- offering gentle, prodding, specific questions as the most powerful confrontation
- providing a safe environment for the debriefing of specific details of past hurts and traumas
- learning to accept and even see the "good" in the shadow
- limited use of catharsis work
- using a group process whenever it is appropriate
- being active rather than reactive

- being nonritualistic while respecting rules, boundaries and rituals
- sharing and using one's own life history, without overwhelming the client
- using physical and emotional responses without projecting or losing the counselor role
- sharing one's feelings in a mild way to reflect connections but not drowning the client in those feelings
- respecting and maintaining boundaries around sex, money, friendship and time
- supporting honesty more than confronting dishonesty
- noticing, labeling and affirming feelings more than confronting behaviors
- linking consequences to behaviors and linking destructive behaviors to the client's feelings and history of past hurts
- supporting people through recovery in a nonjudgmental, nonshaming manner
- always envisioning the preciousness of people
- being creative and eclectic rather than structured and single-focused
- working toward a goal of "growing up" as an integration of childness and adulthood
- acknowledging, affirming and cherishing the differences in women's and men's systems without losing the importance of shared humanity, needs and vulnerabilities
- using other community resources and referrals that share a common belief system.

RECOVERY: THE INTERDEPENDENCE WAY

Interdependence recovery involves taking present realities as seriously as past influences. It means *trusting* the process of growth and *taking risks*. Our interdependence approach is not a search for blame. It is about recognizing feelings toward other people and situations realizing that most offenders have also been victims and have also been deeply affected by trauma and enabled by the world we live in. Self-empowerment comes from a *nonblaming* posture of reconciliation and allows us to first accept and assign responsibility and then forgive.

As interdependence counselors, teachers and parents we respect the objective realities of a person's life as well as the more subjective inner thoughts, feelings, values and premises. We value and affirm a person's view of his or her own experience. We are concerned with both external changes in behaviors and internal changes in feelings, thoughts and premises. Self-deception is a tool that enables us to survive. All of our defenses, even our addictions, are coping mechanisms. We prescribe a gentle approach to reality acceptance, breaking the distortion of past and present. We must accept that both our perceptions and the reality of our lives have an impact. Simply changing our perceptions does not heal the hurt from the reality of the past. We cannot think and affirm our way through recovery with unresolved hurts and trauma buried in the past or continuing in our present, nor can we process and deal with the hurts if we are actively involved with addiction.

The interdependence perspective allows us to see the addictive nature of many self-destructive behaviors. *Addiction is about despair, trauma, neglect, poverty and isolation.* Co-dependency is a cultural issue that manifests itself as a chronic syndrome in certain individuals and organizations. Crime, drugs, violence, relationship and environmental problems have a core cause, with roots planted in our view of children and each other. We see children as extensions of ourselves, as ways to fill the emptiness and give meaning to our lives. We use our children to meet our needs for affection and nurturing, and they become the objects of our pent-up anger and frustrations. Instead we need to accept that we do not own our children and they are not of us or about us. As Kahlil Gibran says, "Our children are a miracle of the gift of life itself." We cannot appreciate the miracle of our children until we embrace the miracle of our own childness.

True interdependence recognizes that all creatures and creation are interwoven and that we all have a place to *belong*. Humans, with our capacity for imagination, creativity and industry, have been granted the *guardianship* of our planet. This stewardship requires embracing the interdependence of creation and living a life of *balance*. It requires taking responsibility for our excess dependency on externals and our over-consumptiveness. We must notice the intricacies and fragility of our world and its inhabitants. It is a process of knowing ourselves and gaining self-respect, which in turn can lead to respect and protection of vulnerable groups and our environment. The process is a *gentle* one — gentle with ourselves, our choices, our mistakes and others. Self-gentleness allows us to be gentle with our home, the earth.

The Maypole Dance: A Symbol For Interdependence

Our goal is to recognize our uniqueness and preciousness on our way to becoming other-directed and service oriented. *Kindness and caring are not co-dependency, they are spirituality.* Interdependence is a posture toward life and each other that weaves the concepts of identity, integration and intimacy into a design of creation. The Maypole dance is our symbol for interdependence recovery and illustrates the vibrant and dynamic oneness of creation.

The foundation of the Maypole is our physical, intellectual and emotional being, with our sexuality emerging as a basis of our identity. Our spirituality is the core, represented by the pole, the major structure for the dance. Each ribbon is a life-giving line attached to and flowing from our spiritual pole. The ribbon lines are postures toward ourselves, our families, our community and our planet. They include gentleness, honesty, modeling, empowerment, vulnerability, trust, belonging, balance, risk, forgiveness, humor and guardianship. The dance is performed in an atmosphere that is nonhierarchical, nonviolent, nonblaming, nondirective, nonprejudiced, nonparochial and nongendered.

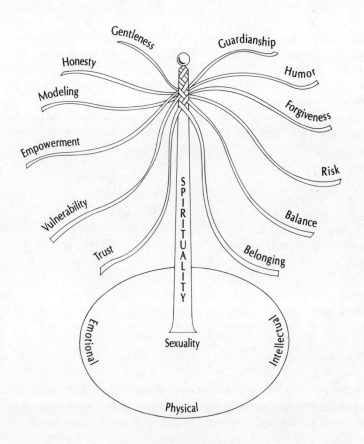

Interdependence Maypole Dance

The design of creation is woven through the four 'I's" of recovery:

1. **Interdependence** is represented by the entire Maypole dance, including the foundation — *us;* the core — *spirituality;* the approach — *gentle, responsible, interconnected;* and the atmosphere — *loving, trusting, belonging.*
2. **Identity** is the foundation and core: our physical, intellectual, emotional, sexual and spiritual capacity.
3. **Integration** is the movement and breath of the dance as the ribbons are interwoven, creating integrity, an integrated wholeness from which our identity and intimacy flow.
4. **Intimacy** is the decorated pole — a movement toward understanding, shared history, common goals and honest acceptance.

BALANCE

The ambiance of the Maypole dance is a state of harmony. The aura of balance abounds: Balance in life. Balance of commitments. Balance in decisions. Balance of choices. Balance of foods. Balance in caring for others and taking care of ourselves. Balance with play and work. Balance of intensity and relaxation. Some of the time we may feel out of balance, off balance. It feels unsteady, unsure, unsafe, off base or not grounded. Other times we may feel in balance, on target, centered, steady and sure. Living is a process of balancing life choices.

Balance is the dance of life. When we feel *in* balance, steady and sure, we can take a few dips, twirls and extra steps without falling. When we feel a little *off* balance, out of step or not in tune, a swirl, an extra move or step may result in a fall. We might need to keep a steady beat and follow a simple rhythm for a short while, get the basic steps down, gain some confidence before moving on. We may have to repeat the steps time and time again. We might need to go over the moves on our own, take some lessons and dance with others; we have to do it *for* ourselves, not *by* ourselves! The exciting part is that we are not practicing or preparing for a big event, major production or grand finale. Each step and every move along the way counts. This is it. This is *not* a dress rehearsal. This is the *dance of life!*

The beauty of the Maypole is in the process rather than the product. It is the vibrant, colorful dancing — of creating a spiral of life that nurtures our childness to be woven into adulthood. The Maypole dance can only be performed with the integration of childness and adulthood. The dance needs the playfulness and energy of childness integrated with adult wisdom and experience to interweave the ribbons. *The future of the world does not lie in the hands of children, it lies in the hands that hold the hands of children. We cannot hold the hands of children until we hold the heart of our childness.*

In recovery the dance becomes the posture and movement of prayer:

> *Child noticing enhanced by adult gratitude.*
> *Child honesty moving toward adult forgiveness.*
> *Child acceptance protected by adult action.*
> *Child newness enriching adult experience.*
> *Child naivete blended with adult wisdom.*
> *Child vulnerability creating adult strength.*
> *Child imagination enlivening adult realization.*
> *Child curiosity merged with adult knowledge.*

As we approach each priority of recovery we do so from the perspective of the beliefs of our interdependence Maypole dance. *In recovery we hold these ribbons in community while creating the dance of life.*

SUGGESTIONS • AFFIRMATIONS • THOUGHTS

SUGGESTIONS

Integration Exercise

In childhood many of us suffered a dis-integration of our identity, our emotional life or our feelings from our bodies. Some of this dis-integration took the form of dissociation as a response to the violence, abuse or neglect. Some of it took the form of splitting off various aspects of our self, breaking apart our trust, childhood, sexuality, feelings, values and behavior.

Recovery involves much more than integration of wisdom and resources and support. Recovery also involves the integration of those damaged aspects of self. Even seemingly disparate parts must be integrated. In recovery we integrate our sexuality with our spirituality, our fear with our courage, our strength with our vulnerability. We integrate our anger and pain, our sadness and joy, our shame and our guilt, intention and action, values, beliefs and behaviors. One of the key areas of integration is that of childness and adulthood. To achieve interdependence we must achieve a level of adulthood and maturity. Much of what we call recovery is really growing up. Growing up, the movement into adulthood, is not done by giving up the childlike qualities, rather it is done by integrating that child into our adulthood.

This integration means that in growing up we lose nothing. We only gain a sense of adulthood. In the past few years we've done exercises that help groups integrate a sense of childness into adulthood. This is the only exercise we do in lectures that involves any regression, and the regression — the going back into a place of childhood — does not include going back into a place of pain or trauma. We do not speak during this regression, even to ourselves. We believe it is very important to avoid bringing people back into cathartic or hurtful places except in a safe place where they can find attention, nurturing and closure. Large groups and lectures are not safe places.

If the following exercise causes uncomfortable pain or opens up something you feel you should be talking about with others, you can discontinue the exercise. You can do it later with a group in a therapy setting or come back to it after you have done some debriefing of whatever it has opened up.

Be gentle and respectful to yourself and listen to your inner messages. For this exercise have two sheets of paper and something to write with. Now, put the paper and pen or pencil aside. We'll describe the exercise that you are going to do, and then you close your eyes and do it.

With your eyes closed, imagine yourself standing at the top of a stairway. Take yourself, in your mind's eye, down the stairway, down inside of yourself. If you have a hard time imagining things, you might just sense or feel what it's like to be at the top of the stairs, and feel what it's like to go down inside of yourself. Once at the bottom of the stairs, picture a hallway going further into yourself. At the end of the hallway is a door. Walk up to the door and open it. Outside the door you see a beautiful garden. If you can't image a garden, feel what one might look like or might feel like. In the garden, look, see yourself as a child again. Any age will do, whatever feels comfortable for you right now. Walk over to the child and take the child's hand in your hand, and spend just one minute noticing what it is like to be next to that child with the child's hand in your hand. You can spend the minute walking around the garden, sitting or standing. You can go to the child's favorite place, or your favorite place, a park or around the block. Do not speak to the child, just notice what it's like for you to be with the child that you were for one minute.

After the minute is up, come back to the garden where you started, with the child still in hand. Go to the door through which you entered the garden and bring the child out and down the hallway to the stairs. With the child still by the hand, go up the stairs, one step each at a time. At the top of the stairs, where you started your journey, spend another few seconds feeling what it's like to be with the child that you were, hand in hand, at the point that you started this exercise.

Now open your eyes and take one of the pieces of paper and your pen or pencil. This part of the exercise is writing. Write a letter from the child that you were with to the adult who you are. You can write anything you want to write — what you notice, what you feel, what you want, what you need, what's going on. Use the hand that you don't normally use for writing. If you are right handed, use your left hand. This is called opposite-hand writing. It may feel awkward and uncomfortable, but that's often how children feel when they're writing. Begin the note, "Dear _____." If the writing starts to feel too painful, and you feel as if you should be with a group or need some support in writing further, you can stop writing. If writing seems too difficult, just write a short "Hi." That's enough for now. If you feel you can write more, write as much as you'd like to. Remember, you can always write more later.

Now write a letter from the adult to the child. Use the other piece of paper, and put the pen or pencil in the hand you normally use for writing. You can write anything that you want to write — what you notice, what you feel, what you can offer, what your life is like, what you need and what you feel for the child. You can even write what you need from the child.

Now hold the two letters, writing side up, one in each hand, and deliver them symbolically by holding them face to face, writing against writing. Fold both letters together once. Good job!

Now fold the letters one more time. Next fold the letters once more. Put the letters in your two hands, and place your two hands against your stomach or chest, with the letters between your hands and your stomach or chest. Close your eyes and feel what it's like to deliver those letters to you, inside of you. Hold against you the feeling of childness, and what childness means to you, the rights you had as a child, the right to your curiosity, creativity, naivete, newness, trust and questioning. The right to notice, to look at the world with awe, the childlike innocence, the childlike spontaneity, the magic of your childness. Hold that against you and feel it inside you, mingling and entering with what it is to be an adult. The experience, the strength, the guardianship, the nurturing, the wisdom, the protecting, the sense of gratitude. Feel all the things of childness, blending with the things of adulthood. Feel yourself having both: all the things of your childness integrating with the wonders of adulthood. When you feel the two together within you, when you feel you are both the child and the adult all at once, all at the same time all of the time, and when you can hold on to that feeling, open your eyes.

You can carry the two letters with you, folded, for a period of time. Plant them in something that you wear occasionally or tuck them in your journal. Marvel has done this exercise many times. She keeps her folded papers in various places to stumble onto occasionally, as a gentle reminder of her journey. Keep them as a suggestion that childness and adulthood are each folded into the other so that we can enjoy and protect. Live a life with a posture of prayer, humor and joy. Prayer is childness entering adulthood.

SUGGESTIONS • AFFIRMATIONS • THOUGHTS

SUGGESTIONS

- Take a look at what you own. Decide what owns you and get rid of it or change your relationship with it.
- Learn more about co-dependency.
- Celebrate Earth Day every day!
- List the places where you feel safe.
- Find a support group.
- Grow something.
- Send your defenses a thank you note, they got you here.
- Notice creation.
- Be a student. Become a mentor.
- Try celebrating Native American Day rather than Columbus Day.

AFFIRMATIONS

- Noticing beauty is my favorite prayer.
- My vulnerability is the loving gift of me to those I trust.
- My recovery is the joy of self-discovery.
- I am recovering from my prejudices.
- I am a unique and precious being.
- I accept my reality — painful and joyful.

THOUGHTS

- Our dominion over earth is not ownership, but guardianship.
- Recovery is growing up — a child gaining adulthood, not an adult losing childhood.
- The earth is dependent on us as we are on it.
- Adult integration is the healing of childhood dis-integration.
- Integration moves us toward integrity, integrity toward wholeness, wholeness toward holiness.
- Recovery is really discovery of our birthright — curiosity, creativity, affirmation and nurturing.

Directions For The Journey:
The Quest of Quixote

R ecovery is a lifelong process. If the basic
system we came from was a low-functioning family, the norm of our life is
the dysfunction and we must maintain daily vigilance
for positive change. When we neglect our recovery program we go back to the stress of dysfunction. Some
recovery is learning to live with pain, our handicaps,
our disease and addictions. Some is learning to live
with joy, our strengths and intimacy.

Occasionally recovery comes quickly, a remission
from addiction, an insight that changes our perspective
or premises. More often recovery is a daily process
that involves discipline, support, facilitation, play and
work. Some recovery is part of a maturation process —
we grow out of a dysfunctional stage. Recovery is in
large part achieving maturity, growing up, learning
how to be a functioning adult with a sense of childness
intact. In recovery our values resurface and we become

realistic about what life has to offer — we stop perpetuating our childhood experiences. Most of our dysfunction is a reaction to or reenactment of hurtful childhood experiences. In recovery we grow away from
cynicism, whining, shame and distrust. We give up constantly seeking
the grand experience and ultimate answer or fix in favor of recognizing
that most of life is just life. As Woody Allen once said, "Ninety percent
of life is just showing up." We would add that most of the rest is just
hanging around. We learn to find our excitement in the little things. We
become fluid, not rigid; we often find meaning in the dysfunction. We
grieve our losses and discover life as a mystery to be embraced rather
than a problem to be solved. *Each day is like the page of a good book, to be
savored and to enrich the excitement of what may follow.*

As we become healthier we tend to move toward healthier relationships and find healthier work environments, therapists and support
groups. We also react in healthier ways to the low-functioning systems
we remain in out of necessity.

Protecting our family of origin is a symptom of the family dysfunction. Healthy families do not need protecting. We protect a dysfunctional family because it feels as though our survival requires us to
remain in the system. It is difficult to move out of a sick system. Even
birds and animals abused in the nest or lair have a harder time leaving.
The world looks scary when our families were scary.

In recovery our lives may seem worse, but we often feel worse before
we feel better. We may even experience a sense of impending doom
prior to talking about the scenes of neglect or abuse. We may experience
waves of guilt and shame before discussing how we've been used or
abandoned. The courage to move through the fear and shame, to disclose
the truth of our past and ourselves and discover our guides, provides
payoffs in our journey. We've been courageous. We move away from the
pathology of our past to the shining of our reality.

Recovery is a return to the values of adolescence and the creativity of
childhood. We discover and reclaim our developmental process to discover true adulthood. Like any journey, the recovery journey has rocks
and swampy areas. When we break the trail for our recovery and move
from addiction and co-dependency, we may run into the following:

- **Preoccupations** — with our addictions or self-destructive behaviors,
  fantasies or guilt.
- **Distraction** — with recovery issues, the past or future, what people
  think, with our families' reactions.

- **Obsession** — thoughts will roll over and over in our minds, we'll ruminate and worry to extremes.
- **Physical discomfort and tiredness** — physical tension and tremors may be present, sometimes our immune system weakens, we feel physically and emotionally drained.
- **Agitation** — pacing, foot swinging, higher arousal states.
- **Irritability** — impatience, quick anger projected inward and outward, toward self and others.
- **Restlessness** — sleep discomfort, difficulty in staying in one area, difficulty sitting through meals or conversation.
- **Feeling lost, isolated, disconnected** — believing no one cares; old friendships become strained and new ones are difficult to form.
- **Sense of loss** — grieving, emptiness and depression arrive as we let go of the old systems and destructive behaviors.
- **Anger and rage** — the stored anger surfaces but often gets misdirected.
- **Confusion** — too much awareness for us to process each issue; we develop new roles and give up old defenses and coping mechanisms that leave us lost.
- **Blocked feelings** — we sense we need to be angry or sad and it won't come; we get numb, emotionally constipated or overwhelmed.
- **Memory loss** — it feels as though we've lost our childhood; some of our memory about present things seems to diminish.
- **Shame, feeling diminished** — debriefing accesses shame, embarrassing stories; we feel exposed, bad for talking about the secrets.
- **Loss of control** — as we see how powerless we were and notice our own pathology, we feel more and more out of control.
- **Projection** — we tend to project our recovery problems and feelings toward the people immediately around us.
- **Dissociation** — we separate aspects of self, feelings and reality as we move through the pain and trauma of the past.
- **Defensiveness** — we attempt to avoid overexposure, hide feelings, feel too much and ward off attack by using our defenses.
- **Depression** — we experience self pity, turn feelings inward, beat up on ourselves and have low energy.
- **Hopelessness** — we believe nothing will get better — but this is a symptom, not a reality.

Each of these is a normal response to the therapeutic process and journey of recovery.

Staying with the journey means waves of good and bad times with gradual movement toward more serenity and hope. We learn separateness and detachment, surrender and acceptance. We learn our self-destructiveness, pathology and addictions, and intimacy problems are not about *who we are* but are about *what happened to us*. We find our humanity and become more affirming and understanding. We discover psychologist William Glasser's five basic needs: freedom, love, belonging, worth and fun.

On the journey we can travel to:

- look at helplessness to find powerlessness
- become fluid, not rigid
- make meaning of experiences
- draw away from cynicism
- stop bonding through complaining.

We get better when we give up the belief that our families will "change." Of course all families *will* change — some will get worse!

The more covert the abuse issues we are dealing with, the longer it takes to work out in recovery. The severity of our symptoms does not depend only on what happened to us. It also depends on:

- what age we were chronologically and developmentally when the abuse occurred
- what we were told and believed about what was happening
- the severity, frequency and unpredictability of the abusive events
- whether we could alter a behavior or role that lessened the abuse
- whether we had a confidant with whom to share and debrief what was happening.

The last point is especially important. It is the therapy process: finding a caring person or persons with whom we can share the details and feelings about what we are going through or have been through.

THE CO-DEPENDENT POLAR BEAR

Polar opposites are set up by neglect and abuse. Children react by complying or defying, acting in or acting out, hyper-arousal or malaise. This polarization is the mark of a person struggling with co-dependency. *Balance is the mark of recovery.* Each trait of co-dependency includes its opposite. We may swing back and forth between the victim or offender posture, perfectionism or chaos, depressive self-denial or narcissistic self-involvement, under- or over-responsibility, hyperactivity or immobility. Some people find one polar position and remain in it. We truly are polar bears and have difficulties finding our temperate zones.

The following is a partial list of traits of a person struggling with co-dependency: *

1. **Self-doubt.** Constantly questioning, doubting own ideas, thoughts, feelings and behavior. The opposite of self-doubt would be excessive self-assurance to the point of arrogance, never questioning oneself.
2. **Difficulty caring for oneself.** We frequently do a better job taking care of others than ourselves. We practice self-neglect as an art form, sometimes neglecting our appearance, needs and nutrition, which leads to an unbalanced lifestyle. The opposite is a total self-focus, a hyper-concern about anything that might interfere with self-obsession.
3. **Burnout.** The result of not taking care of self is burnout, which is the mark of later stages of co-dependency. Burnout at work, burn-out as a parent, burnout at home, burnout as a spouse or burnout with community involvement. We work ourselves to the point where we have no energy left and nothing left to give. The opposite is never allowing the collapse or break, and laziness so we don't have to collapse.
4. **Poor body image.** We experience dissatisfaction with our appearance, body shape and size. Feeling ugly, too short, too bald, too fat, too tall, too skinny, too flat-chested, too thick-thighed. Physical shame sets up isolation and the self-destruction of fad diets, unnecessary surgeries, expensive treatments, narcissistic body shaping and resort pampering. The opposite pole is narcissistic self-love.
5. **Feeling like an imposter.** Studies have shown that many professionals feel like imposters at what they do. They feel as though they are fooling everybody and are constantly believing that if they get found out or get caught, people will know they are inadequate and they will lose their job and relationships. The opposite extreme is feeling overly smug about who we are and what we do.
6. **Unsatisfactory relationships.** Our relationships don't quite fit our lives or needs and never live up to our expectations. We obsess the problems of relationships. The other extreme is to pretend our relationships are perfect, when in fact they are empty or falling apart.

---

*The original list, in Terry Kellogg's *Broken Toys Broken Dreams*, has 100 items. This abridged list shows the working spirit of interdependence.

7. **Distrusting self.** Not trusting our instincts, feelings, thoughts or ideas, and feeling or believing that other people know more than we do or have the answers that we don't. We have little self-confidence. The opposite is being overconfident in our ideas, never doubting our own feelings and instincts nor listening to others.

8. **Perfectionistic.** We attempt perfection to hide the broken self and our broken integrity. We hide behind the image of being "all to-gether." The opposite is to screw up most of what we do, goof off and set up others to expect nothing of us.

9. **Dissatisfaction.** We are in constant churning, continual crisis or chaos. We are never at peace with ourselves. There's no resting and very little letting go. The opposite is to act complacent, have a flat affect and no movement in our lives.

10. **Sleep disorders.** We toss and turn and don't sleep well, or we use sleep as our avoidance.

11. **Fears.** Fears become worries, obsession, anxiety and phobias. The absence of a feeling of safety in our lives keeps us from really being ourselves and risking. The opposite is a fearless, reckless life-style.

12. **Nasty mood afflictions.** Our anger and resentments sweep through us and out toward people around us. We project many of our bad feelings about ourselves onto others and our own inadequacy gives rise to noting inadequacies in others. The opposite is a *pretend* passivity.

13. **Constant chaos or crisis.** As long as we are in a whirlwind, nothing can touch us. Our problems are too big, but we feel truly alive as long as we're in a state of intensity. The opposite is to avoid any stress, never make waves and avoid any variations or unusual situations.

14. **Enabling relationships.** We become disrespectful in relationships with others. We enable the people we are with to continue their destructive behaviors. They do the crime, but we pay the fine and do the time. We remove the harmful consequences of other people's inappropriateness. The opposite is to take no risk, involvement or responsibility in any relationship.

15. **Passive-aggressive.** We don't get angry, we get even. We get side-ways. We go away. We withdraw. We shut down emotionally or physically, but all in order to punish the people around us. The opposite is constant aggression and becoming bullish.

16. **Shamefulness and shamelessness.** We feel terrible about ourselves and cannot acknowledge these bad feelings, so we act shamelessly.

Our behavior either becomes a shameless manifestation of our repressed shame or direct projection of this shame.

17. **Mood swings.** We experience emotional ups and downs. Highs become manic, and lows follow. We lack evenness of temperament. Things are either great or awful. We move through grandiosity to self-hate.

18. **Manipulative.** We do things in roundabout ways and control covertly or indirectly. We take the side approaches rather than directly noticing and dealing with issues. The opposite is not being political, being the "bull in a china shop."

19. **Defensive.** Our defensiveness pushes people away. We do it out of a need for self-protection, but instead it leads us into more self-destruction. We can't acknowledge making mistakes because we feel as though we are a mistake. We can't accept criticism because we believe people are abandoning us. We escalate any feedback or evaluation. The opposite is not defending or standing up for ourselves.

20. **Invulnerability.** We feel too vulnerable, so we try to act invulnerable. Being ourselves, being real or being close means we can be hurt, so we try to keep control at a safe distance, denying the things that might penetrate our armor. The opposite is being too vulnerable, the walking open wound.

21. **Instant gratification.** What we want, we want now! If we want to feel good we want to feel good now. If we're hungry we have to have it right now. We lack the ability to delay our needs. We look for the fix. The opposite is always delaying or avoiding gratification.

22. **Acting childish.** We try to regain our lost childhood by becoming childish rather than embracing childness. We pout and throw tantrums. Our playfulness doesn't involve consideration of others, but it becomes mean or vindictive. We act cute for attention, for approval or to manipulate. The opposite of this is pseudo-maturity, never playful or spontaneous, denying any sense of childness.

23. **Judging ourselves.** We judge ourselves through externals, appearances, wealth, by how others see us. This is a no-win situation since we are usually our own worst critics. Nothing we can do will ever satisfy us. Nothing we can own will ever be enough to make us feel successful in other people's eyes. The opposite is not to care at all about what others see or feel about us.

24. **Lack of emotional fluency.** We don't affirm our feelings or those of others. We don't speak in the language of feelings. We have a hard time processing feelings. We don't embrace feelings. We try to get rid of them or distract from them. The opposite is using

emotions as a way to control others or processing feelings ad *nauseum.*

25. **Fear of intimacy and abandonment.** Fears cause us to withdraw in relationships. We feel abandoned even when we're not being abandoned. When close, we fear the intimacy. When distant, we fear the isolation.

26. **Being critical, whining and complaining.** A posture toward life that keeps us judgmental, negative and pushes people away. We negatively bond with people through our complaining. The polar opposite is never complaining and accepting everything passively.

27. **Inability to let go.** We have to complete everything perfectly. Everything has to be done a certain way, no sense of surrender, no acceptance. Worrying too much is how we look like we care. The opposite pole is not caring, letting go too quickly, never completing what we begin.

28. **Judging and comparing ourselves.** We judge our children by comparing them to other children. We judge our house by comparing it to other houses, the things we see in magazines and on TV. We judge our relationships by how we see other people's relationships. We judge ourselves without mercy. The opposite pole is no self-examination or scrutiny.

29. **Defiant/counterdependent.** We become defiant to authority or tradition. We refuse to allow any patterns in our life. We operate totally on impulse and won't accept direction. We break the rules for the sake of breaking rules and we feel as though the rules are impinging on our freedom of expression and that traditions, the old way, won't work for us. We despise scheduling or having to be somewhere. The polar opposite is compliance for the sake of compliance.

30. **Helper role.** We adopt the role of helper but we can't ask for help ourselves. Being the helper gives us more control. We are the listener, the one with the advice. Many people can come to us, but we go to no one. The polar opposite is helplessness.

31. **Blaming and projecting.** When things go wrong we can't take responsibility, so we blame and project. It must be someone else's fault. When things go well we want the credit. When things go wrong we deliver the blame. The polar opposite is taking all the blame.

32. **No sense of humor.** We lack the ability to laugh at ourselves. We lack the ability to be spontaneous and laugh with others. The opposite is excessive reliance on humor as a way to avoid our pain or the seriousness of things around us.

Most of us can relate to several of these symptoms. So often we focus on the problems rather than the solution. The following includes our guidelines toward recovery:

THE 12 PRIORITIES: A FEW BASIC PREMISES AND GUIDES

The following 12 chapters each has as its theme one of the 12 Priorities of Recovery. No theme has a particular destination, time line or completion date. Each priority is a foundation step for the next focus of work. Begin with Priority One and continue to work on it while gradually adding Priorities Two through Twelve. In recovery we work concurrently on themes as we add new dimensions. Following is a list of twelve key life themes building one upon the other, the recovery priority list.

Priority 1. **Identity.** Self-relationship, the developmental formation and awareness of who we are including our history and our present, our reality and goals, likes and dislikes, values and flat spots.

Priority 2. **Emotional Fluency.** Our feelings, the ability to label, embrace, affirm and share feelings in self and with others.

Priority 3. **Friends and Family.** Building a support system, a group of people who nurture, care, notice, touch and affirm us. This is building a *family of creation* to balance our family of origin.

Priority 4. **Physical Balance.** Caring for, liking, nurturing and challenging our physical selves, protecting and enjoying our bodies.

Priority 5. **Spirituality.** Meaningfulness of life, values, a lifestyle that gives life and flows with love, guardianship and relationship to creation, the process of becoming ourselves.

Priority 6. **Sexuality.** Our relationship with ourselves as men and women, the sexual expression of that relationship and our response to touch, needs, drives and desires.

Priority 7. **Play and Recreation.** Experiencing the world in a childlike, noticing way, re-creation through recreation, the soaring of our spirit in activities, movement, learning and experiences.

Priority 8. **Nutrition and Food.** The gentle nourishing of our physical being in a way that reflects guardianship, love and care.

Priority 9. **Intellect and Creativity.** Learning, seeking, questing, reading, listening, teaching, awareness and gratitude, to grow in insight and risk-creating.

Priority 10. **Career.** Learning to labor with pride, finding work that suits our identity, feeling positive about the productive areas of our life.

Priority 11. **Community.** A sense of the oneness of people, of life, of all things, the true interdependence expressed in a relationship with others.

Priority 12. **Passion.** An intensity of caring, noticing and protecting what we value and believe.

As you move through the 12 Priorities, be aware of the following helpful recommendations. These suggestions and premises are the basis for beginning the adventure through the priorities:

- being drug free
- attending meetings and support groups
- doing worksheets
- striving for balance
- practicing forgiveness.

Being Drug Free

Regardless of what life issues you are facing, whether you are recovering from an eating disorder, co-dependency or alcoholism, it is important to be engaging in the recovery process drug free. Don't use any life-threatening substance — alcohol, nicotine or any other drug.

We recommend this to all the people we work with and often get a response similar to Mario's. He said, "Well, I came here to get help with my disordered eating problem. I'm not an alcoholic. Why do I need to stop drinking?" Our reply to Mario and others is, "If you don't have a problem with drug use, then it won't be difficult not to use. And if you do have a problem, then you will know very soon." Recovery is more than treating an addiction, which is usually a symptom. We need to treat addictiveness. Better yet, let's treat people!

Becoming drug free can come from a decision rather than an addiction. Given the hard facts — costs of drug use and abuse; the fact that drugs anesthetize, medicate and alter how we feel and impair our judgment, memory, balance, coordination and sense of well-being — why use at all? To be chemically free from life-threatening drugs, including nicotine and alcohol, is to model interdependence. Do as we do, not do as we say. In recovery our feelings are even more important as guides. Our internal forces, insights and messages are awakening. It is essential to be drug free, especially during the therapy aspects of recovery.

Meetings And Support Groups

We recommend finding a 12-Step meeting to help build a *family of creation.* Such a group facilitates spiritual healing and is a way to find ongoing support for not acting out our addictions or self-destructive behaviors. Meetings vary in approach, format, length, issues addressed and health. Some groups work the 12 Steps, others do not. Some do cross talk, others listen and affirm. Some are open, some are closed, some follow the 12 Traditions of Alcoholics Anonymous, others do not. We prefer groups that work the 12 Steps, with occasional topic meetings; have no cross talk; adhere closely to the 12 Traditions; are open, mixed and nonsmoking meetings — but who are we to judge? Find one that works for you, one that feels supportive and safe.

You can find addresses and telephone numbers for local meetings in the Yellow Pages, or see Appendix A for mutual support group contacts. Other support groups, of course, can offer the support and care we need on our journey. We discuss 12-Step groups because they are available everywhere and accessible to everyone — all you need is the desire! Marvel has many years of experience participating in support groups, which have actually become her *family of creation.* The members celebrate family holidays and celebrations together and have blended with her family of origin. Often families of origin are not available to us emotionally or physically, so we must reach to others.

The goal of joining a group is to learn to take responsibility for yourself: your feelings, thoughts and statements, which are shared and directed to the whole group or one other person. Being able to do this happens over time and with practice. Some groups are for sharing your experience and there is no cross talk, while other groups encourage exchange and discussion between members. Here are some guidelines for getting the most out of a group experience:

1. Be aware of feelings. Try to express your feelings. There is a difference between talking *about* feelings and *feeling* feelings. Sometimes we have to talk about them before we can feel them. If you are not used to expressing feelings, give special attention to how people feel and try to use feeling statements: "I feel sad" or "I'm afraid."
2. Use "I" statements. Instead of saying "we" or "you," speak for yourself. "I feel comfortable."
3. Speak directly to another person. Instead of "Tom seems angry," say, to him, "Tom, you seem angry to me," or "I imagine you are angry right now."
4. Speak freely and openly. Depending on the style of group, people need not ask permission to speak, intervene, move around or contribute in any fashion.
5. Respect other group members' group time. Everyone needs an opportunity to share if they choose to.
6. Use statements whenever possible. Before asking a question (or answering one) consider the statement behind your question and

try to express the direct statement. For example: "Why are you looking at me?" is better expressed, "I'm not comfortable when you look at me like that" (a statement).

7. Avoid the constant question "Why?" Asking "why" leads to analyzing and often leads one away from feelings and into intellectualizing.

8. Be descriptive — avoid judgments. Describe the person's behavior and your response. In this way you do not shame another person. You take responsibility for your own reactions and won't project your stuff on others. For example: "You talk too much. You're off the wall!" projects disgust and will shame. "When you are speaking at great lengths, I start to feel confused." This statement is responsible; you are taking responsibility for your own experience.

9. Be there then. When sharing about your experiences of the past, try to recapture and experience the feelings you had then. If you have not expressed them, they are probably still with you.

10. Be here now. When you give feedback to others in the group, be in the here and now sharing your now experience.

11. Confidentiality is primary. It is essential that we all honor the confidentiality. What happens in the group stays in the group; information about who is in the group stays in the group.

12. Be honest — not just saying whats true but also what is difficult to say and being honest with feelings.

Worksheets

You will find worksheets in the companion volume to this book. We have designed the worksheets to help you help yourself to focus and support your process of recovery. "It only works if you work it!"

Balance

Balance is our recovery goal. The recovery journey can swing from one extreme to another. For example, if you are in an overly dependent relationship, with no sense of your own identity, in recovery you may go to the other extreme and become very independent and possibly isolated. This is a very common experience. The recovery goal is the balance — interdependence — being able to depend on others without losing ourselves.

Forgiveness: The Ultimate Goal Of Recovery

We are often reluctant to go back to childhood and examine the developmental roots of our low-functioning lives. This is a continued form of the denial we learned from the family system. We tend to be hard on ourselves, trying to take full responsibility for who we are and what we do. At first glance this seems a healthy posture, but it may prevent the possibility of change. The dysfunction is often based on feelings and events that lie buried in the past and are still being denied (with denial of the denial).

Sometimes people get "stuck" in blaming their environment and families for their problems and inappropriate behavior and never seem to get past this blaming posture. This situation is rare, however, compared to the number of us who keep trying to move forward while dragging a loaded trailer with no wheels and driving with our eyes closed to the context of our lives. We continue to struggle with the same issues and eventually watch our children carry on these struggles. A common belief is that doing family systems or family-of-origin work can cause irreparable damage to cross-generational relationships; that things will worsen with the anger. This can happen when we are not guided through the process of forgiveness and is rare compared to the families where intergenerational healing is taking place.

Family systems therapy is a healing process and a part of spiritual recovery. As a participant in recovery, you are actually beginning a process of *forgiveness*, not blaming.

Forgiveness is a process, not an event. It consists of the following phases, which Terry uses as part of his Kellogg's Lifeworks Clinics:

Phase One Is Recognizing The Wrongs That Were Done To Us.

Forgetting is not forgiving, and denial precludes the possibility of forgiveness. We tend to repress or "forget" painful events, so in this stage there is an unraveling process of seeing and remembering the painful experiences. These include the covert dysfunctions, secrets and denial that we unknowingly replicate or act out. Often we believe the wrongs done to us are about some failing in us. Or we accept them as normal, having few healthier experiences to compare them to.

Phase Two Is Recognizing We Have Feelings About The Wrongs.

We not only tend to repress memories, but also feelings. Early learning teaches us not to show or express our natural emotional reactions to the hurts and losses we experience. These feelings become the basis of acting-out behavior, or we may somatize them to the point of illness. We learn to medicate (with drugs such as alcohol and nicotine) or look for fixes of food, shopping or intensity. This inability to understand keeps us isolated and in denial. The "I don't care or feel" posture is a kind of death of the self. Simply acknowledging we have feelings about what happened enables us to begin the healing process.

Phase Three Concerns Embracing Our Feelings About The Wrongs.

Nothing changes until it becomes real. Our feelings include cognitive and physical reactions to the world and ourselves. Embracing the feelings is embracing the self and becoming real. M. Scott Peck, in *The Road Less Traveled*, wrote, "The only path away from our suffering is to embrace the suffering." This embracing includes a physical healing and new energy in our bodies. Denied feelings are a psychological and physical drain. Our bodies tighten and tension and stress increase. An appropriate sense of feeling gives us clearer insights and more energy to follow the path of becoming the person we were meant to be.

Phase Four Is About Sharing The Feelings With Others —
Sometimes With The Wrongdoer.

Sharing the feelings is sharing the burden. We open up to others and embrace and release our shame by learning that we can depend on people. Sharing feelings is the act of love, of sharing oneself. The forgiveness process is not a fix for relationships. It is the spiritual healing for self that is part of recovery which will facilitate better relationships overall. In the sharing we lessen our isolation and reduce the hold that the wrong and wrongdoer exert over our lives.

Sharing with family requires judicious evaluation. Sometimes it may help heal. Other times we may get abused in return or the family denial will again break our hold on reality. Some family members may be too fragile (but less often than many of us believe) or may be no longer available. Not sharing because we think they are too old and can't handle it is ageism! The process doesn't require direct confrontation or sharing because our goal is not to change others — only ourselves. Role play, imagery, psychodrama, writing or discussion all work well in this stage.

Phase Five Requires A Decision Of What To Do With
The Relationship With The Wrongdoer.

Remembering this is a process and not an event may mean we let this decision evolve over a period of time. Usually we need detachment, a breaking of the enmeshment that occurs with the dysfunction and abuse.

This detachment sometimes requires a period of separation. Stage five may meet the most resistance from family members because it involves a change in how we operate in the system, which has an impact on the entire family. We often feel more guilty during this process, and it helps to remember the guilt is a by-product of the family dysfunction. A healthy family encourages its members to be living where they are happy and doing what makes them the happiest.

Most of us can maintain an improved relationship with family because we have a better sense of self. The detachment actually can help us spend time in the system. It is easier if there have been changes made by the wrongdoer, for example, when an alcoholic parent is working a recovery program. The key is our growth and our becoming sufficiently aware of self to establish clearer boundaries.

Phase Six Involves A Sense Of Serenity And Acceptance About The Wrong And Our Relationship With The Wrongdoer.

This is the final stage. Acceptance does not mean we no longer have feelings about what happened. There may always be pain or anger at the abuse or neglect. It means the feelings no longer control us or force us into a denial system. Our relationships no longer suffer from inappropriate, defensive or avoidant behavior.

Sometimes we get stuck in a stage and don't complete the process. This decreases the opportunity for healing the relationship and we reflect this in being stuck in our lives. We also have to be prepared to reenter the process as we receive new data or insights into how we've been hurt. In beating ourselves up about how we've hurt our own children, we may recognize it was another way we were hurt in our childhood and we have been trying to write checks out of an empty account.

Recovery itself is a lifelong process of self and other forgiveness. In the process we become less and less controlled by the past. A blame system is a refusal to move through the forgiveness process. Forgiveness, though painful, may help us find ourselves so that we may begin to seek others.

THE QUEST

As we travel, teach and participate in our own quest, we continually encourage the people we are with to work on their journey too. Following are many of the commonly asked questions people present to us as a part of their search for recovery. The questions range from simple to complex. They are asked by people who are just beginning their recovery and those who have traveled many miles down the road. We have chosen to answer them concisely, without detail, since many of the answers could be a book in themselves!

What is recovery?

Recovery is the *discovery* of our birthright. It is rejoining the path that leads to becoming the person we were meant to be.

Should men and women attend separate groups?

Both mixed and gender-segregated groups are helpful. The goal is to feel safe and be vulnerable in both situations, remembering that the world is a blend.

What is co-dependency?

Co-dependency is a child's reaction to family dysfunction. Children who are unable to depend on their survival figures and are not nurtured through the developmental stages tend to have problems with dependency, intimacy and identity. Co-dependency is not about a relationship with someone else; it is an absence of relationship with self.

What is addiction?

Addiction is a recursive, pathological relationship with any mood-altering event, person, experience or substance that causes significant life problems.

What are the first issues in recovery to address?

First, if you are in a physically abusive situation, find a safe place. If you are in a safe place, begin by looking at addictiveness and active addictions, especially chemical dependencies, which prevent us from moving on. The following chapters of this book address other priorities of recovery.

Do I go as a couple?

If you are in a relationship, we recommend you go through the intake work together and then do the family of origins work separately. Recovery priorities one and two might best be done on your own and then work together on the rest of the priorities. Couples can share literature, workshops, tapes, 12-Step meetings and information, while having their own therapists and groups in the beginning stages.

What if my spouse or partner isn't interested?

This is a common problem. Plan your own recovery program. Inform your partner about what you are doing and invite him or her along. Don't drag your partner along unless you have to, but don't drag too far or too long or you won't make it there yourself! Even when our partner is in recovery, we often don't think it is the *right* recovery or it isn't *fast enough or happening in the right way!*

What if a family member needs help and refuses to get any?

Going as a family takes the pressure off the member who needs help. Usually this person is a symptom-bearer of the family problem anyway. If the person still refuses to go, options include: setting up or noticing consequences of their refusal; a respectful intervention that offers positive alternatives; letting go and focusing on our own recovery which will usually require some grieving (see Priority Two, Feelings).

What is an intervention?

An intervention is the process by which we interrupt a person's destructive behaviors. It can be a friendly suggestion, a gentle comment or an angry demand. Formal interventions can be arranged with professionals.

What is a formal intervention?

Please see the Comments section toward the end of this chapter for an extensive review of the intervention process.

What is treatment?

Treatment is a structured program of education, group process, therapy and community support that is offered for varying lengths of time in both residential and outpatient settings.

How do I know if I need treatment?

Treatment may be necessary as a process for a person to work through the delusion and denial that are part of addictive disorders. Some people may use treatment as a safe place to deal with past hurts and traumas.

Do I need testing?

There are many types of testing that may be appropriate for someone entering recovery, including psychological, physical and personality tests and inventories. Testing possibilities include career and vocational, IQ and special learning, physical and neurological, health risk, fitness, addiction and co-dependency inventories, personality disorder or mental illness. Testing can help in diagnosis and treatment program suitability, since it is important to establish what we are recovering from. It is appropriate before using medications or entering treatment or intensive therapy programs; when there is a familial history of mental illness; or if your present recovery program doesn't seem to be working.

Do I get a second opinion?

We would say yes, but you may not want to get a second opinion!

What do I look for in qualifications of a professional?

Numerous health professionals treat various emotional, relationship and family problems. Physicians, psychiatrists, psychologists, psychiatric nurses, social workers, psychotherapists, addiction counselors, marriage and family therapists — to name a few. The training and license requirements vary greatly from field to field and in each state and province. Fees and insurance reimbursement vary according to the profession, geographic location, individual practitioner and insurance policy. Following are a few suggestions of how to choose help.

- The most important factor is that you are creating a relationship and need to feel comfortable and safe with the person you choose.
- Ask questions:
  - length of sessions?
  - time line?
  - prices?
  - diagnosis?
  - approach or belief system?
  - therapist's own recovery?
  - training for specific issues?
- Select a therapist or group that does not have a "far out" theory or approach or gimmick and does not use rigid techniques or the same diagnosis for each client — for example, *everyone* must find a magical child, *everyone* must do rage work, *everyone* is suffering from depression or mother or father loss, *everyone* must do regressions, and so on.
- Look for someone who has helped others in similar circumstances as yours and is not too intrusive *or* passive.
- Choose someone who models the elements of interdependence as outlined in Chapter 1, who networks and refers to other helping professionals, has access to a variety of recovery settings including groups, family work and individual, and supports your participation in other appropriate recovery programs and seminars.
- Frequently it is helpful to begin with a same-sex therapist.
- Keep in mind you don't have to "marry" the first therapist who comes along and you can make changes when appropriate.
- Remember you are purchasing a service as well as creating a relationship with another person.

How do I choose a treatment center?

The information regarding choosing a therapist also applies to choosing a treatment center. In addition, however, keep in mind the following points:

- Treatment centers, regardless of whether they are for profit or not for profit, are highly competitive business entities with beds that need to be filled in order to stay in business. Frequently staff members are underpaid and the turnover in personnel is high.
- Inpatient treatment may be appropriate when outpatient programs and therapy have been ineffective over time.
- Get an assessment for your treatment from an objective professional.
- Begin with a therapist you trust. Many agencies offer outpatient treatment, group therapy and numerous short-term intensive programs. Residential treatment for four or more weeks is not a cure-all but may be helpful.

A good basic rule is, "Buyer beware!" You are the customer and are purchasing a service and the competition and marketing for providing medical service is aggressive. You always have many choices, although when you are hurting and needing help it may not seem as though you do. Unfortunately someone with co-dependency can be maintained in a victim role by treatment centers. Problems include misdiagnosis; having clients over-stay to continue to collect insurance; early discharge if benefits run out; over-charging, especially for psychiatric services; providing unnecessary services; excess nonproductive client time due to program disorganization; prescribing unnecessary medication; heavy confrontation and emotional battering of clients; undertrained, underpaid and overworked staff who are also expected to do marketing; and using intervention as marketing.

Unfortunately many treatment centers are more interested in filling beds than providing quality service. Many treatment centers are sometimes arrogant about what they offer and use abusive tactics, particularly during family week, which has been made into a primary marketing tool.

Treatment programs are available that offer quality service for reasonable prices and are staffed by warm, caring and talented people. Don't settle for less. You are worth taking care of!

Have I been abused?

If you are wondering, you probably have been. Most of us were, maybe not intentionally or by the people we thought abused us. For further information review the abuse lists in *Broken Toys Broken Dreams*.

Am I depressed?

Symptoms include experiencing changes in sleep patterns, decreased energy level, increase or decrease of appetite, loss of sense of humor, difficulty with play, change of activity level, experiencing hopelessness, suicidal thoughts or diminished interests. If you have several of these symptoms you may be depressed and need to seek help from someone who does not *immediately* prescribe medication. These symptoms may also be from previous trauma.

What am I recovering from?

We need to have an appropriate diagnosis and possible testing. Addictive and compulsive behaviors, post-traumatic stress disorders (PTSD), depression, adult children issues and co-dependency are common recovery issues.

Is all this about childhood?

Recovery is often about past hurts, traumas and false premises, whether we were traumatized yesterday or as a child. Therapy issues are frequently related to what happened or what we learned in our families of origin. We will have to look backward to go forward.

What should I do about my family of origin?

A few suggestions for dealing with our family of origin while in therapy:

- Don't confront too early, if at all.
- Do emotional work on past hurts and anger before you bring your family in.
- Learn detachment, take separation time if needed.
- Give up hoping that they will change.
- Anticipate possible punishment, rejection or resistance to your changes.
- Invite them along.
- Request support, don't settle for less. We can't expect them to *understand* but we can expect them to *accept* what we are choosing.
- Don't hang around if they are abusive.
- If a major inheritance is on the line, be practical and go slow!

Where do I go for recovery?

It depends on what you can afford and your unique needs. Crisis services, community health centers, social service agencies, private clinics and therapists offer workshops, programs, therapy and groups. Talk to people in recovery to find which services are best in your area. We highly recommend 12-Step programs, especially ones that work the Steps. There are 203 different 12-Step programs in the United States and Canada, it only takes two people to start a meeting and it costs a dollar per meeting if you can afford it.

How long do I attend 12-Step meetings?

We recommend attending meetings at least until you *want* to attend meetings. Your attendance is crucial early in recovery, it may vary some in later years.

What types of therapists are there?

There are numerous ways to categorize therapists. Much depends on who is doing the categorizing.

Beware of . . .

- PhDs and other lettermen — who have little people sense and little empathy.
- Listeners and nodders — who charge a great deal for sleeping with their eyes open.
- The recovery elite — who have the answers and are recovered and put down other therapists. "They did it themselves," have a seductive/ well-structured approach often based on false assumptions and talk too much about themselves, their relationships and recovery.
- Exploiters — manipulate and use clients, attach like a lamprey and never let go.
- Instant pioneers — who upon discovering a concept began preaching and teaching as if they were part of developing it.
- Former addicts — who are well-intended and poorly qualified and often do projection (for example, recovering alcoholics who still smoke and eat compulsively).
- Caretakers and other ambulance drivers — who need you to be sick so they can be OK.
- Psychophant — an elephant with a degree in psychology! Always being nice, ingratiating, but offering no real help or direction.

Seriously now, many PhDs, credentialed counselors and recovering addicts are wonderful, insightful therapists. Our real goal is to have clients question, search and find someone they like and who seems to be helping. If you are a therapist and think you fall into any of the above categories, this is not intended as an indictment. We have both been there, sometimes still are and believe change is possible. What we all have to offer is important, as is continuing our own growth.

THE THREE 'C's' OF RECOVERY: CAUTIONS, CONCERNS AND COMMENTS

Notes On Large Group Work

Do not do catharsis work in large groups. In groups of *more* than eight or ten people, do not do:

- painful or emotional work
- regression work, where you go back to places of deep pain or trauma
- work that uses repetition of words or body posture that bring up deep, painful feelings
- imagery or writing about abuse.

We believe in these powerful and helpful processes — but only when you are the only one doing the work in a small group. Do it with a trained therapist and in a group that is focused on *your* process. You deserve this special attention for this painful work. Show self-respect and say "No, thank you" when asked to participate in these activities in a group larger than eight or ten people.

Cultural Misogyny

Misogyny is a term that has been applied to men who fear and hate women. In the interdependence model misogyny is a word describing a culture that fears and hates vulnerability. Co-dependence is a by-product of this cultural misogyny. When children are used and abused, neglected and enmeshed, when their vulnerability is turned against them and their feelings are not affirmed, they learn to fear and hate that vulnerability. This fear and hatred of vulnerability gets projected toward people, other living things and the planet itself. A culture that abuses its own children is set up for that abuse to continue and to be acted out against all vulnerable groups and things. Cultural misogyny is reflected in our infant mortality rate, the homeless and other groups including children, gays, Native Americans, differently abled, Vietnam veterans and others. Vulnerable groups do not fare well in our culture.

A further example of cultural misogyny is that the people who work with vulnerable groups do not fare much better than the groups do with regard to compensation, training, support, public positions or prestige. In interdependence we recognize that this reflection of vulnerable groups is a rejection of our spirituality, responsibility and oneness with these groups and the planet as well as a symptom of a rejection of ourselves. We propose a healing process that would enable us to embrace ourselves and all of creation.

Formal Interventions

A formal intervention is only appropriate when a person has an active chemical dependency or life-threatening behavior. It should be facilitated by an objective therapist and involve significant people in the addict's life who have the genuine concern for the health of the addict and who have previously approached the addict with caring suggestions and concerns. Participants should not have a secondary agenda such as revenge or "getting even" for past behavior. They should not have financial gains to be made by getting rid of the person. Employment and career issues should not be involved unless there is severe career impairment, violence or a life-threatening situation.

An intervention should never be based on interrupting a situation or relationship because an individual or group of people don't approve of it. The caring people should prepare specific information, usually in writing, not based on subjective or secondhand information. It should be presented in a caring, nonjudgmental manner. The specific data should be followed by suggestions of positive alternatives through which the addict can maintain their dignity by participating in recovery choices. Rigidity in the intervention process reflects more about the pathology of the people doing the intervention than the addict's need for help.

The danger with interventions is that they can be used as marketing techniques for treatment centers, which hire professional intervention specialists in their marketing departments — an ethical conflict of interest. They can also be used as a "big brother" approach to frighten, badger and pressure people into conforming to someone else's lifestyle choices or to react to their disapproval.

Interventions can do more harm than good. They are very serious and must be handled with utmost respect.

SUGGESTIONS • AFFIRMATIONS • THOUGHTS

SUGGESTIONS

- Stick to it even when uncomfortable unless you are being put down, abused, shamed or used.
- Attend meetings and do the readings.
- Talk to people you trust or meet in programs about who a helpful therapist may be.
- Don't do your therapy or emotional work in large groups or lectures.
- Join a 12-Step group and find a sponsor.
- Don't rush recovery — give yourself a lifetime to do it.
- Don't rush out and confront your family.
- Inform people you care about what you are going through.
- Find a good therapist even if you don't need long-term therapy. It's good to have someone you know and who knows you to call on when needed.

AFFIRMATIONS

- My questions are a part of my recovery quest.
- It's OK not to know, it's OK to ask.
- Reading and listening provide the input for my recovery choices.
- My therapy can offer me choices; I must do the choosing.
- I am a child and an adult.
- I am willing to take the risk of recovery.
- I will move through my hurts.
- My journey is paved with hope.

THOUGHTS

- Therapy is withness.
- Brief encounter therapy is a way of utilizing our tools and insights to help others we encounter.
- Don't attend 12-Step meetings in which members "therapize" each other.
- Men in recovery often need rituals and ceremonies to access feelings.
- Intervention should not be used to impose values or a lifestyle; rather it should be used to support a person in receiving help for a life-threatening disease.
- Twenty-eight days of inpatient treatment is not a miracle cure — recovery is still a lifelong process.

PRIORITY 1.

Identity:
Know Thyself

V olumes of written material and numerous tapes have been produced on recovery, yet over two thousand years ago a
Greek philosopher said it in only two words: "Know
thyself." The essence of our recovery is to discover
our identity, to know us.

The other day we were having lunch with our friend
Bill, who has recently started his recovery journey. His
enthusiasm for what he was discovering was boundless
and he had many questions. Suddenly he stopped short
and simply said, "I don't get what everyone means about
finding 'self.' What is self anyway? I know my name
and when and where I was born and who my parents
were and what my occupation is and some of the things
I like to do. Isn't that enough?" Our answer to his
question was simply another question: "Does it feel like
it is enough to you?" He shook his head and asked what
he needed to do. We wish we had a simple solution but

we don't. We do have some ideas about why people don't have a sense of self and suggestions on how they might begin finding their identity.

The absence of identity is the core of co-dependency. When our natural dependency needs are not met we begin to rely on externals. Babies enter this world totally dependent; their job is to do nothing more than let parents and caregivers know what they need. Besides food, warmth and having physical needs met, children require emotional attention, care, touch and having their feelings noticed, correctly labeled and affirmed. The caregiver's job is to meet these dependency needs. Whenever needs are expressed and not met, the normal response is to repress, hide and feel ashamed of the needs. This leads to lost noticing and possible hiding of need — even from ourselves. We change what we need, how we respond, who we are, according to each new situation. Our natural and evolving nature is lost in unsafe environments. Our repressed needs will be met in unhealthy ways and we begin to depend on externals, which become addiction. Soon we begin to find our identity in the addiction, even in recovery.

OUR PATHS

Co-dependence sets up enmeshment — unhealthy identification with someone else's identity. The antidote for enmeshment is identity. We are no longer on our unique and individual path of becoming who we were meant to be. We can lose the path in many ways. Some of us were abused and beaten off the path. Others were intellectually abused, became confused and couldn't find the path. Some were neglected, abandoned and lost the path. Many of us have been scripted and set up or enmeshed into living out another's dreams and expectations of life and have ended up on someone else's path.

Scripting, being used, enmeshment and neglect creates a damaged identity. Violence, abuse and trauma disintegrate identity. We end up wandering aimlessly, hiding in fright, or fighting and offending in an attempt to find our path. When we are not on our own path, we cannot read our internal compass. We depend instead on external messages. We become addictive in an attempt to fill the emptiness, loneliness and pain caused by our use and abuse.

We did not choose to be hurt and we do not choose our addictions or self-destructive behaviors. *Co-dependency and addiction mean not having choice. Recovery through identity building means having choice.*

Many of us feel young and scared inside while trying to live in a grown-up world. So often it seems as though we are little kids fumbling around in big bodies striving for adult needs and wants and desperately seeking contentment by seeking intimacy. According to Erickson's stages of development, identity is a necessary prerequisite to intimacy. We need identity and intimacy with self before we can gain and sustain intimacy with others. Too often as adults, we are grasping and groping for intimacy with others — before we have intimacy with self or before we have found our own identity. We need to have identity in order to move through our adolescence regardless of our chronological age. In order to push on through adolescence we must seek identity and travel our own path.

SELF-WORTH: WHERE DOES IT COME FROM?

Self-concept is *how we see and identify* ourselves. Self-esteem is *how we feel* about our self-concept. Frequently people describe themselves in terms of their family, career and how they look. For example, a woman may say, "I am a mother, wife and teacher, I am of average intelligence, I have green eyes and brown hair, I am five feet, three inches tall and am about fifteen pounds overweight." Our feeling about this kind of description is affected by the messages we received as children and the messages we hear from our society. Because our society is focused on image, our identity is tied up in body type, shape, size, weight and physical abilities. Very few of us are going to meet the societal norms of being "beautiful" or "handsome." If we accept these expectations, we are setting ourselves up for frustration, hurt and low self-worth.

Identity is affected by culture, social messages, race, religion and economics. Oppressed groups are more vulnerable and hurt by the messages they receive from the dominant group, whether the focus of discrimination is about race, religion, poverty, sex, sexual orientation, body size or being differently abled. When people are oppressed and beaten down in education, jobs, housing, medical care and opportunities, a negative self-concept is inevitable. They begin in a one-down position. Uniqueness and preciousness are denied and the result is low self-esteem and a shame-based identity. *Shame is the felt sense of low self-esteem.*

BOUNDARIES

Boundaries have been described as everything from suits of armor to peanut butter jars to zippers. We are told to image these items as external to ourselves as a form of protection. These images may be helpful for self-protection but they misdirect us into believing our boundaries are external.

Boundaries are a construct of identity. They appear to be external because we reinforce them by setting limits. We can't set our limits until we know our limits. We can't know our limits until we know ourselves.

Once we know ourselves we have our limits. Boundaries define an entity.

Most of us are hurt from the inside, so wearing a suit of armor is not going to help us. External boundaries become rigid and reflect anger and arrogance and often are used to attack other people. Internal boundaries move with the flow — a gentle noticing, a careful backing away.

Boundaries are interwoven. Our sexual, spiritual, physical, intellectual and emotional boundaries are inseparable. Boundary violations in one area affect all areas because they are woven one with another. True identity creates gentle and flexible boundaries.

IDENTITY BUILDING

Identity is supported through a system of feedback from primary caregivers about who and what we are. They reflected our identity back to us in how they saw us and what they said to us. Many of us received very negative messages from parents and caregivers, and our identity was hurt by the painful things said to us as babies, children and young adults. We believed these negative messages and reacted in one of two ways: We either internalized the information as true, or rebelled against it but continued to tell ourselves how bad, useless, ugly or awful we were. As part of our healing we need to find new people to give us feedback so we can internalize positive, loving and caring messages to live by. (Chapter 5 explores how to find a *family of creation* who affirm who we are and what we stand for so we can begin creating a positive self-image.)

Building identity comes from knowing our history and culture, our family system, our joys and traumas, our roles and the rules, premises and myths by which we operate. Identity work means exploring memories, making lists, keeping a journal and doing affirmations. We need to ask questions, chronicle our history and do discovery work. Recovery is a search not for identity, but for the courage to embrace who we are.

Journal-Keeping

Our journal is the story of us, told to us by us. It is a record of our lives, creativities, passions and recovery. We begin our identity building by keeping a journal, which is simply writing about everyday thoughts, activities and feelings. A journal is a place to record words, phrases, stories, events, poetry, sayings, quotes, ideas, doodling, drawings or whatever pleases us. It can be short or long; spelling and grammar don't count. The only thing that matters is doing it — but it isn't homework and doesn't have to be done daily.

Some people have trouble writing and putting things down on paper. If you have this problem, try the technique of *flow writing*: Keep your pen moving, either repeatedly writing the last word over and over again or simply drawing a continuous design of your choice. Drawing, making up designs, stick drawing, drawing old toys, dolls and houses can get you unstuck as well as provide feeling and insight.

Too often our self-criticism blocks journal-writing because we get caught up in performing or doing it perfectly, which is impossible, so we end up not doing it at all. Be gentle with yourself and view your journaling as you would a friend's personal writing. You would probably tell your friend something kind and encouraging about keeping the journal. Try being a friend to yourself.

Sometimes it helps to have a friend who is also journaling. Recently both of us have begun journaling again. We had started and stopped many times, feeling guilty because we were recommending that audiences and clients journal while we did not. It's not uncommon to stop for a while, so don't judge yourself if you do. We share a section of our journal with each other, which has helped motivate us to write. Finding a friend to share stories with is a joy.

Often therapists or group facilitators request clients to keep a journal and bring it to sessions to share. This is a helpful activity for self-disclosure. We also encourage you to keep at least one part of your journal just for yourself. When you write and know it will be shared with others, you may tend to write slightly differently than if you know you will be the only person to read it. If you decide you want to share it, go ahead and do so, but realize that developing privacy is part of building identity. Make a note at the beginning of your personal journal that says something such as, "This journal contains personal notes. Please don't read it. If you do, you do so at the risk of hurting both of us. Thank you for your consideration and respect for me."

Autobiography: "Me — My Very Own Story"

Another important step in beginning to discover our history is to write an autobiography, a history called "Me — My Very Own Story." It can be part of your journal and you may want to leave it open-ended so you can add to it as you learn more about yourself.

Learn and write about how you were given your own name. Were you named after a relative? Did your name come from a popular novel or movie? Who named you? What does your name mean? Do you like your name?

Besides discovering and writing about your given name, write about your nickname. Who gave you the pet name? Did you like it? Do people still call you by it? Is it reminiscent of a certain time or place in your life? What and how were you doing when you received the nickname? Many people in recovery take on a new name or nickname. Marvel has a friend who entered treatment with the nickname Grizzly Bear and left with the nickname Teddy Bear. Over the past three years he has collected more than 130 stuffed teddy bears!

A helpful way to recall our past is to visit with relatives and friends, ask questions, listen to stories, look through photos, watch home movies, read old letters and return to visit past neighborhoods, schools, churches, synagogues and communities. Rather than seek specific answers, keep an open mind to whatever information you might learn. This will encourage people to share more easily. You might ask your parents open-ended questions about their families rather than beginning with direct questions about themselves. You will not only learn important intergenerational information, you will learn about your parents' perception of their lives.

Memory

In the process of journal and autobiography writing, it is easy to become overly focused on memories and trying to remember everything. *Recovery is not a search for memory; memory is a by-product of the recovery process.* Psychodrama, role play, sculpture reconstruction, writing, photos and visiting geographic sites all assist in memory. Regression work, hypnosis and other therapy processes can help us recall events and traumas from the past. Generally, as we recover and are able to deal with what we need, we will remember what we need to. The present memories we have are often only the tip of the iceberg.

Regression — going into old places physically, emotionally or cognitively — can stimulate memory. It may bring memory of what happened or memory of a fear or a threat. Remember, these are past memories. Try to move through memory to a place of balance.

It is important to look at how we remember. Everything that we've ever experienced is stored in our mind, but we often can't get at it because it is at an unconscious level. Often our memories are physical and emotional rather than intellectual. We hold our memories in our bodies. As we reconnect and use our bodies the insight may arise.

The connection between the mind and the body means that bodywork can help access the unconscious. Bodywork such as massage, rolfing and movement often release feelings and memories. Body postures can tell a great deal of what has happened in our lives. Even weight, pain, sensitivities or hiding of self can speak of past events.

Often our memories seem more emotional than intellectual or physical. This is because children do not learn cognitively, but they learn emotionally. *Our feelings are often memories.* When we give the feelings form, sound, movement or words, we can see the reality of our past. We can learn to trust our feelings and bodies just as we do our mental images. Remember, however, that this work with body and feelings requires us to be in a safe setting with skilled, caring people.

Our history can be found in our present. As we learn to read what we are doing in our lives today we will see our past. We are constantly trying to tell ourselves where we've been by leading ourselves to the same places over and over. Our adult lives and problems are often a reenactment of or a reaction to unresolved childhood issues. Memories can help us give names to these problems.

Look, List And Learn

Discovering very simple things about ourselves can be insightful and revealing. A powerful tool is to make lists of people, places and things in your life — in your past, present and future. List the movies you enjoy, your favorite colors, places you want to visit, people you don't like, people you do like, food you lust after, food you can't stand, childhood friends, music you relish, things you dread to do, favorite activities, sports that thrill you and sports that bore you to tears, special moments and treasures . . . this list could go on and on and on. Make wish lists, hate lists, illness lists, fear lists.

Affirmations

Affirmations are messages of care and nurturing that we give to ourselves. Sometimes giving and hearing these messages is difficult. It doesn't work to stand in front of the mirror and repeat twenty times, "I like me just the way I am." Generally we must first receive the message from other people who genuinely care about us. If we are being put down by the people around us, we need to hang out with new friends who will affirm us. (We will explore this in Chapter 5.)

Too often people confuse affirmations with compliments. Giving a compliment is usually about externals — how someone is dressed or looks or what they own. Affirmations call attention to internal qualities. Effective affirmations have more depth and take more energy: They *notice* who people are and what they stand for. Affirming means noticing

the sparkle in their eye, the bounce in their step, their cheerful disposi-
tion, their kind tone or their giving nature.

It takes some practice to affirm someone since many of us never were
affirmed as children. The negative thoughts many of us give ourselves
will persist unless we make an effort to replace them with positive
thoughts. Affirmations take time to learn, practice and most of all
believe. Keep trying. You're worth the effort!

Recognizing Rights

In building identity we recognize our rights as human beings. These
rights were lost through trauma and dependency needs. Following is a
list of your rights and the rights of others.

I have the right to:

- Be myself.
- Refuse requests without feeling selfish.
- Have my feelings noticed, labeled and affirmed.
- Be competent and be proud of my accomplishments.
- Feel and express anger.
- Ask for affection and help (I may be turned down, but I can ask).
- Be treated as a capable adult.
- Make choices and mistakes — and be responsible for them.
- Change my mind.
- Say, "I don't know."
- Say, "I don't agree."
- Say, "I don't understand."
- Say, "I don't care."
- Say, "Yes" or "No."
- Say, "Oh."
- Not have to justify my behavior or decisions.
- Be responsible for my behavior and decisions.
- Delay and consider decisions — ask for more information.
- Have my opinions given respect.
- Have my needs be as important as the needs of others.
- Tell someone what my needs are. They may not do anything, but I
  have the right to state my needs.
- Judge my own behavior, thoughts and emotions and be responsible
  for their initiation and the consequences.
- Make a decision about when and how to help others.
- Take pride in my body and define attractiveness in my own terms.
- Grow, learn and change.
- Value my gender, age and experience.

- Be eccentric and idiosyncratic.
- Sometimes make demands on others to insist on change.

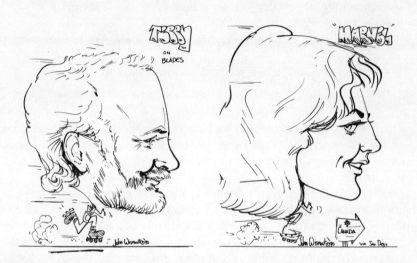

The identity-building process means a shift from external to internal focus, but it is important not to get stuck there. Once healthy identity is present we can become other-directed without losing a sense of self. Most of us will be able to return to our families of origin and not get pulled back into the old rules, roles and behaviors. This shift happens over time, in small steps, after we recognize the old patterns and have enough identity and recovery to make healthy choices for ourselves.

SUGGESTIONS • AFFIRMATIONS • THOUGHTS

SUGGESTIONS

- Keep a journal.
- Write your autobiography.
- Write a paragraph on early childhood memories.
- Glean information from parents and siblings.
- Write down your rules, roles, premises and myths.
- Create an album of old photos and memorabilia and the new 'stuff' you collect.

- Do lists — of interests, people, places, things, events, like, dislikes, shameful and joyful experiences.
- Take a family of origin class or workshop.
- Have your caricature drawn! Since we would never recommend something we wouldn't do ourselves, have a look at ours.
- Do affirmations.
- Visit relatives — never longer than three days! Ask to hear stories and tales.
- Make a decision to like yourself and your humor.

Felt Sense

Self-image is the image that we have of ourself. It's an important part of our self-concept. Our self-concept, our self image is made up of two parts, the image we have of our self and the feelings that we have about that image.

All relationships have a felt sense to the relationship; if wherever you are right now, your best friend walked into the room, you would immediately feel something — elated, excited, moved, overjoyed. If you're having a fight, or angry, but you would still feel something and that is the felt sense of the relationship at that given time. We can't decide to change how we feel about ourselves. We can decide to like ourselves. Some of that decision might include a decision to take better care of ourselves. Eventually, the feelings about ourselves will catch up to the decision.

An exercise we frequently use to help people sense the feelings of relationship, involves closing your eyes and picturing an empty chair facing you, across from you. Place someone or a pet you care about a great deal in that chair. For one minute, feel what it's like to be sitting across from that person. If you can't picture a person who you care about, imagine what it would be like to sit across from someone you care about. If there's no particular person, invent someone, or take someone from your past. For one minute, just sit across and look at the person, and experience what it is that you feel about being across from that person.

Let yourself have the felt sense of the relationship. And now, keeping the empty chair across from you, we want you to repeat the exercise, but this time the person that we want you to put in the chair is you. Spend one minute sitting across from yourself in your mind's eye, just feeling what it's like to be across from you.

Now that the exercise is over, write down the differences that you had when you were sitting across from your friend and when you were sitting across from yourself. Did you have a harder time feeling? Were you harder on yourself, more critical? Did you have a difficult time seeing yourself or holding yourself in the chair? Deciding to care for, like and be gentle with ourselves will eventually result in a warmer felt sense of our relationship with ourselves.

AFFIRMATIONS

A — *Achievement* — the satisfaction of arriving at excellence in some area of endeavor.

F — *Friends* — the broadening of one's social base by having learned to make friends and maintain them.

F — *Feelings* — the self-understanding gained through having learned to share one's feelings with another person.

I — *Identity* — the sense of knowing 'who I am,' and being recognized as a significant person.

R — *Responsibility* — the confidence of knowing "I can stand alone and make responsible decisions."

M — *Maturity* — transformation from a child into an adult.

S — *Sexuality* — acceptance of responsibility for one's new role as a sexual being.

- I am a risk taker.
- To know me is to love me.
- Occasionally I laugh at myself but most of the time I smile at myself.
- I am unique and precious.
- I am interesting and interested.

THOUGHTS

- The antidote for enmeshment is identity.
- Boundaries are a construct of identity.
- Our self concept is the lens through which we view the world.
- Our self-image is the reflection we receive back from those around us.
- We need to know ourselves in order to forget ourselves.
- "Know thyself" said Plato upon interviewing his first co-dependent students.
- "To thine own self be true" said Shakespeare shortly after his decision to write under someone else's name.

PRIORITY 2.

Emotional Fluency:

Feelings, Facts,
Fantasies And
Falsehoods

WINDOW PANES OF RECOVERY

Adult behaviors and actions are reflections from the windows of childhood. We can catch glimpses of how the child has been neglected or abused by looking through the windows to the past. Looking into the eyes, noticing feelings, we see glimpses of lost childhood.

Phobias and terror are windows to the frightened child.
Depression and isolation are windows to the hurting child.
Self hate and self hurt are windows to the shame-filled child.
Apathy and hostility are windows to the angry child.
Intimacy disorders are windows to the abandoned child.

The window shutters are our defenses that each one of us has been blessed with in order to survive. Over time, the shutters become weathered and worn and no

49

longer can keep the winds, rain and cold out or the fear, hurt, shame, abandonment and anger in. Good friends and therapists can help us release and open our shutters so we are able to see out and repair them so we can discover boundaries and choices.

Through feelings we experience the relationships and fantasies of our existence. Our feelings are the physical and cognitive responses to external reality and internal thought. Our feelings are affected by events outside of us as well as how we perceive these events. We emotionally respond to what others do or say and we respond to our own ideas, creativity, thoughts and imagination. *The word emotion is used to describe a particular feeling or a strong feeling — the word portrays how our feelings can create motion in our lives.*

Language Of Feelings

Dr. James Averill of the University of Massachusetts has challenged us to new ways of viewing and discussing feelings and emotions. He indicates there are approximately 2,000 words in the English language describing feelings and between 300 and 500 words for emotions. Maybe some of these are *basic* emotions, possibly not.

In 390 A.D. Nemesius' classification of emotions included desire, pleasure, fear, distress and anger. In 1984, Tomkins listed anger, interest, contempt, disgust, distress, fear, joy, shame and surprise as fundamental emotions. Throughout time philosophers and researchers of emotions continue the quest of identifying and defining emotions. The information and insights have amazing similarities over the past 2,000 years. We have chosen to discuss in detail later in this chapter the emotions, anger, fear, shame, guilt, sadness and joy. These emotions are outlined because of their significance in the recovery process and how commonly they are referred to, but we do not intend this to be a complete list of the emotions any of us experience, nor the definitive list of basic emotions.

Feelings are greatly affected by the language we use to describe them. The range of descriptive words varies from two — pain to pleasure — up to six or eight and on to 2,000 words. What gets included is somewhat at the whim of the theorists, their background and the times that the list is being made.

In the addiction field it is common to talk about mad, sad, glad, scared, shame, guilt and sometimes lonely. Often missing on the list is disgust which may be akin to revulsion, disdain, aversion or "yucky." Maybe people with addictions and addiction counselors leave it off because of their yucky feelings about *aversion therapy* which is sometimes used in addiction therapy. Each feeling provides a gift or benefit. The benefit of these feelings of disgust or revulsion is the gift of choice, of the ability to make a choice and to steer clear. If something is revolting we are likely to avoid contact which may be positive self-protection.

COMBINATION WINDOWS

Some feelings are not feelings, but combinations of feelings. Jealousy is primarily fear with a dash of pain and anger and maybe a smidgeon of disgust. Envy seems to have few redeeming features, seldom making the list of the basic eight, but we believe it is what consumptive America thrives on. Most advertising is based on some people having something and others not, so they better get it to be happy. In some ways it keeps our economy on the move, but we don't envy people with a lot of envy who have to keep over-consuming to feel OK. Anxiety is usually unattached fear. When anxiety attaches, it becomes worry. If it over-attaches, it can become an obsession or in the extremes a phobia. Co-dependence usually evokes a feeling of being empty. We are not empty, we just feel it. There is a big difference. Emptiness is probably why we have so many eating disorders, relationship problems and intensity addictions. We are always trying to fill or distract ourselves from the emptiness with something that doesn't stick and doesn't fulfill.

TOXIC LABELING

The language of feelings can help create a feeling of balance or may create problems with feelings. It is helpful to describe shame. It helps us embrace and deal with it. We are not really interested in labeling feelings — good or bad — positive or negative — even though there is a definite plus and a minus aspect to feelings. Some feelings feel better than others.

Labeling shame or rage as toxic is somewhat destructive since experiencing or having them is a common human experience and believing they are toxic makes us feel as though we were poisoned or are poison. The feeling itself is not toxic nor destructive; it is an internalization of the feeling that becomes a problem. Shame is over-rated and over-focused on anyway. It is similar to disgust, except it's inward. Fear is a more debilitating issue.

Survival is a much greater need than self-esteem. Fear is about survival; shame is about self-esteem.

FEELINGS IN THERAPY

Many styles of therapy encourage discharge, the release of our emotion. Therapists provide a setting for catharsis, use serum therapy, touch, massage, sculpting, psychodrama, imagery or some other method to engage us to release feelings. This is effective at providing temporary relief and can even alter brain chemistry at the time to provide a high. When we express a feeling that is not attached to the reality of the cause of the feeling, there is less real healing. The catharsis and emotional discharge can even become an addictive process, since the release of emotional tension also releases endorphins, adrenaline or dopamine and gives us a chemical high.

Catharsis — intense emotional expression — is an important part of recovery but catharsis for the sake of catharsis is empty work. We need to express our feelings as big as they *are*, not as big as we want them to be. Most of our therapy is learning to express feelings in a mild way, to appropriate people in safe settings, as they come up. Catharsis work is a very small percentage of the feeling work of recovery. Catharsis gives us a look at our emotional intensity and the depth of the feeling, but emotional health is to embrace rather than give back or be rid of the feeling. Some therapists try to help people get rid of feelings rather than express and embrace feelings.

All abuse includes a level of emotional abuse, since we are not able to or allowed to process our feelings about it. Trauma is an event outside the range of normal human experience that we cannot process and express the feelings about. PTSD is caused by re-experiencing the emotional response to the trauma in different settings. The numbing or flooding of feelings, acting out the feelings, having our lives controlled by the fear of our feelings or the avoidance of what may bring the feelings to light — all prevent us from choice and balanced living.

FEELINGS AND FAMILY

Emotional problems tend to be intergenerational because feelings are easily projected. Impatience, rage, fear, anxiety, sadness, shame and guilt can all be passed down through the generations. The feeling of shame can produce a blame system and the blame then creates the second generation of shame. The fearful person who worries is successful when the people around the chronic worrier are worried more than the worrier! We can easily project fears, anger and guilt by what we model, say, do or repress.

Emotional enmeshment can occur as a result of repression. We become tangled up and stuck in another person's emotional reality. Our feelings are no longer responses to our life's journey but to the feelings and problems of another's journey. Projection does this, but we can either react to or avoid the projection. The more serious enmeshment comes from denial. A person who is angry but pretends everything is OK is incongruent. For example, children feel and react to parent's anger but are confused by the overt cheerfulness. The child will exhibit the symptoms of the unexpressed adult anger with temper tantrums, whining, irritability, hyperactivity or boredom.

We can get enmeshed in a hostile attitude toward life, a fearful posture toward intimacy or the world, internalized shame and self-criticism. We can even get set up to act out a cheerful Pollyanna attitude — "There can't be anything wrong" — which can set us up for very large crashes. Problems and pathology never get resolved or dealt with in this type of denial system.

Enmeshment can involve depression, paranoia, phobias or rage. All of these are intergenerational issues fueled by denial and suppression. Parents must model healthy openness and appropriate expression of feelings, since children enmesh in the denied emotions and act them out. The denied feelings can take on many faces: withdrawal, boredom, physical illness, anxiety and all forms of addictive behavior.

Unhealthy dependencies on substances, places, events or people are primarily about feelings. The dependency changes how we feel or distances us from our feelings. Anything that relieves unwanted feelings can become addictive — love, sex, food, drugs, sports, crime, gambling, shopping, work, intensity, TV and so on.

EMOTIONAL FLUENCY

We are emotionally fluent when our feelings, words and behaviors all match. This is emotional congruence, a state of dynamic balance. Learning emotional fluency is important for addiction and co-dependence recovery. We need the congruent modeling that we missed in childhood.

Emotional fluency requires us to have our feelings noticed, labeled and affirmed. To have our feelings noticed, be given labels for them, hear that the feeling is OK and learn appropriate expression doesn't sound that difficult, but it's something few of us received. How many of us in childhood, when sitting on our steps crying after a friend hurt us deeply, had a primary caregiver come up and say, "I know how badly you must be hurting about this and I think it's important for you to cry it out. If you want me to be with you or hold you, I will. If you need to be alone for a while, I'll be available." It seems simple yet it happens so rarely.

Feelings are varied, complex and overlapping. We seldom experience one feeling at a time. Many emotional experiences involve a range of feelings with varying intensity — jealousy, impatience, grieving, intimacy and love — to name a few. It may be possible to sort out and express or process each feeling, but balance is important. It is easy for us to over-process or over-explain our feelings, thus losing the spontaneity and gifts that come from them.

Our feelings can get us in trouble, especially if we don't learn to suppress them in certain settings. Often we self-destruct through the over-expression of feelings, not being able to stuff them, getting too overtly angry at employers or co-workers or getting so scared we can't function. *Balance of expression and suppression of emotions gives us emotional fluency.*

Some of us are so out of touch with feelings that we need others to notice them; often others can tell what we feel long before we can. The old saying "No one can tell me how I feel" is not true. Many people can speak and act quite angrily and yet be unaware that any anger is present. It is also not true that "No one can make me feel any particular feeling." Our feelings come as direct and usually predictable responses to other people's behavior. People *can* hurt us or make us angry. We don't always get to choose our emotional reactions, but we can choose how to frame and express the reactions.

It is also a fallacy that we create our own reality and our feelings are a product of this creation. We can influence our feelings by our perceptions and references; we can also create postures and pastimes that generate different feelings than our current ones. "I am what I believe and believe what I am" has limitations. Reality, especially the reality of our childhood, has a profound effect on our emotions. *Nothing changes until it becomes real.* This applies to the feelings and what creates the feelings. We need to attach the feeling to the reality, and both must be made real to create a lasting and postive change.

Children of low-functioning families tend to be reactive and to polarize responses — remember our co-dependent polar bear. This is also a symptom of PTSD. In response to trauma we can experience emotional flooding, being overwhelmed with feelings that roll over us in waves; or we can experience emotional numbing, a disconnection from any feeling of reality, which produces a flat affect. We can remain in either of these postures or swing back and forth between the two. Our anger can be constantly present and exhibit itself as impatience, irritability and frustration or it can remain hidden as passivity, withdrawal or boredom. We may blow up or we may go away — either extreme is dysfunctional. We miss the middle ground of recovery: daring to fight, to express our anger in appropriate ways toward the source of our anger or to notice it and move on. Our fear sets up destructive risk-taking or overly cautious avoidance. The need for balance and middle ground is essential in our recovery. Many of us have been stuck in either a survival or a defensive reaction, and in recovery we often go to the extremes. Our guilt becomes excess scruples. Overconcern for others swings to "I don't give a damn about anyone but me." That doggone polar bear keeps lumbering back!

THE GIFTS OF FEELINGS

We have many feelings and each has various hues and shades. We generally need to develop a healthy identification and expressive relationship with such feelings as fear, anger, shame, guilt, sadness, joy and hope. Each of these feelings, when embraced and expressed, offers gifts.

Fear

The gift of fear is wisdom and freedom. Embracing our fear gives us the opportunity to notice what is life destructive and what is life enhancing. Both involve risk. Fear gives us the pause to reflect and make judicious evaluations. The opportunity to use our wisdom gained from listening to our fear gives us choice. Freedom is the ability to choose. Repressed or denied fear controls our life just as constant fearfulness and phobias do.

Shame is often called the master emotion, yet fear is its equal. Repressed fear can create phobias, anxieties, death obsessions, hypervigilance, terror, anxieties, worries and obsessions, with the frequently attendant rituals. *Two primary issues of co-dependency are the fear of abandonment and the fear of intimacy.* The dysfunctional, polarized approach to fear involves overreacting to fear, coming into it and avoiding any risk. We become like wallflowers, standing along the wall watching the dance of life but afraid to join in because we may be rejected, laughed at or not do it well enough. If we do get rejected we end up back where we started — nothing lost, but the fear of rejection prevents many of us from risking and putting ourselves out there again. This fear of being ridiculed, laughed at or not performing well can control our lives.

The other approach is the daredevil who says, "I"m not afraid of anything." We have fear but we disconnect from it and lose touch. We can't ignore it but we defy and challenge it, taking life-destructive risks: "I'll jump the Grand Canyon on a bicycle with a parachute." Does this prove courage or a lack of common sense? The bully keeps hiding the fear behind aggression. Our fear can be the pause to reflect, and this gives us an opportunity for choice. Listening to the fear tells us what is life destructive or life enhancing. This is the source of our wisdom.

Pain and terror are windows to the frightened child within. Fear creates a need to control. Scary families produce controlling people. Phobias are more about control than fear. We fear having a panic attack during a time when we do not have control: while flying, on ski lifts, during storms, on freeways, in crowds and so on. Usually they are unattached childhood terror and fear that attaches to the object of the phobia. Phobias are enmeshed anxieties. Some may be a result of a particular trauma, such as a near drowning that creates a fear of water. Most phobias do not connect so directly with a particular incident, but are still the result of trauma.

Fear can be the barometer of our spirituality. When we trust the process and hold a sense of meaning and higher power we will still have fears, but the belief in and feeling of safety will flow from our spirituality. Blended thoughts and fears become worry, the source of most of our stress and stress-related illnesses. Unfocused worries become anxieties, free-floating and often attaching like magnets to whatever we pass by. Worry that is overly focused on a particular issue or setting can become a phobia.

Worry can be a fearful style of facing the world that we learn in our family of origin. Nothing worries kids more than worried parents. We know a family where the father is a real worrier. Fred frets about the safety of every move his wife and young son make. Before they were married, Sarah used to try new and exciting things, take reasonable risks and was a superb snow and water skier. In response to Fred she seems to be overly cautious and timid with herself and their son, which greatly limits both their activities. Sarah says she misses going water skiing but wouldn't *dare* do it, since Fred would be worried and get upset. The "dare" is not about the activity but about Fred's reaction. The issue appears to be Fred's worry. But underlying his worry is Sarah's worry or fear of abandonment, which prevents her from participating in the lifestyle she used to enjoy and results in her being overprotective with her son.

When we fight against worry or fear, we empower it. We must give in to it, embrace it and find its core message — often childhood fear, trauma, neglect or double binds. Moving through the worry to its logical conclusion can be helpful. The best antidotes for fear and worry are play, relaxation, physical activities and affirmations. Our fear can be a spiritual problem — we don't trust the process of life or the comfort of a Higher Power. We try to control too much and the controlling sets up an increasing fear of being out of control.

Abused children learn fear in order to survive. Fear based in survival becomes a deeper issue than shame. Children who are abused or abandoned, threatened or molested fear for their lives. Since survival is a more basic need than positive self-image, the fear controls our lives and recovery even more than shame.

Fear that becomes anxiety affects our ability to risk, to move forward and commit. It creates hesitation and lessens risk and spontaneity. We become defensive and obsessed with security, rituals, money issues or keeping things organized. We lose our objectivity and insight and can no longer focus on tasks and topics before us. We don't notice or heed warnings and miss important aspects of our daily lives. This creates agitation and hypervigilance.

In recovery we don't get rid of our fear, but we embrace and learn to share it. We can reduce our anxieties and worries by looking at the real causes of our fear, especially childhood issues we haven't faced or finished. Unresolved childhood fear sets us up to recreate anxieties and fear in our lives so we can attach the repressed feeling to current situations and explain the feeling without having to look back. This applies to all feelings.

Fear is a very difficult feeling to express and is the most commonly denied feeling. The denial sets up more acting out and escalation. Embracing the demon lessens its power to control. Sharing the fear can make it manageable. Knowing other people have the same fears helps cut it down to manageable proportions. *Obsessions are the mental aerobics of a fearful mind.*

As we embrace fear, our wisdom and our courage to risk increases. We hope the affirmations and suggestions at the end of this chapter will help you find wisdom, freedom and courage.

Anger

The gift of anger is strength and protectiveness. Our anger is a source of energy and strength, which enables us to create change. It helps us defend and guard what we value and can be the process by which we resolve relationship differences. Many of us were not allowed to be directly angry as children, so our anger came out as temper tantrums or withdrawal. Victims of child abuse have an especially difficult time with anger because it makes them feel like the offender. They often believe violence and anger are the same thing.

Anger is a difficult feeling to express, especially for co-dependents. People don't like anger; it's both unpleasant and unpopular. Many of us would rather whine, complain, criticize, be sarcastic or pseudo-nice. Few of us deal directly with what we don't like.

Our own anger can kill us. It could well be one of the leading causes of death: Many people become chemically dependent in an attempt to medicate their anger. Many angry people commit violent and self-destructive acts; much suicide is the result of anger. Many stress-related diseases are about anger. A study of Type A (hostile, aggressive) personalities found that many of them were at a severe health risk, and many were dying, but it wasn't a result of being Type A. The risk was correlated with only one trait of Type A: the anger level, regardless of whether the anger was expressed or repressed. It seems that either way it was the same anger being recycled.

Anger is associated with high blood pressure, arthritis, cancer and brain tumors. There is no limit to the damage our anger can do when it is repressed. There is hardly any limit to what can happen when it is expressed inappropriately.

Virginia Satir once said, "Relationships often don't make it because people can't accept differences in others." We suggest in our intimacy workshops that it is actually our inability to learn to *fight* about the differences. The opposite of love is not hate, nor resentment, nor hostility nor anger. *The opposite of love is apathy.* Apathy occurs when the anger has festered and killed the caring.

Anger can be a source of strength. People who have made changes in the world have been angry people: Martin Luther King, Indira Gandhi, Winnie and Nelson Mandela, Gloria Steinem, Ralph Nader. They have turned their rage into outrage about something in the system that hurts people or that doesn't work. Ralph Nader changed the lives of 200 million people with his anger, and he isn't 200 million times angrier than anyone else. We can turn rage to outrage. Our anger can give us the strength to make a change.

Adolescent rage is the biggest learning disability in our culture. Adolescent rage often becomes adolescent boredom, apathy, not noticing, not caring. Angry children will not learn well, fare well, live well and certainly will not act well.

Anger can be a torch of outrage; it can illuminate the past, shed light on reality, burn the terror of our childhood and light the path of recovery. It can become a winnowing flame guiding us to the window of our becoming-self. Anger can be maintained as a bonfire of strength and passion. Our rage can become outrage at abuse and injustice. When we repress the anger, we become resentful, hostile, apathetic and passive-aggressive.

It's not easy to live with angry people, but for many of us it is a reality we have to deal with. Here are some suggestions for how to behave when you are around angry people, and how to understand the anger:

- Verbally commit that you'd like to help them through it.
- Notice it out loud, around them or with them.
- Problem-solve with patience.
- Don't blame or ridicule.

- Be open-minded.
- Use active listening and be empathetic.
- Remember: most anger, even directed at us, is not about us.
- The more we get defensive, the more the anger will escalate.
- When we view someone else's anger as a win-lose situation, we create a power struggle.
- Let go of who's right or who's wrong. This attitude can escalate the problem.
- People argue, not necessarily because one is right and the other is wrong, but because they are different from each other and see things in different lights. Remember, difference is not bad.
- When angry, it is very important to work through the anger.
- Learning to take time-outs can help.
- Much of our anger is about the unchangeable past.
- Writing it out, expressing it, sometimes will enable us to write it off, to leave it. It is not that we won't ever be angry at it again, or that we can't use the anger, but when we keep repressing it and recycling it, the anger has us, we don't have it.
- Anger can prevent intimacy.
- The appropriate sharing of anger can build trust and intimacy.
- It may be a good idea to leave, or to take a break.
- If it feels safe enough to share how you feel around the person's anger, and you think the person might listen, you can help him or her know the impact of the anger on you. The angry person may be more tempted to monitor the anger in the future.
- Even angry people, unless they have severe personality disorders, don't like to think that other people are uncomfortable with them or scared of them.
- When you can't validate the behavior around anger, you can usually validate the feeling or what it comes from.
- If someone we are with or close to is angry about us, we can look at the possibility of altering our behavior around neatness, niceness, cheerfulness, openness or noticing the other person more often. Change is not co-dependency.
- Men and women often try to deal with anger very differently. Women are taught to hurt rather than to be angry. Men usually end up going away. It seems that men would rather talk it out after they are done being angry. Women like to talk it out until they are done being angry.
- We can get easily enmeshed in other people's anger. We carry baggage that doesn't belong to us.

- Enmeshed anger is anger that time doesn't heal:
    We feel unappreciated and unloved.
    We have chronic ailments. We constantly bicker and are impatient.
    We want to get back at everybody. We feel incomplete and down
      on ourselves.
    We feel sexually disinterested.
    We exhibit compulsive behavior, especially eating.
- Most of our anger at our children is diffused or deflected anger
  from our marriage or our childhood. Of course, when our children
  become adolescents, they do become like alcoholics: always present-
  ing us with what we can't control, they give us a great target for
  our anger.
- Much of our anger at others comes from our anger at self. The
  biggest fight most of us have seems to be with ourselves; but the
  real fight that we need to deal with is the one with our parents or
  the fight our parents had with each other. This fight is one that we
  often get enmeshed in and carry internally.
- Recognize that many of us act out our self-anger through compulsion, depression, the self-provoking things we say and do, our self-
  destructive tendencies.
- When we are angry, we need to treat ourselves with gentleness and:
    self-forgive
    make healthy decisions about ourselves
    self-affirm
    learn to be assertive without being aggressive
    do things to make us feel better about ourselves.
- We need to work on changing and accepting self, much more than
  we need to work on changing or accepting others.
- Anger kills our humor and our prayer, two of the most important
  facets of recovery.

Sadness

The gift of sadness is healing and empathy. Sadness is the healing feeling.
It is part of vulnerability, which leads to strength and intimacy. Our
ability to experience sadness enables us to heal from loss and hurt and
to be protective, the guardians of what we cherish. When we do not
affirm sadness, we may internalize it and allow it to dwell within. Then
we feel small and wounded, depressed, victimized, lonely and isolated.
Sadness experienced is a path to intimacy with others and an expression
and affirmation of our dependency needs.

Men have been taught not to feel hurt and not to express hurt; women have been given permission to feel and express sadness but are often called overly emotional when they do. Many of us suffer from emotional constipation and cannot seem to find our tears. This may be the result of rules or messages about crying, or perhaps from trying too hard. Tears are the most common physical reaction to sadness, but certainly not the only way to express our hurt. A simple, congruent statement about hurting can be as profound and healing as tears.

Sadness is the washing of our souls. Our tears are the rain for the dryness of our spirit, a cleansing healing solution for past hurts and antiseptic to prevent the festering of our wounds. Our pain can bring peace, it can wash away loss. Our tears promote growth, they moisten the soil of us for new intimacies to grow. Feeling sorry for ourselves can move to feeling sorrow for self. Our loneliness can become the sense of aloneness that prompts us to reach out, to risk. It becomes a felt need for connection. When embraced it teaches us our need for closeness and for others. It teaches us to be with ourselves and enjoy a true life of integration.

Much of our sadness comes from loss. In order to deal with the losses in our lives we must go through the grieving process. *When repressed, sadness is isolation, despair, hopelessness and self-protection. When embraced, sadness provides healing and leads to intimacy and connectedness.*

Grieving

Sadness is the key stage of the grief process that precedes acceptance and serenity. The grief process involves many states, emotional and physical. Grieving is not hanging on to loss but the process of connecting to the new. All of life involves change and all change involves loss. We grieve the losses in an ongoing process of emotional sharing and physical sensitivity growing toward deeper connections. To grieve is to be sensitive and empathetic to the becoming adult, nurturing and healing to the hurting child. *Grieving fuels the forward movement of our lives.* We are grown from our grieving in the field of our emotional health.

The grieving processes include:

- *Denial* — Denial is the anesthetic that enables the shock to be absorbed gradually. Denial is necessary; but when it becomes unyielding and lasts too long, we cannot move on and the healing doesn't happen. Denial can keep us attached to the loss and prevent new connections.
- *Fear* — Most loss creates fear, fear of what we will do after the loss; fear that we caused the loss or will be blamed; fear we will never

heal, understand, reconnect or be happy again, fear of more loss The fear can control and feel too big, immobilizing us.

- *Bargaining* — The process of moving through the denial may look like bargaining. We say things like, "Maybe it wasn't that bad" or "If you (God) bring it back I'll enter the convent" or "They'll be better off, I didn't care that much anyway," and so on. Bargaining helps to accept the loss in stages.
- *Anger* — A common and early response to loss is anger at the person or object or whatever is gone. It may be anger at God for the loss, at ourselves for not preventing the loss, or anger at having to go through it all. Anger can give us strength to get through it.
- *Guilt* — We feel responsible for the loss and begin to blame ourselves. We think we didn't cherish, love or protect enough; we should have reacted sooner; we should have told the person we loved them, not fought with them, given them more time, shown more care, worked harder — all of the "shoulds" ride with us through this stage. We can learn to cherish what we have from the guilt of our losses.
- *Shame* — We feel bad about who we are and believe we deserved the loss, or that the loss came as punishment because we deserved to be punished. The loss is proof we are not good enough and it reminds us of the abandonment, the unavailability of caregivers who set up the original internalized shame. This shame flows out of its hiding place during grieving and can be healed in the sunlight of its new exposure.
- *Depression* — A stage of low energy, loss of appetite, sleep problems, loss of interest and flat affect. Some of this slowdown is allowing the healing, some of it is the crash that comes with too much intensity and pain.
- *Emptiness* — We feel empty, lost and alone. There is a vacuum, a hollow place inside and a sense that no one cares. The emptiness can move us toward healthy fulfillment.
- *Sadness* — The pain and tears often come in this stage. The healing is setting in. We may feel overwhelmed and think it won't ever go away, but it does, at least for a while.
- *Acceptance* — A sense of, "This is what I have been given and I will do with what I have left." The loss is real, to be felt and accepted.
- *Forgiveness* — This is the forgiveness of self for the time we beat ourselves up for what we have or haven't done; forgiveness of the person gone or those who were involved in the loss and forgiveness of God.

- *Reconnections* — The filling of the empty space. New intimacy and care, including a renewal of interest in life and activities. A willingness to risk new loss.
- *Serenity* — A feeling of peace and joy, with the knowledge that we can experience loss and healing and find deeper sense of self in our new living.

The most important aspect of grieving is the awareness that we are in the stages of grief — we tend to discount our reaction to loss and feel sick and stuck. Someone close to us who says, "Oh, that energy loss is a part of grieving the loss of your marriage," for example, can give us the permission to come through it.

Every major change in life requires grieving — even when the changes are healthy. Few of us were given permission or support to grieve losses — of friendships, places we've lived, completing phases of our lives.

When Marvel was in grade four her best friend of nine years moved away to another province and she felt terrible. The message she received was, "You are making a mountain out of a molehill. You'll still get to see Michele every summer, besides there are lots of other girls and you will have another best friend before you know it." Although she has always had lots of friends, it was 25 years before Marvel felt as though she had a best friend again.

Even when a person close to us dies, many of the messages of our cultural heritage say we are supposed to mourn for a few days, go back to work, keep busy so we don't think about it (or feel it) and get on with our lives. When we don't grieve or cry we are told we are handling it so well. Many of us medicate our grief and remain stuck in it.

Reframing depression or rage into grieving can help us heal. The processes of grief do not flow in a particular order or one at a time. Going through one does not mean we are finished with it. Some losses we don't finish with ever, but we just learn to continue to grieve as needed and move on with our lives. As Pat Conroy once wrote, "There is no repairing a damaged childhood, the best we can hope for is to make the sucker float!" We can grieve loss and float, but the damage leaves us handicapped and the grieving may return. Of course it is not what we have that matters, but it is what we do with what we have that makes the difference. The core of all therapy is grief work, dealing with loss.

Guilt

The gift of guilt is the ability to see we have an impact on others. Guilt is different than shame. It can be the denial of our uniqueness. Guilt is the veneer of co-dependency. When we don't have our rights and uniqueness, we tend to try to be what other people want us to be. We try to find out what they need, who they are, and respond and react to them.

We now recognize there is a part of the guilt that is healthy: a sense of right and wrong; a sense of knowing that some things are OK and other things are not; a sense that what we do really does have an impact on others; the ability to go through the confession process, to do restitution, to be forgiven, is a very important process that many of us need. When guilt is excess, when guilt gets repressed, it becomes "scrupulousness" overreaction, anxiety. When guilt is healthy, it's part of our conscience formation — the ability to know that what we do has an impact on others.

Guilt can be used to control. Many clients we've worked with say Mom and Dad never fight, never argue, never yell at each other in front of the kids, although even parents who do not yell at each other in front of the kids will yell at the kids in front of each other. Saint Mom and Dad give a very clear message that we are wonderful, and we love you so much that you would never do anything to hurt us. What would hurt us is if you don't become exactly what we want you to be, like us, like what we couldn't be. This is not love. It is guilt and enmeshment. It is spiritual abuse. Love is when you help someone become the best person he or she can be.

Shame is often described as being about who we are, whereas guilt is more about what we do. Shame says, "I *am* a mistake"; guilt says, "I *made* a mistake." We believe that guilt and shame are not so separated. The integration of our guilt and shame is a very important part of recovery. We need *both* feelings.

The guilt is about what we do, the doing. Shame is about who we are, the being. What we do comes out of who we are. Who we are and how we see ourselves is largely based on what we do. The doing and the being are interwoven, just as shame and guilt are. Our capacity for guilt arises out of our capacity for shame. If I feel bad about myself and never deal with that, eventually I will be doing bad things out of that bad feeling of myself. If I continue to do bad things with my life, eventually I will feel worse about myself. Excess guilt eventually becomes shame. We can only feel bad about what we do for so long, and then we feel bad about who we are.

When we embrace healthy guilt, it becomes our conscience, the voice of others within us; it gives us the message of our impact on what is outside of us. Our guilt is an extension of our capacity for shame. It is the message that our doing is separate, but interwoven with our being and identity. Guilt is the ability to see the consequences of our behavior.

Shame

The gift of shame is guardianship, and a sense of shame is the bedrock of our honor. Since our feelings are healthy and we don't get what we don't need, shame, too, must be healthy and we must need a sense of it. Shame can be many things: It can be the felt sense of our capacity for harm — to self, others and our environment. It can be an innate sense of destructiveness — our fall from grace, original sin; an awareness of limitations, incompleteness; a heightened sense of self-awareness and introspection. When it is repressed, it affects our physical relationship with ourselves, our sexuality, our belief systems; it creates dependency issues, a need for control, manipulation and perfectionism. The problem is not the shame but our denial of it. When denied, shame becomes internalized as self-hate. In therapy we access the shame.

Shame becomes a path to recovery. It is a basic quality of our humanness. In Genesis we didn't fall from the Garden, but we were given the keys to the Garden. We were made the guardians of the Garden. Without a sense of shame, without the felt sense of our own capacity for destructiveness, we are not very good guardians. Embracing and sharing our shame is our most valuable path to intimacy. There is no intimacy without vulnerability. We are never more vulnerable than when we are telling what happened to us that made us feel bad about ourselves, what we've done that made us feel bad about ourselves or what we haven't done. In sharing the shame we find our truest vulnerability, which enables us to be loved and love more deeply. A sense of shame gives us humility, honor and pride.

The Latin word *pudor* can mean shame or honor, depending on how it is used. Recovery is in the balance between our flaws and our perfection — original sin and original love, shame and honor. The curtain that we draw around ourselves, the masks that we wear, the hiding of ourselves for fear that people will not love us, accept us or care, is not just the shame, but it is a shame shrouded in denial that sets up the false self, the need for immediate gratification which empowers addiction. Shame itself does not damage, but it represses the ability to share, to feel and express. Sharing our shame is the ultimate sharing.

The process by which we learn to embrace our shame, so our shame does not embrace us, is forgiveness. *We have no real freedom until we have choice; no choice until forgiveness takes place, no forgiveness until we are no longer in denial.* When we try to get rid of our shame, we become like the offender, projecting and getting rid of feelings — usually at other people. When we embrace our shame, we become real and find the messages that shame can give us. Before our consciousness of self, our awareness

of our awareness, we were a part of the natural order. We were in the
Garden. But with the knowledge of good and evil — with the self-
awareness that we could manipulate and create, as well as destroy — we
now had the potential to either destroy or protect the Garden. Our
sense of dominion over all things of earth is not permission to use as we
please. It is not an ownership; it is a stewardship. The sense of shame
came with the self-consciousness. This new awareness is the guideline.
When we lose the sense of shame, we will practice arrogance and abuse
of the Garden, rather than humility and protection of the Garden. Our
self-awareness moved us from a passive role in creation to a role that
enabled us to grow, envision, create and manipulate to our liking.

This gift of self-awareness made us co-creators. We had potential for
our destruction, but we also had the pride, the gift and the power of a
celebration of life and the Garden. Without the balance of shame, the
ability to embrace our own vulnerability, we practice a fear and disdain
of vulnerability in and around us and we have become the destructors
of the Garden. This is the biggest problem facing our culture. Unless
we do something about the destruction of life and habitat for life, we all
need to be ashamed of ourselves.

Our internalized shame is self-hate. Expressed shame is the healing
balance, pride and sanity. We need to refuse to hide shameful feelings
and keep secret the shameful events, both the ones we have done or
those that have been done to us. When we finally acknowledge our
flawed, vulnerable self, we will recover the purity, honesty and sanctity
of our humanity that lies in our childhood.

Shame facilitates spirituality. It is an awareness and a feeling of our
flaws, of our incompleteness, that creates a craving. We have a feeling
of loss, of missing something. When we deny and repress the shame, the
craving becomes a craving for a "fix," for instant gratification, for addiction. When we embrace the incompleteness, the imperfection, the craving becomes a craving for a completeness through a Higher Power,
through meaningfulness in life, through our spirituality.

We must recognize what the triggers are for us to feel shame. We
must learn to label shame and to be gentle with it, even though the
shame requests that we be hard on ourselves. If we are gentle even
about the times we are hard on ourselves, the feeling of shame dissipates
and the strength of the shame lessens its hold on us.

When we can acknowledge our dependency needs we can release the
internalized shame that had such a firm grip on our identity. Humor also
shortcuts internalized shame. If we can laugh at ourselves easily and
well, we will never be controlled by the shame. Some of our favorite
people have a great deal of shame; sometimes it hits them in waves. Their

ability to talk about it, to label it and to laugh with it and at it, seems to keep them in balance. They use the shame to keep them in balance.

Cultural groups frequently experience a collective shame. For example, this is what happened in Germany after World War II. When a culture acts shamelessly, when a culture acts aggressively, when it doesn't take care of its vulnerable members, everyone feels it. Sometimes this cultural shame gets acted out and sometimes it gets hidden. Our country's cultural shame is reflected in our aggression and in the fact that much of our armaments are hidden and stored in underground weapon silos.

Children who have too much shame projected on them, too much abuse, neglect or abandonment, become shame-based. Most of their behavior comes from their bad feelings of self, especially behaviors that feel good and give them a temporary relief. The behavior is a harmful consequence and they will get caught, punished, hurt or damaged. Shoplifting, sexual acting out and drug use tend to make sense to a shame-based child. They feel good. In the very harmful consequences of these behaviors there is a reason to continue using and abusing. The consequence reaffirms their view of themselves: They *deserve* the harmful consequence. So many of our adolescents have such deep shame, they are acting out in our culture with crime, drugs, suicide, pregnancy, withdrawal, underachieving and even overachieving. We need to share our shame and reduce whatever produces the shame. We don't get rid of it and can't really give it back, but we can embrace it — even when it comes from the projection of someone else's shame. The embracing and sharing of all feelings provides the healing.

Shame is our guardianship. It is the felt message of our capacity to harm. It is our path to seeing the consequences of our doing. It is the bedrock of our honor, the access to our vulnerability and the doorway to spirituality. *Shame is the recognition of our flaws and imperfections and it gives us the opportunity for completeness as children of our Creator.*

Sometimes we mess up our lives to explain our sense of shame — "Oh, that's why I feel bad about me — I just wrecked another relationship." This prevents us from finding the true source of our damaged self-worth, which goes deeper than day-to-day mistakes.

Abused people feel shame. They tend to be hard on themselves and others, creating more shame. Out of shame comes blame, rage and hiding, which produces and spreads more shame. Shame empowers addiction because it involves a denial of our dependency problems — chemical dependency, sexual dependency, food dependency, co-dependence. In recovery we learn to depend on others and that loosens the grip of internalized shame.

Joy

The gift of joy is nurturing, health and healing. Joy is the emotional result of the recovery journey and the felt sense of our deepest friendships. Joy comes from identity, intimacy, prayer, noticing and gratitude. It is the child spark of noticing with awe, the miracle of creation. Joy comes when we are hearing life in concert and moving with the harmony of the universe.

Many of us are afraid of joy, for we fear the crash that must come. We think there is a cosmic balance scale of pain and joy — if we hit an eight in joy we look for a nine or ten of pain. Many of us were raised in families where joy wasn't allowed, or a time limit was placed on it. When children are joyful they make noises of glee, but so often we are told not to make joyful noise, to be quiet.

Discovering joy is watching a child, a wedding, a starlit wilderness evening, listening to an honest voice, seeing life created and creating, listening to the recovery miracles at a meeting, watching a newly baked banana cream pie emerge from the mouth of an oven, stopping long enough to taste, touch, hear, smell or see — all that brings joy.

Joy, the life spark of the human spirit is a healing presence. Laughter is the body's natural curative.

Hope

The gift of hope is a positive push toward a belief in betterment, a brighter future. Hope is a feeling we seem to have lost over the centuries. Thomas Aquinas included it in his list of basic feelings in the thirteenth century, but today it is omitted from most of the basic emotions lists. Of course times dictate what feelings may be basic, and in the thirteenth century hope must have been a big need. Probably Thomas Aquinas had eternal hope in mind, the hope of afterlife. Maybe it was a reaction to the plagues, when all that many people had was hope. We see in the present a need for hope and a more spiritual orientation for our species — *hope* for our planet.

RULES ON FEELINGS

In a weekly group Geoff repeatedly told stories that brought tears to the entire group, including the therapist, yet Geoff never shed a tear. Finally the therapist asked if there was a rule about crying in his family. Geoff replied, "I don't know, no one ever cried." When asked if he knew where his father was, he replied, "In his office in Los Angeles." With the support of the group, Geoff called his father and asked for permission to cry. His father, taken aback, first asked him if he needed money or an attorney. Eventually he said, "If you need to cry, go and do it." Geoff hung up the phone and sobbed. He was finally beginning to heal the wounds of childhood. Many of us need permission to break the rules that prevent our sharing and healing. Often we can't get it as directly as Geoff did. The permission must come from within when we can't find it from others.

Emotional fluency, learning the language of feelings, often involves breaking rules and going through periods of embarrassment and discomfort. Our sadness is difficult because it brings us back to feeling weak, to vulnerability. In our vulnerability we were hurt and used; the feelings that remind us of vulnerability are difficult to embrace and share. Rules about feelings are both overt and covert. In Marvel's family the overt rule was: You can cry about hurts. The covert rule was: You can cry, but not too much; and once you have cried, it is over, be done with it, move on and get on with your life. The overt rule in Terry's family was: Men can cry. The covert rule was: Men can only cry for what happens to other people. Crying for oneself was not allowed. This rule prevented the healing of the tears. The ability to complete the grieving process was lost. We need to discover the rules and what we learned about feelings, and learn the language of feelings to be emotionally fluent.

SUGGESTIONS • AFFIRMATIONS • THOUGHTS

SUGGESTIONS

Feelings List

Following is a list of words describing feelings. We have included them for you to learn to notice, label and affirm in yourself and others.

loved	unimportant	ineffectual	antagonistic
alive	regretful	helpless	vengeful
wanted	bashful	resigned	mad
lustful	self-conscious	apathetic	indignant
worthy	puzzled	ashamed	hated
respected	edgy	shy	unloved
pitied	upset	uncomfortable	friendly
empathetic	reluctant	baffled	regarded
awed	timid	benevolent	confused
elated	mixed up	nervous	wide awake
enthusiastic	provoked	tempted	at ease

zealous	liked	relaxed	tense
courageous	esteemed	worried	comfortable
enchanted	affectionate	perplexed	contented
infatuated	excited	troubled	daring
tender	patient	disdainful	smart
vibrant	alarmed	strong	shocked
independent	good	contemptuous	panicky
capable	jolly	annoyed	trapped
happy	silly	kind	horrified
great	disgusted	inspired	afraid
proud	amused	resentful	scared
gratitifed	secure	bitter	terrified
admired	popular	detested	consoled
sympathetic	peaceful	fed up	infuriated
important	frustrated	appealing	angry
concerned	determined	dumb	cynical
appreciated	stubborn	sad	joyful
threatened	pleased	depressed	hurt
delighted	interested	sick	lonely
eager	relieved	disconsolate	quiet
optimistic	glad	dissatisfied	prayerful
miserable	venturous	fatigued	exhausted
hopeful	worn out	peaceful	impotent
brave	intelligent	useless	abandoned
brilliant	wise	weak	degraded
unpopular	suspicious	hopeless	humiliated
listless	envious	forlorn	alienated
moody	repulsed	rejected	virtuous
lethargic	dejected	guilty	kind
gloomy	unhappy	embarrassed	meek
sexy	bored	inhibited	superior
discontented	bad	generous	bewildered
tired	disturbed	frightened	center-staged
indifferent	disappointed	anxious	reflective
unsure	torn	dismayed	erotic
impatient	inadequate	apprehensive	relieved

Feelings Pictures

Following is a series of pictures illustrating feelings for those people who prefer pictures to words. They will help you learn to notice, label and affirm feelings in yourself and others.

Aggressive Agonized Anxious Apologetic Arrogant

Bashful Blissful Bored Cautious Cold

Concentrated Confident Curious Demure Determined

Disappointed Disapproving Disbelieving Disgusted Distasteful

Eavesdropping Ecstatic Enraged Envious Exasperated

Exhausted Frightened Frustrated Grieving Guilty

Happy Horrified Hot Hungover Hurt

More Suggestions

- Do a daily inventory of feelings. Note how you felt, how you expressed the feelings with people around you.
- Share your feelings each day with a person of your choosing. Use direct and brief emotional statements.

    I feel sad because . . .

    I am scared about . . .

    I get angry when . . .

- Use terms that fit the feeling.
- Avoid sharing thoughts or making statements as if sharing feelings. If the words 'like' or 'that' follow an "I feel" statement, usually it is a thought rather than a feeling.

AFFIRMATIONS

- My tears are raindrops for my spirit.
- My sadness moistens the soil for new intimacies to grow.
- My vulnerability is the source of my strength.
- My grieving fuels the forward movement of my life.
- My anger is a bonfire of my strength and passion.
- My rage empowers my outrage against abuse.
- My fear is the threshold of my courage.
- My sense of shame is the bedrock of my honor.

THOUGHTS

- There is no healing without the feeling, no leaving without the grieving.
- Vulnerability is the path to intimacy and strength.
- We create our emotional reality just as reality creates our emotional responses.
- We choose feelings and feel choices.
- An addiction is a failed attempt to feel better or not feel worse.
- It is as important to know when to stuff the feeling as it is to express it.
- Giggling creates the best of times.
- Boredom is anger without passion.
- Discovering my body uncovers my emotions.
- The opposite of love is not hate. The opposite of love is apathy.

5

PRIORITY 3.
Friends And Family:
Lean On Me

There are three basic ways to find the support we need. The first way is very easy: You simply *wait* around until someone gives it to you. Wait for someone to notice your needs and then meet them. When we were totally dependent beings as infants, we had to wait until someone figured out what it was we needed — and even then most of us cried out for help in one way or another. It's about as useful as staring at the telephone and waiting for the darn thing to ring. This way seems easy, but it isn't very effective, except to keep us in a victim posture.

The second way to seek support is both more difficult and more reliable: You take a deep breath and a big risk and you *ask* for help. This is very scary for many people, since it means putting yourself out there and possibly being rejected. Worse yet, someone might see you are not as *strong* as you would like to appear to others.

Ironically when we need help the most is when we struggle the most with asking for it. At these times it helps to realize that our strength lies in our vulnerability. It also helps to remember that if someone asked *us* for assistance, we'd feel pretty good.

The third way to seek support generally comes after we have learned to risk rejection and have been able to ask for help. It is to *give* support. Many of us try to give away what we don't have. This kind of giving can be a way to distance self from others and never appear weak or needy. We can only genuinely give if we can genuinely receive.

RELATIONSHIPS

Most people enter therapy because of relationship problems. Difficulties in a relationship stem from many things: addiction, depression, control issues, co-dependence, fear — but it is the relationship problems, not the underlying problems, that motivate people to seek help. Albert Schweitzer once said, "There are 2 billion people in the world, and they're all dying of loneliness." You are not alone.

Even though our relationships with others flow out of our relationship with self, a self-relationship is also a product of our relationships with others. Our relationship with caregivers, especially in our childhood, determines much of our identity and self-relationship. When these relationships were damaged, our identity suffered damage. The wounds show up in other relationships. The damage can be healed, but seldom by those people who hurt us. We must find healing and affirming people who help us achieve confidence and healthy identity so we can return the gifts received in our continuing relationships with others.

CONFIDANTS

Our friends and support systems are vital for mental and physical health. Touch deprivation is the most common and one of the most serious forms of physical abuse. We need to be touched, held, hugged; we need friends for play, emotional support, parenting, affirmation, noticing, challenge, feedback, discussion, stimulation, disclosure, listening, laughing and even to complain to. The people closest to us become our confidants; we can share our secrets and feelings at a level with confidants that we can't share with other people.

Some of our clients suffered rather intense and severe trauma and abuse in their lives. In therapy they resolved their problems rather quickly. We call these resilient clients. The trauma or abuse or neglect didn't seem to affect them as deeply as we would have expected. Other clients who suffered less abuse or trauma had a much more difficult time resolving it. We wondered what caused the difference in response, and came up with several answers: the age at the time of abuse; the severity, frequency and predictability of the abuse; and what the person believed about the trauma. One key concept that affected the level of trauma was whether or not the client had a confidant — someone with whom the client could share the trauma. Many people never talked about it before they entered therapy. Others had friends while the trauma was going on, or someone they could talk about the trauma with, and they did their therapy along the way. Most of the therapy process is simply finding a person to be our confidant so we can talk about what has happened to us, so that we can embrace the feelings and share them. From this we can learn how to build a support system.

Childhood confidants may have been friends, coaches, teachers, counselors, camp leaders, ministers, a family friend, an adult, a neighbor or a relative who understood and knew what was going on.

Sometimes the confidant may have been the nonabusive parent. Parents can be confidants if the abuse is occurring outside of the family. Usually, however, when we think one parent is our confidant, we have actually become the parent's confidant. A parent who was truly acting as a friend or confidant would prevent the violence or abuse, not just talk about it.

SOCIALIZING

There is a great deal of focus on relationships, why relationships don't work and the importance of intimacy in our lives. Often this focus on relationships misses the fact that before we should have intimacy we should have friends; before we have friends we need acquaintances; and before we have acquaintances we need to know how to socialize. One of the most important things we can learn in a family is how to socialize, chat and make small talk. We need to know how to get along with people, how to have a balance of interaction and how to communicate with others. Adolescents who lack social skills are very vulnerable to joining the drug-using or acting-out groups, where all you need to belong is the ability to get high or crazy.

In low-functioning families very little is said about problems. We didn't chat, we didn't talk about the small things, but we also didn't talk about the big things that were hurting us, that controlled our lives that we responded to in self-destructive ways. We enter therapy and learn to talk about those big things. We learn to talk about incest, suicide, attempted murder or neglect. It helps to talk about these things in therapy, but it doesn't do much for small-talk skills. For example, when we casually mention at a party that Dad tried to kill Mom three times, it's a real conversation stopper!

Much of our ability to socialize comes from our ability to be informed and have a variety of interests. It also comes from our ability to ask questions, to show interest, to listen to people and to show that we can communicate.

Many of us in our recovery are impatient with the patterns of conversation around us, the shallow level of interest that our friends have. But until we learn to communicate easily with others, we will never be able to find the people who want to talk about things at a deeper level and people we are truly compatible with. We need to learn to pace ourselves, to notice the little things that other people notice and talk about general subjects — weather, sports, business, children, clothes and movies. We often advise our clients to read *People* magazine so that they can learn to talk about things people are interested in.

Many people, both athletes and nonathletes, are very interested in athletics and watch a lot of sports. Watching a sporting event once in a while makes it easier to talk to people about sports. We don't have to know much to show that we're interested, just watching once in a while is enough. If we close ourselves off to spectator sports, we're closing ourselves off to the possibilities of getting to know someone and getting to chat so that we can have a deeper relationship and connection.

Every particular interest group — whether rock-climbing, sailing, spelunking, bicycling, chess, photography, computers — do lots of visiting about other things. Sometimes the interest is really just an access vehicle for socialization, for meeting and talking to people. If you find a group that shares your interest, you will find a person with whom you already share the basis for a relationship.

FRIENDS

When we come from low-functioning families, we often have internalized shame that keeps us from being able to be interested in others. We are sure they wouldn't be interested in us, and we fear we will get hurt or they'll see what we're "really like." We tend not to trust people and we tend not to want to accept them. We have a hard time seeing how people are charming or wonderful. We feel threatened by others. In recovery we find out that people aren't threats. They are interesting, and they are scared too. Just like us.

Most of our relationship problems are caused by family-of-origin issues. Sometimes we have a problem depending on people because people in our family weren't dependable. We then become overly dependent. Or we become "independent" and hide our dependency needs. Sometimes we fear getting too close to people because it touches our pain and we have worked so hard to avoid that pain. We fear that if we get too close to people our secrets will come out, or we will be too vulnerable, and we learned to fear our vulnerability. We are also sometimes afraid that other people might get vulnerable and need us. We fear that we will either be used again by trying to "fix" them, or we'll be inadequate and unable to help.

Vulnerability is a path to friendship and intimacy. It includes our ability to share and show how we feel, especially our fear, pain and shame. It includes our willingness to be honest about sexuality, to be dependent and small and give up control in asking for help, support, caring and nurturing. To trust the giver creates our strength and friendship and enables us to give the same to our friends who become vulnerable.

Vulnerability needs to be balanced by mutuality rather than complementarity. Relationships that are complementary say, "I have a need, you fill it. I will be vulnerable, you be strong and powerful to take care of me." Mutuality says, "We both have needs and we both have the ability to meet each other's needs, and at times one of us will have greater needs than the other." Mutuality is based on interdependence. In our relationships many of us are crisis oriented. We listen to and care for a host of friends. It's not really about their needs so much as our style, a way of having a place, being needed, protecting our own insides. This caretaking approach to friendship breeds anger. Rescuers eventually get used and feel unappreciated.

In relationships we must balance expectations with realities of the present and changes from the past. Updating friends on changes in our life is essential. Damage can be repaired with forgiveness and acknowledgment. Friendships often end because of excess demands or a sense of betrayal, but most friendships simply evaporate due to lack of interest, changes in lifestyle, spiritual postures or not enough time. Friends who always view us as who we were, not as who we are now, are very difficult to maintain as friends. If we feel abandoned, we need to ask directly if that is what is going on. The pain is the same, but it occurs over a shorter duration. When abandonment is dragged on, our pain gets dragged on with it. Grieving the loss is enabled through the knowledge of what is happening so we can move on and risk elsewhere. Friends outside a committed relationship are sometimes a source of enrichment. Some of these friendships can be causes for antagonism and jealousy. There is no formula that works for jealousy. What is needed is openness and honesty, a respect for feelings, and discussion of the jealousy. The jealousy can be about feelings shared, sexual intimacy,

affection, time, stimulation, recreation or dancing. The biggest risk we
can take is with discussing the jealousy issues and doing it without
manipulation and control.

If our life lacks balance and we have too many unmet needs, we tend
to get jealous and complain a lot. To celebrate another's success is the
deepest sign of friendship.

We need to develop boundaries in our friendship around touch, what
is said, jokes and teasing. We need to learn to trust our discomfort, fear,
agitation. Friendship is a balance of:

- giving/receiving
- laughing/breathing
- listening/sharing
- noticing/caring
- working/playing
- joking/praying
- studying/kneeling
- thinking/feeling
- calm/passion
- abundant/rational
- noisy/serene
- dirty/clean.

In recovery we learn to embrace our vulnerability, allow ourselves to
get close to people and be able to touch our vulnerability and see theirs.
We learn that we don't have to fix other people when they're vulnerable;
we just have to hang around, be close and maybe even affirm.

REENACTMENT

Many of our relationships are based on what we see in our parents'
relationship. If there was anger, hostility, passivity or distance we often
reenact that. We can also reflect or react to our relationship with our
parents. So much of adulthood is a reaction to or reenactment of unresolved childhood issues. The reenactment is setting up the same
qualities in relationships with others that we had in our family: distance
control, enabling, hostility, argumentation, passivity. The reaction is to
go in the other direction. Instead of being controlling, we become out
of control. Instead of being argumentative, we become passive. Whatever we do, we are controlled by the unresolved relationship issues of
our family of origin.

SIBLINGS

Many of us were abused or hurt by siblings. In therapy we often forget to talk about sibling relationships, sibling abuse, neglect, abandonment. The quality and nature of our relationship with our siblings is elemental. Much of our socialization with others is a reaction to or built on how we socialized with our siblings — even more so than with our parents. In larger families the younger siblings get more parenting from their older siblings than from their parents. Studies have found that only children tend to socialize differently than people with siblings. If you are a parent with one child, it is important to give the child opportunities to socialize in safe and protective environments with children of different ages.

The sibling abuse that occurs is often a reflection of the marriage problem, or a parent's problem. Sibling abuse has a profound impact on our ability to trust and be vulnerable with those around us. Siblings in low-functioning families who are distant, hostile, angry or abusive toward each other are not fighting or distant because of the anger, but because of the stored pain. If the siblings allow themselves to be as close as they want to be or feel with each other, they feel too much of the pain. If we get too close to a brother or sister, we see the hurt child that he or she is, and we will touch the hurt child that we are. After we leave the family, we often maintain that distance. It is still to avoid our own vulnerability, our own store of pain or our own hurt child because we still see the hurt child when we get close to our brothers and sisters.

FAMILY OF ORIGIN: WHERE IT ALL BEGINS

Many books have been written about relationships, sex-role rigidity, why men avoid intimacy and why women love too much, why they get abandoned, why men don't trust women, why men don't commit. These books are essentially red herrings. They keep us from looking at the real problem: our family of orgin. If we came from a low-functioning family, we didn't see intimacy modeled. No one was real enough to get close to. What chance do we have for intimacy? We don't know what it looks or feels like, we never experienced it and we don't have it with self.

Our family of origin issues are the core of our intimacy problems, and we must go back to our family for the healing. We project our problems with our parents and our siblings onto our relationships with others. We can't get close to them because we might feel too vulnerable, touch our pain and see the hurt in them. A lot of us are hurt children. We are like siblings from a very large low-functioning family who can't quite get close because it will hurt too much. Siblings in recovery often support each other. In recovery a sibling will perceive the hurt child in the other sibling, and that will touch the hurt within and help the grieving begin. Siblings in recovery can hold hands, can touch their pain and can move through the grieving together to build intimacy.

Woody Allen once said that in our relationships we try to find what we had in our childhood and what we didn't have in our childhood. That makes relationships difficult. There is no chance for friendship in a relationship without risk. We have to put ourselves out there, take the risk of rejection, of feeling foolish or of being made fun of. Whatever we put out there, if we lose it, we just go back to where we started. We haven't lost anything really. What we've learned is more about taking risk and maybe more about the selection process about who to risk with. Many of us have been burned and we're not willing to risk again. We need to go through the debriefing and the grieving process about how we've been hurt and burned so that we can get the energy to risk again. Sometimes we need individual professional support or an open group, so that we can find out that we are truly lovable and precious and we have something to offer before we can risk again outside of the settings that are safe. Some safe settings are therapy, 12-Step groups, therapy groups and programs that are set up for people to meet people, clubs and hobbies. These are low-risk environments in which to meet people. Many of us need to find the low-risk areas before we are ready to take more risk in other places.

FAMILY: FUNCTIONAL VS. DYSFUNCTIONAL

Over the past decade we have heard a lot about dysfunctional families — so much so that we wonder if there are any healthy families. The joke goes, "Ninety-seven percent of all families are dysfunctional and the other three percent are in denial!" This has given many people permission to break the secrets of what occurred in their families of origin, ask for help and get into recovery.

Are *all* families dysfunctional? We prefer to say that *all* families have problems, and all families function. Some function better than others and all function differently at various points in time. Families are dynamic and ever changing. How a family handles problems determines how functional they are. A trait of a low-functioning family is the inability to recognize its own strengths. Often we get so focused on what went wrong that we overlook what went right. We overlook what strengths we have drawn as individuals from our families. We reenact both the problems *and* virtues of our family of origin.

Every family member has a unique experience and an often conflicting interpretation of what happened in their family. Views vary according to our individual bonding, roles, time of arrival in system and interpretations.

Too many of us came from low-functioning families, families who are no longer available to us or cannot provide what we need. We need to build a new family, a *family of creation*. A family of friends and parent figures, a family of acquaintances who care about us, who can offer us something and to whom we can offer something back. A *family of creation* can include our family of origin, or certain members of our family of origin, or it can be people of all ages we have found in our life, be-friended, adopted and become close to. Members of our *family of creation* don't even have to know each other. The important thing is that they know us.

> Our *family of creation* consists of the people who accept us for who we are, and who believe in us while nurturing our journey. They support us on our unique path. A family brought us to life and our *family of creation* can bring us to life. In the family we learn to live and play, love and pray. Family are the people we can always come home to. Our roots are planted in the family: of origin and of creation. When we are firmly grounded we can spread our wings and soar.
>
> Roots And Wings
> *Words On Growing A Family*

HEALTHY FAMILY TRAITS

The following is a list of traits and qualities of a healthy family, both of origin and of creation:

1. *Notices, labels and affirms feelings.* This is the key to healthy parent-ing: using feeling words, linking feelings to reality. Often when we are hurt, depressed or suffering from an energy loss, it takes someone else to point out, "Look at what happened: Your young-est son just moved away to college, your dog died, you just had an argument with your best friend — of course you're going to have low energy and feel depressed." Sometimes we don't attach our feelings to the events in our life, so our feelings feel crazy. In a healthy family we have people who let us know we're grieving and that what we're feeling is normal. They support us and affirm the feelings, even· if they disagree or don't affirm the behavior. Sometimes they'll even notice what we're feeling around us, when we tend not to hear when it is directed to us.

2. *Shares openly and honestly about feelings.* The honesty is rigorous, and not perfect. Our *family of creation* doesn't share *every* feeling and whim — this can be a way of dumping and it can be too scary.

People use feeling words. They place feelings in their appropriate setting without dumping or projecting. They use feelings as a way of connecting, not as a way of pushing away. They make choices about the time, the place and the feeling shared and how it is shared.

3. *Has an abundance of communication with each other and the world.* Small talk, big talk, feeling talk, discussion, socialization with each other, taking time to listen and to share, keeping an open mind with the world, with others outside the immediate circle through letters, calls and reading. A healthy family needs to recognize that we cannot *not* communicate with those close to us. It is a group of people who use covert, nonverbal communication responsibly. Communicating with love and respect is a key function of this healthy family.

4. *Teaches active listening.* Listening with the eyes, listening without distraction. So many times people in our lives pretend to listen. Active listening involves repeating some of what's said — maybe not just paraphrasing it, but saying it a different way. This shows that we understand what we're hearing. We have an expressive and open body posture. We don't over-lecture or over-advise, but simply stay active with listening skills.

5. *Provides an environment of trust and safety.* Healthy family members keep their word, whenever possible; they give explanations when things change or go wrong. They support and defend each other without enabling or fostering helplessness or dependency. They support us to do rather than doing for us. They help us find a safe setting to the best of their ability. They help us notice. They gently point out things, places, behaviors that may be dangerous to us, yet give us the freedom to make our own choices. Without being punitive, punishing or shaming, they support us into growth or change.

6. *Allows space to grow, provides encouragement for the uniqueness of individual members.* They respect our ideas and allow our ideas to be different. They give us room to grow, both physically and intellectually. They allow emotional space, again being available, but not intruding on our feelings. They provide encouragement for our uniqueness. They cherish the uniqueness. A *family of creation* celebrates the differences of each person within the family.

7. *Respects privacy of thoughts, feelings and space.* A healthy family doesn't prod, except gently. They allow us our privacy in some of the things that we just don't share. They allow us time with our feelings; they allow us our physical space. They don't intrude. They don't get too

close. They don't stay too long. They don't follow when we need to be alone. They just keep acknowledging that they are available. They keep letting us know where they are. They don't have to be close all the time. They just need to be available.

8. *Openly expresses spiritual beliefs and values.* The open expression is a way of modeling a prayerful posture toward life and teaching spirituality. Our families don't force us to believe exactly the same thing, or to practice the same beliefs in the same way. They just model what they believe and what they practice, and invite us in. Some families might have more ritual around prayer and worship, some families less; but the key is that we have a common belief system about the world that each member can share with his or her own unique approach. Each person develops a sense of value formation, of rightness and wrongness. The common spiritual belief of the family is respected. Each person is allowed to become the person he or she was meant to be by the Creator.

9. *Teaches risk-taking.* Teaches by modeling, by taking risks intellectually, physically, politically — in the community, in relationships, in intimacy. We can have no real growth and very little intimacy without risk. A healthy family is willing to take risks with us and for us — risks to protect, risks to enlighten, risks to be close.

10. *Recognizes, celebrates and acknowledges the strengths of the family.* A healthy family acknowledges its positive attributes and strengths, the things it has learned or its ways of learning, its sensitivity. It is as dysfunctional to *focus* on the dysfunctional as it is to deny the dysfunctional. In the celebration of each other and the qualities we share together, we reach the true meaning of family.

11. *Teaches respect for the environment and each other.* The Earth is our true parent. In learning to care for our planet, we are showing caring for ourselves and each other. Environmental respect flows out of self-respect, but also replenishes it. To respect each member of the family — including the ones who don't seem to be contributing so much, or seem to have more problems that get recycled within the family — gives the family members a true sense that this is a place where they can live, be themselves and not be abused or abandoned.

12. *Is sensitive to and protective of vulnerable groups.* Healthy families do not participate in "isms" like racism, fatism, sexism, ageism. People and groups are respected and cherished, as well as defended and protected. This protectiveness flows out of knowing that our own vulnerability is noticed and cherished.

13. *Stands up for and supports each other.* Members actively defend each other without enabling. Support is given on several levels, in-

cluding emotional, physical, financial and intellectual. Hurting
members get more protection while the healing is taking place.

14. *Practices rituals without rigidity.* In a healthy family some things are
done because they have always been done that way. We can count
on some things being the way they are: Sunday morning church
and breakfast; Friday evening movie and popcorn; Tuesday late-
afternoon tea and discussion; a new book on the coffee table
every week; holidays or solstice celebrations. It doesn't matter
what it is, we tend to bask in familiarity. Members may complain
about ritual. As children we often detested the rituals. What? We
have to go to the lake the third week of August? Every summer
we go to the lake. But as we move away from the systems that
we've been in, we look upon the rituals with fondness; we cherish
the memories, the sameness of the rituals. The ritual is not rigid.
It doesn't exist for the sake of the ritual, but for the benefit of the
family. And not everyone must particpate in the same way — or
at all. It is available for each of us to choose.

15. *Values history and tradition.* Chronicles the family members' lives.
The history of the family and of family members is known and
recorded in memory, journals, photos, videos, letters and memorabilia. The traditions and past are valued, not worshiped; known,
not obsessed. Each side of the family is known; secrets are few.
The life of family members is chronicled and held as a gift to be
given to the member, as a story of who we are.

16. *Embraces change.* Change is accepted, expected and welcomed. People
in social systems are dynamic and ever-changing. As we change,
the family changes. Our acceptance of the family is not based on
our staying the same. We are loved for who we are inside: evolving,
growing creatures; not for how we are at a given time.

17. *Develops a playful and humorous posture toward life.* Family members do
not take themselves or the family too seriously. Gentle teasing,
playful tumbling tricks and joking create a song that harmonizes
with the spiritual, humorous posture toward life and each other.

18. *Models giving and service to others.* Giving of time, material, money,
both within the family and to needy people. Abundance is shared.
When abundance is absent, we give our time: volunteering, tith-
ing, giving of what we do creates a fullness. *We only have what we
give away.* Keeping a low profile, but not needing to do it all
secretly, anonymously, or practicing a false humility; allowing giving and services to be matter-of-fact, not hidden or self-aggran-
dizing; not giving to the point of resentment or loss of self; giving

from what we have, not out of our emptiness; not as an attempt to have fullness, but as a flowing out of our fullness.

19. *Challenges with physical and intellectual activities.* Family members are provided with opportunities for physical and intellectual challenge, without being pushed too hard. Settings within and outside the family are utilized to challenge both our minds and bodies. Rigorous physical and intellectual puzzles, games, activities and competition are provided without the results being over-focused on. Time is reserved for particular family members as well as for the entire family. Mealtime, weekend time, vacation time are valued and shared, without rigid rules about how they are shared. The importance and value of time itself is modeled, appreciated and respected.

20. *Has an open-door policy with the world, but maintains a sense of family.* Family members' involvement with outside resources and other families is encouraged, not seen as a threat. The family has a free flow of traffic with nonfamily members. Every once in a while a Mack truck may come through and blow the house away, but we rebuild and open doors again. Information and people flow in and out of the family. Family members, with all the influx of people and information, still have a sense of special belonging within the family, what it means to be a part of this particular family.

21. *Is neither child- nor adult-focused.* Children are important; their needs are met, but the family doesn't revolve around their needs and wants. Adults model and enjoy healthy adult intimacy and activities that do not always include children. Children are not hovered over or forced to do adult things. Vacation planning is done with a balance of adult and child activities, games and places.

22. *Models forgiveness and healing.* Wrongs are felt and acknowledged. Reconciliation occurs. Mistakes are accepted. Hurts are felt and shared. Grieving is encouraged.

23. *Limits consumption and electronic distractions.* Overspending is discouraged, regardless of income. Without being cheap, each family member is aware of money, its value and place. Waste is discouraged. The center of the family is activity, rather than cable or Nintendo. TV use is limited; music, computers, electronic games are balanced with creative and physical pastimes and activities.

24. *Encourages critical thinking and questioning.* The family quest is to question, evaluate. Family members arrive at individual conclusions. Questions are answered honestly and seriously. Media information is evaluated, not just accepted. The "system" is questioned, as are the rules and the world. Learning is more important than grades. Thought is more valued than prestige.

25. *Competes without being competitive.* To be able to compete is to be able to do the best we can in a setting or situation. To be competitive is having to win at the expense of someone else; having to beat someone down to feel better about ourselves.

26. *Adults model adult intimacy and are available to children's needs.* Adult relationships are the key to a healthy family; through adult modeling children learn intimacy and are encouraged to build intimacy from their image of it. When adults do not maintain or work at intimacy, they tend to bond with the children, and the children never see real intimacy modeled. Children who get used by and bonded with adults can have a hard time finding intimacy in their own lives. Our biggest intimacy blocks are not the relationship with the parent who wasn't there, who was mean or cruel, but with the parent whom we were closest to, especially when they were using us to meet their needs. In a *family of creation* there are significant others. When we have friends who are in a significant relationship with each other, we don't make excess demands that might pull the relationship apart. We are able to be with couples and enjoy and see their intimacy and use it as a base for finding our own.

27. *Is open about problems and seeks help from outside the family.* All families have problems. A family becomes low-functioning when it maintains excess denial. Drinking, anger in the marriage, legal and financial problems can be discussed with other members, with children, with friends; but we do not have to be responsible for fixing the problem. We can understand, affirm and support without taking responsibility. When we share problems with children, we need to make it clear that the adults will do their best to work the problem out and take care of it. Problems also have to be shared with appropriate language, at a level appropriate to the child. We must also be careful that our relationships with others don't become so problem oriented. Many of us learn to bond through complaining, through playing "Ain't it awful?" We need to bond through healthy activities. Then, when the problems occur, we share them appropriately.

28. *Allows and notices consequences of behavior.* Most behavior has a consequence built into the behavior. Sometimes the best we can give is to notice the consequences or help people link it back to the behavior. Children very seldom really need punishing, maybe never. They do need the consequences of their behavior. Friends don't need to be punished by us, but sometimes they miss the connection between what's going on in their lives and the behav-

ior that set it up. In a caring way, when we make that link, we help people understand and learn and grow. When we remove the consequences from people's behavior, we enable them to continue self-destructive habits.

29. *Approaches conflict with an intent to affirm and learn.* When members of our family have conflict we don't need to solve the conflict or get enmeshed in that conflict. If we approach it with an attempt to learn about the person, about ourselves and about the conflict, often everyone grows. The growth comes from understanding and awareness. Some conflicts can't be easily resolved, but can be clarified. Double-binds, anger at situations or people, victimization: When clarification takes place, choices open up.

30. *Responsibilities are earned, not assigned.* When we enforce jobs, we often find resistance. As children mature, they earn rights. Along with the rights come responsibilities to participate and help the system work.

31. *Provides information and access to information.* Teaching is a function of parenting and friendship. We teach what we do; we teach what we know; we teach about the world and about us. Mostly, however, we teach how to question, how to learn — where and how to find information — and we teach how to teach. The best teacher is always the student; the best students also teach.

32. *Is nonblaming and gentle about mistakes.* Permission is given for imperfection. Errors are seen as a chance to teach and learn. Members are encouraged to go beyond what they know and are comfortable with, even though more mistakes will be made. Each person is taught and encouraged to have a balance of risk and caution; more caution when there's the possibility of injury. When things go wrong, family members react together to unravel and move through. When the problem comes from noticeable irresponsibility, there is noticing, teaching, comforting and support, as well as honesty with feelings, but there doesn't have to be blaming and punishing. Much blame that we project comes from our own fear, a need to control. Healthy families accept that about 20 percent of everything goes wrong and doesn't work.

33. *Notices and supports work.* Work is modeled and the joy of work is expressed. Work is a means to self-expression, not self-worth. Family members notice, show gratitude and encouragement for work and productive activity. Work is taught in balance.

34. *Operates through love and responsibilities rather than rules.* The more rules, the more power struggles. Rigid rules mean the breaking of rules. Flexible rules bend. The fewer rules, the more members

are allowed to grow in judgment and trust themselves: the more
prepared for the world. The more rules, the more enforcement is
needed. Rules need to be overt, whenever possible, for it is the
covert ones that get us in trouble: don't cry, don't make waves,
don't bother Dad, don't be successful.

35. *Allows and encourages grieving and losses.* In healthy families losses
are acknowledged openly and processed together. People are noticed and supported for whatever state of the grieving process
they may be in. Things lost, pets, friends are not replaced immediately and automatically to eradicate a loss. What was lost is
special and the person is given time to heal.

36. *Understands child developmental stages.* Children will do things when
they are ready. When children are pushed too much too early,
they react by becoming pushy or anxious. When they are not
offered the opportunity to grow and risk with each developmental
stage, they regress and feel insecure. Knowing the uniqueness of
each child and what developmental stage he or she is in, is as
important as knowing the developmental stages themselves.

37. *Has a balance of family exchanges and connection.* Triangles are avoided.
Communicating play, touch and support is widespread. Special
relationships are minimized. The deepest love may be in the marriage, if it's a family of origin; but the bonding of adults and
children is not to fill the parents' need and is relatively equal
among the children. We will always have special friends. Some
friends we just play tennis with. Some friends we pour out our
hearts to. Some friends we call and some friends always call us.
This is not about equality, but about caring and availability. Our
relationships are egalitarian. We each play our own role. Each is
important, but not the same. Each is not necessarily perfectly
equal or balanced but equally respected.

38. *Respects ownership and models sharing of property and money.* Individual
ownership is respected, while sharing is reflected. Some things
are community; others are private property. Boundaries around
space and property are modeled and respected. Money is property
and each member is supported in earning money inside or outside
the system. Financial irresponsibility is not extolled as generosity.
Generosity is valued. Loans may be made, but as business, and in
a spirit of love.

39. *Views children as a miracle of the gift of life.* Each family member
shares in the miracle of childness. Children and vulnerable family
members are not owned; the goal is not control or discipline.
Family members are not of us, about us or reflections of us in the

world. Each person is a miracle of the gift of life itself. When we embrace our own miracle, we can truly appreciate the miracle of those around us. When we embrace our own childness, we can embrace the childness of the adults and children around us.

A family can be a place of loving and support, whether it be family of origin or creation. The above list of traits and suggestions may help your family be a healthy place of possibilities.

SUGGESTIONS • AFFIRMATIONS • THOUGHTS

SUGGESTIONS

- Learn to chat — develop interviewing and visiting skills with people. Learn to ask questions with genuine interest, questions that engage conversation without being intrusive. Learn a bit of information to share about sports, world events, geography, travel, food, business, careers other than your own, nature, causes or other topics of general interest.
- Seek out mutual help groups — people who know just how you feel (see Appendix A for a list of self-help organizations and addresses).
- Hobbies — develop interests that include others and seek out clubs to join; the Chamber of Commerce, the Yellow Pages or city new-comers' groups often have lists of organizations in your area.
- Find a mentor or coach or become one.
- Search out volunteer or social action groups and join up as your energy and recovery allows.
- Do a group recovery program and meet after the meeting.
- Join a religious or spiritual community that is compatible with your beliefs.
- Do "hosting" — better yet, do co-hosting! — of an exchange student, a block party, tea for two, a discussion group, snacks after the game, the team meeting.
- Show up! — when you are invited or the public is invited, even for a short while.
- Travel — take an adventure with a group or, if you have well-developed social skills, travel alone and plan to meet people.
- Reach toward, not away.
- Drop a line — to catch more than fish. Write notes and letters to people you want to stay in contact with.
- Phone home — and other meaningful places.

AFFIRMATIONS

- My friends reflect my soul.
- We bring out the best in each other.
- I am a warm and caring friend.
- I feel safe in my *family of creation*.
- My friends please me.
- I am easy to meet and wonderful to know.
- I discover my strengths in family.
- I enjoy sharing stories with others.

THOUGHTS

- Balance is easier when we have someone to lean on.
- A friend is a present you give yourself.
- Some friends are mainly tennis partners, some friends share our soul.
- Family meetings — their purpose is not to work out problems or assign responsibilities, but to practice sharing and listening.
- Remember: Friends use each other — usually taking turns.
- A friend is someone you can complain to — we "whine" and dine them.
- Some members of our *family of creation* won't know each other, others won't like each other (just like home!)

6

PRIORITY 4.

Physical Balance:
What Every Body Knows

We don't have bodies, we *are* bodies. Through our physical being we interact with creation. Maintaining physical balance is a major step in recovery. It involves activity, movement, challenge, play, dance, massage, fitness, strength, endurance and flexibility. When we choose to care for our body, here, today, we show self-respect through hygiene and learning to do the best we can. Most important, physical balance is gratitude and gentleness with our bodies.

You may be wondering why the physical/body priority is so high on our recovery list. Why does it precede spirituality?

The answer is simple: Because our bodies are the manifestation of creation, the vehicle by which we relate to all other creation, the tool of the guardianship of creation and the means by which we co-create. We once heard someone say, "Maybe we are not human beings

93

having a spiritual experience, but rather spiritual beings having a human experience." Many of us have been taught that the bodies are the temple. We are the physical embodiment of our Creator's love. We must nurture and cherish our bodies. If we destroy the temple, where will we worship? In this sense *caring for our bodies is spirituality.*

FAMILIES, CULTURE AND RELIGION

Therapy and treatment programs offer ample support and tools for emotional, intellectual and spiritual recovery, but the physical aspect is barely acknowledged. This is a reenactment of family dysfunction as well as religious and cultural norms: to repress, neglect or ridicule everything from the "chin down."

In our families many of us were shamed about our bodies. We were told with words and looks that we needed to lose weight, were too short, were supposed to have been born a boy (or a girl), looked funny, had freckles, red hair, big ears, no breasts, big breasts, looked like a monkey with long arms, short legs, buck teeth, big bottom and so on. Very few of us had our bodies affirmed in healthy ways by our parents, relatives, teachers or other significant adults as we were growing up. When our bodies were noticed and complimented, it was often done seductively, or stated in a way that our good feelings were from the outside and we became an extension of them; our uniqueness was not affirmed. We have internalized these hateful and hurtful messages and have continued them on our own.

PHYSICAL ABUSE

Some of us were abused in our families. Physical abuse is both the most common form and the most minimized type of abuse. We only have to reflect back on an instance when we were hit by a parent, sibling or other person. We need to ask ourselves this question: If we were responsible for the guardianship, care and safekeeping of this young child, would we have treated this child in the very same way? *Many of us would not treat a child in this manner because it would be abusive. The violence we do to self, others and our planet will only change when we recognize and heal the violence that has been done to us.* This recognition will heal and change our collusion, our altered tolerance level for violence and abuse. Following is a partial list of abuse issues from *Broken Toys Broken Dreams:*

- hitting, slapping, excessive spanking
- kicking, biting, pushing, shoving, pinching, choking, shaking.

- use of objects in hitting: branches, boards, belts, saplings, whips, straps and so on
- knocks on the head, excess squeezing
- being physically restrained, tied up and tortured
- burns with cigarettes, matches, stove and fires
- threatened with violence and hitting
- lack of space, lack of privacy, no rights to property
- tossed around, constant mussing, hair tossing and pulling, excess tickling
- deprivation of food, shelter, clothing and warmth
- being physically tested beyond your abilities
- not being protected from:
    sibling abuse (older, younger, or same age)
    being beaten in school by bullies or teachers
    excessive housework
- children/infants not being put in car seats or seat belts
- lack of personal hygiene modeled and taught
- excessive scrubbing and abrasion of hands and ears
- being exposed to unsanitary living conditions, rats, roaches, dirt, insects, plumbing that didn't work, odors
- lack of dental and medical care
- clothing that was improperly fitted, inappropriate, dirty, worn out
- lack of information about body, being teased about body
- excess emphasis on external appearance
- being shamed or teased about body functions or formation
- physical punishment by relatives, ministers, strangers
- constant moving, relocations
- being in close proximity to nicotine smoke
- being locked in house, rooms, closets
- not being protected from someone else's rage, anger, temper, hitting walls, thrashing, destroying property
- not being protected from one's own rage
- not being taken care of when sick or ill nor supported when sick
- having pets, people or things that we become attached to be destroyed or removed from our lives
- overexposure to the elements
- pushed into violent sports
- no sense of ownership or learning about property, money, spending and the cost of things
- witnessing violence

- living through earthquakes, tornadoes, storms, wars, excessive crime
- and the most common physical abuse of all, touch deprivation.

When we have been used and abused, we lose a sense of our physical being and become shut down. We get out of sync with our natural energy flow. Our repressed feelings from being hurt in childhood become physical tension, lowered energy levels, tightening of joints, jaws and muscles, stomach aches, lower back pain, indigestion. We have numerous chronic physical ailments as a result of the trauma in our lives. Emotional, intellectual and physical trauma and stress are commonly manifested in our bodies.

Cultural messages regarding bodies leave most of us feeling inadequate and unattractive, which we translate into being unacceptable and unlovable. In workshops when we ask people to write down one thing that they like about themselves, they generally describe something about their personality or intellectual ability: "I like that I am caring, bright, considerate or have a sense of humor." When we ask them to write down something that they do not like about themselves, very often it is about their bodies, appearance or body weight. Much self-deprecation is about our bodies.

Body-image studies indicate that very few women accept and like their bodies and that fewer men today than 20 years ago are satisfied with their body shape and size. It is as though men are now being asked to join the beauty contest — there are many more men's beauty maintenance products, new men's magazines full of "vanity" advertising. Men are expected to have a larger wardrobe than a decade ago, and men are now being asked to take their clothes off on stage. From the perspective of men's and women's sex-role issues, in the name of progress we now get to participate in each other's pathology. Women get to own and run corporations and die of heart disease and other chronic illnesses at an earlier age, and men get to join the beauty contest and end up taking a ride on the diet roller-coaster. No one wins. Neither men nor women own and run corporations — corporations own and run men and women; and diets don't work, so the roller-coaster is a never ending ride of deprivation and a punitive posture toward self.

Many religious messages about the body are negative. Our body is a temporary inconvenience on the route to eternal life. Our sexuality is a necessary evil for procreation only. We have sins of the flesh. People go bananas around sexual issues and physical differences. The body has always been a distinct second to the soul, a temporary burden until we reach a heavenly state of spiritual success. The body is dirty, for it contains the sexual parts necessary for procreation, and causes much sin and shame. The body is a test, to be used until discarded. These messages do little to enhance the celebration of our physical being. One's spirituality is experienced with the body, the smells, sights, sounds and touch of creation. The spiritual posture of enjoying, guarding, noticing and being of creation is done with the body.

BODY ACCEPTANCE

Body acceptance has nothing to do with body shape and size or what we see on the exterior. There are as many thin people hurting and hating their bodies as there are fat people. Men dislike their bodies almost as much as women; young and old people struggle with nonacceptance. The problem has to do with the overwhelming size discrimination that is present in our culture.

Fatism is an "ism" that not many people are willing to discuss. Our culture teaches that fat people are slobs, careless and lazy. Fat people are blatantly discriminated against and mistreated: by medical professionals who focus on the person's need to lose weight and disregard other concerns; by employers who can't look beyond a person's body size to see what skills he or she has to offer; by people on the street who grimace in disgust. Size discrimination has a particularly interesting dynamic. People believe that fat people wouldn't be fat if they didn't want to be; they just need more willpower and control. This is simply not true. Being fat does add health complications, but people do not learn to care for themselves in a loving way when put down and discriminated against. Most of us are hard enough on ourselves — we don't need someone else judging us.

This discrimination goes beyond *fatism*. People with other physical differences are similarly mistreated. People with skin problems, lost limbs or unusual facial or body features are often shunned. Many diseases, situations or normal life changes can affect body posture and appearance. They do not call for being riduculed and abused, but this often happens. The discrimination comes from our fear of differences and becomes a projection of our own self-hate, self-criticism and ugliness. We have been filled with myths and fairy tales that speak of the purity of beauty and the evil and grotesqueness of differences. We are a culture that disdains growing old; ageism emerges out of our fear of our own mortality and our worship and obsession of youthful bodies. We do not worship youth, but rather the looks of youthful bodies.

Discrimination comes from our own lack of self-acceptance and unresolved issues and fears about our own body. When I accept me as I am today, I no longer have the need to put someone else down.

As our bodies change and develop we are given new challenges for acceptance. People who are disfigured or lose body parts in accidents, undergo body-altering surgery such as mastectomy, or have medical conditions such as diabetes need special nurturing and attention. They must grieve the loss of their looks, abilities, normal body functioning or body parts as outlined in Chapter 4. It takes much time and courage and requires a great deal of support to move to self-acceptance after physical change.

RECLAIMING YOUR BODY

We need to reclaim our bodies as our living entity. Many of us have ignored and abused our physical selves and therefore our spiritual selves as we internalize our pain from past hurts and abuse. In our recovery we need to begin caring for our bodies in a gentle and loving way. Therapists, treatment center team members and helping professionals have all been victimized and shamed by the same cultural and family messages regarding bodies. How can they assist us in reclaiming our bodies when they are struggling with disordered eating problems, physical and sexual shame, poor exercise habits and lack of body acceptance? Until we have the support and information to reclaim and to nurture our own bodies in a gentle, respectful way, we cannot give it to others.

Voluntary seat belt use is a powerful sign of self-acceptance. The "click" can be a regular symbol of our mind/body/spirit connection — of treating ourselves with respect. When we fasten our seat belt it means that we care enough about our body's well-being to ensure its safety when given the opportunity.

BEING ACTIVE, ALIVE AND FEELING ACCEPTABLE

Physical activity is a significant sign to ourselves and others of self-respect. Researchers such as Lobstein at the University of New Mexico, teams at the University of Toronto and others are finding that aerobic activity is a powerul booster of self-worth. We simply feel better about ourselves when we get out and move. Almost everyone agrees that physical activity and fitness is a good thing. So why isn't everyone doing it? The excuse we hear the most often is, "I don't have enough time." Well, there are only 24 hours in a day, not an hour less or more, so it comes down to priorities. How do you spend your 24 hours? Many of us spend it chasing after kids, bogged down in careers, watching TV, shopping, working late, volunteering and helping others, being perfectionistic about our houses, cars, clothes and "stuff," being weighed down with family baggage and obsessing about our looks, what we are eating and losing weight.

Getting physical means making physical activity a high enough priority so we fit it into our busy lives. This can feel very selfish and self-centered for someone who has always put other people's needs, thoughts and activities before their own. Thinking of your activity program in terms of *self-respect* and *self-interest* can be helpful. When we are energized, healthy and fit, we have more to offer the world and people around us. This focus on *self* is for the sole purpose of giving it away to others. *We cannot give of ourselves until we have of ourselves.*

Year after year, "Getting in shape" is one of the most popular New Year's resolutions. If it worked last year, then why is it back on the list this year? There are several reasons why we believe it doesn't work. Foremost, if we begin an exercise program to "lose weight," it is just like going on another diet and will have a similar failure rate — about 98 percent. People often think of exercise as punitive — we have been "bad" and need to "beat" ourselves back into shape. Obviously it isn't going to work well. Second, we overdo it — if a little is good, more must be better. If we go too hard, too fast, too much, too soon, we are going to get injured or burn out. Some people believe that it has to hurt to do any good, which is probably a repetition of a message they got in their family. If you see yourself being caught in these situations, take a moment to reassess. *It is more important to change your mind than your body.*

BACK TO THE BASICS

Begin by taking a gentle approach to body care. Develop the attitude that you are worth taking care of. How many times have you heard someone say, "I would be so *happy* if I could just lose 10 pounds," as though every trouble would suddenly disappear when the scale told them the magic number. Accepting yourself here, today, in a loving way is a big step. Remember that beating yourself up hasn't worked in the past, so *give acceptance a chance.*

Physical activity boosts self-esteem and sends a powerful message: "I am worth taking care of." It is a great place to start. You can choose from a number of physical activity programs from *attrACTIVE WOMAN. A Physical Fitness Approach to Emotional and Spiritual Well-Being* that encompass the four categories of fitness: flexibility, strength, skill building and aerobic activity.

Flexibility, Strength, Skill Building, Aerobic Activity

Flexibility exercises like yoga, stretching, and dance all enhance your balance, improve posture, reduce joint discomfort and lower back pain,

and offer an opportunity for peaceful relaxation. Stretching also can play
an important role in injury prevention if it is done slowly and gently. The
most important aspect of stretching is to warm up your muscles and cool
them down. Participate in your activity very slowly to begin with and
then do it gradually faster.

Strengthening exercises include lifting weights (both free weights and
machines) and calisthenics. Developing strength is necessary for performing daily tasks independently with ease and comfort, and it can
improve your posture and confidence. This kind of activity is not aerobic.

Skill-building exercises include most recreational activities: downhill skiing, bowling, golfing, horseback riding, basketball, softball, soccer, football. Most games and team sports are anaerobic because of their start-
and-stop nature. They are especially important for developing coordination and balance and offer many of us, young and old alike, some wonderful social experiences. And besides, they're a lot of fun!

Aerobic exercises are essential for development of a strong, healthy
heart and cardiovascular system. They will help strengthen bones and
improve your endurance. With aerobic activity the fat levels in your blood
change. The beneficial high-density lipoproteins (HDL) increase and the
total cholesterol decreases, so there is a lowered risk of arteriosclerosis or
hardening of the arteries. Aerobic activities help us burn more stored fat
for fuel and therefore are the basis of developing a lean, trim and stream-
lined body. Some of the best activities for aerobic condition are:

- cross-country skiing
- square dancing, tap dancing
- swimming
- jogging or running
- brisk indoor or outdoor cycling
- brisk walking or water walking
- aerobic dance classes.

Other activities that provide a desired conditioning effect if done with
enough intensity include:

- dancing
- roller blading
- racquet sports like squash, tennis, racquetball, or handball
  (a person needs to be fairly skilled at these sports to enjoy them at
  an aerobic level)
- roller skating or ice skating
- horseback riding

- sports involving continuous motion, such as soccer and rugby can be conditioning as well as skill.

AEROBIC ACTIVITY PROGRAM

The most efficient exercises for fat loss are the aerobic activities listed above. In order to feel your best and for great pleasure, enjoy a combination of flexibility, strengthening, skill building, and aerobic activities. We are going to elaborate on the areas of activity that will lead you to a sense of well-being and balance.

Ideally we would participate in a combination of all of the above. Participating in one would be a realistic beginning. Because of the psychological and physical benefits, the most important one to focus on is aerobic activity.

Simply follow the FITT formula: frequency, intensity, time, type.

Frequency — How Often?

Fitness, like sleep, cannot be stored. Five hours of activity on the weekend does not take care of your body's needs for the week. We need a regular activity program to reach and maintain a healthy level of fitness. A program of three to five days per week is optimal for most people. Two basic rules to follow are:

- Aim for being aerobic every other day.
- Avoid missing aerobic activity for more than two days in a row.

Intensity — How Hard?

There is a pace at which activity is vigorous enough to condition the muscles and cardiovascular system, yet not overly strenuous. This pace is called the *target* or *training heart rate* and is often referred to simply as the talk/sing test. That is, if you can't talk comfortably while active, then you're working too hard. If you are able to sing while active, you're not working hard enough. Researchers are now recognizing that all the charts and numbers for pulse taking are not nearly so important as it is for you to listen to your body and your perceived level of activity. On an effort scale of 1 to 10, with 1 being little or no effort and 10 being the most effort you could possibly exert, aim for around 6. You need to pay attention to your body and the signals it gives to you about your pace.

Time — How long?

In the past the basic rule on length of time for aerobic exercise in order to gain cardiovascular fitness was to be active at your target heart

rate for a minimum of 20 minutes. Now we realize that getting out for
even 5 to 10 minutes at a time is helpful. After you've started a grad-
uated program make a 30-minute commitment: 5 minutes to warm up,
20 minutes at your workout rate and 5 minutes to cool down. Now
there are many reasons to be active longer than 30 minutes. Longer
activity will develop your endurance and maybe — just maybe — you
will enjoy having an active body and will want to do it more. Beyond the
minimum time for good health you will discover your comfort zone for
the length of time for you to be active. Above all, enjoy yourself. If you
are really pushing to add a few minutes, give your body a break and
build up time slowly.

Type — What Activity?

What type of activity counts as aerobic? An activity that . . .

- is continuous and steady
- has rhythm, without stopping and starting
- uses the largest muscles groups (legs and buttocks)
- meets the frequency, intensity and time outlined above.

Go slow. Change does not happen overnight. For someone who is
just starting out, going five or ten minutes is enough. Go easy on
yourself. No pain, *more* gain! If it hurts, stop and let up a bit. Our
bodies are incredible machines that let us know what is going on, and
pain is an important signal to respect. If the pain persists, see your
health professional.

A common response to having our bodies ridiculed is to obsess about
them. As the symptoms of co-dependence are often polarized, so are
our reactions to the symptoms and many of our attempts at recovery.
Too often we become overly zealous and overdo it. Some people switch
their addictiveness to exercise and believe this is good. *There is no such
thing as a positive addiction. Addiction limits our choices and recovery increases our
choices. Recovery offers us choice and freedom in life.*

STICKING WITH IT

People often say that getting started in an exercise program is difficult. Far more people start and stop exercise programs, so it seems as
though sticking with it is much more difficult. Here are some ideas and
simple tools to help you stick with it:

- Be active one day at a time.
- Keep an activity log — it can be part of your journal.

- Hang around active people — we can "energize" each other.
- Have body celebrations — begin planning now to do something "physical" on your next birthday; set a goal that will require building toward to celebrate when you physically entered this world!
- Find mentors — look to other active women and men for guidance and modeling.
- Body wisdom — when we reclaim our bodies and live an integration of body, mind and spirit, we can learn much about ourselves and creation.
- Think in terms of being an athlete — athletes are people who can do physically what they realistically choose for themselves.
- Be gentle — too much, too fast, too soon can hurt. You are worth taking care of!

MOVIN' ON

Body acceptance and self-care are essential to recovery. How can one have sexual recovery if we don't respect our body? How do we play, work or pursue community involvement when our life energy is spent obsessing about our appearance and hating our bodies? Can we hope to proceed with spiritual recovery without caring for our place to worship? We need to feel connected in a *whole* and perhaps *holy* way before movin' on.

SUGGESTIONS • AFFIRMATIONS • THOUGHTS

SUGGESTIONS

- Give up the scale. Better yet, give up dieting and refocus all that energy on taking care of yourself.
- Walk, run, bike or skate — almost everyday.
- Join a team — or a physical activity club — running, skiing, cycling, hiking, walking, canoeing, archery.
- Find family fitness.
- Find places — indoors or outdoors, that are safe, comfortable and familiar, where you can be active regardless of the time of year or day.
- Be attrACTIVE — we must be emotionally, physically and spiritually active to be emotionally, physically and spiritually attractive!
- Challenge yourself — push yourself gently within limits of safety.
- Take a risk — don't be foolish, but go beyond where you are now; try something new and do it with others.
- Move to the music — try tap, jazz, ballroom, square, folk, rock and roll. Become a dancin' fool!

- Dance alone, dance together, dance whenever, dance wherever!
- Wear a helmet when you cycle.
- Belt your kids in the car and hug them at home.
- Hang around active people.
- Accept each other's pace.
- Participate more than spectate.
- Try competition — compete without becoming competitive.
- Travel — with your athletic shoes, roller skates, sweats, racquets and swim suit.
- When traveling — check out fitness facilities and safe outdoor recreation possiblities. Try to stay in places that offer activity amenities.
- Plan a physical vacation — bicycle tours, mountain hiking, tennis camp, river trips and ski trips.
- Balance and diversify activities.
- Celebrate your body!

AFFIRMATIONS

- I am active and alive.
- I am an athlete.
- My body is a temple.
- My energy astounds me.
- I am gentle with my body.
- I have a healthy glow.

THOUGHTS

- Instead of "Holy Smoke" and "No Sweat!" we believe in "Holy Sweat" and "No Smoke!"
- Listen to your body — know your pace and limits.
- Getting weighed does not tell us whether we are healthy or fit, but it simply is how much we weigh. Body weight also does not indicate whether we are good or bad people.
- No pain, *more* gain — heed physical signs.
- Physical aerobic activity is a source of life energy.
- *Fatism* is a cultural dis-ease.
- Our bodies in motion can send us powerful messages of hope, strength and power.
- Giving ourselves time to be physically active is not being selfish or self-centered, but it is showing self-interest and self-respect.
- When we care for ourselves physically we have more energy to share with others.

- Pay attention: Be alert, be in the moment. Be conscious of now: of breath, heart, legs, body temperature and all sensations. All movement can be active meditation and prayer, a way of being grateful for creation — and creation includes each of us.

7

PRIORITY 5.

Spirituality:

12 Small Steps For Humans,
A Giant Leap
For Humankind!

S piritual recovery is often said to be the
first priority of recovery. So why is it
number five on the priority list? Be-
cause spiritual recovery is included in *all* the priorities.
It begins with identity building and continues through
our entire journey of healing — emotionally and sexually, in community and career.

Focusing on spirituality too early may lead to an obsessive and escapist style of spirituality. Before we have
a sense of self, a foundation of identity, physical and
emotional healing, our spiritual nourishment flows
through and out of our emptiness and becomes the
insatiability of religiosity. Until we have a sense of
boundary that comes with identity we are vulnerable
to the exhortations, exploitation and extortion of any
self-styled spiritual leader who has a seductive voice
and a convincing message.

Spirituality is a concept of activity and belief, learning and teaching, stewardship not ownership, noticing with gratitude not worshiping with platitudes, reverence and care not ritual and hypocrisy. It rests on physical, intellectual, emotional and social activity. True spirituality is the integration of the wisdom of spiritual people, whether they be scientists, philosophers, mystics, environmentalists, religious leaders or simply a courageous voice coming out of an honest soul.

RELIGION

Many of us have strong religious backgrounds. Some of us still adhere to the teachings of our childhood, while others of us have moved into other forms of religious expression or have given up on religion altogether — often giving up on God and spirituality as well. Those of us who adhere to the religious practices of our family background often do so in a sporadic and rote manner. We continue to do or be something that we have never decided to do or be. We don't have the commitment, faith or passion for what we do or believe. "Going to church" becomes our religion, but we miss out on spirituality.

Religion is a support system for spirituality. Unfortunately where there is little or no true spirituality, religion is like an empty shell — form and ritual but no substance. Spirituality feeds and frees the spirit; it is inspiring and aspiring toward wholeness — holiness. Many religious people are not very spiritual, many spiritual people are not very religious.

Religion can give us the opportunity and setting to experience, learn about and practice spirituality in a community. We are community beings and we all need support systems. We are also creatures of habits and rituals. Many of the rituals of religion enhance the spiritual aspects of life, but over-ritualizing can remove us too far from people experiences. The excess ritual feeds ego and is consumed by its excess. Liturgy, gospel, music and prayer bring out the feelings and awareness of our spiritual core. When these become rigid, detached and legalistic, the symbolic thrusts drive us away from a true simple journey of oneness with creation and the Creator. Religion must serve as the conduit for stewardship but, as with many organizations, the potential for power, wealth, seduction and control becomes the impetus. Spiritual values get lost among the myth and manipulations. We need not disband churches; we can rearm them with the simple messages of their roots.

GOD

If religion is not spirituality, then what is? Our belief in and relationship with a deity seem to be the primary focus of spirituality for most of us. The worship of God seems to be spirituality, but this alone contains certain problems. The first lies in the nature of the God we worship.

The God we worship is often a patriarchal God of power. A God of miracles and constant change, who would alter the course of individuals, nature and nations for punishment, pleasure, reward, or whim, like the anthropomorphic gods of ancient Greece all rolled into a single image. Often the God we worship is a meddlesome co-dependent caricature of a deity, which reinforces our own co-dependent meddlesome tendencies.

In Genesis we were created in the image and likeness of God, but today we have reversed Genesis. We have created God in *our* image and likeness. We are the gods of power, of technological miracles, without considering consequences and the fragility of what we affect. We are the patriarchal system who would use power to reward or revenge, to smite our enemies and give abundance to those who believe in us or adopt our ways. We have lost a God of gentleness, process, creation and vulnerability. For Christians who want to live a Christ-like life, the question is, what was Christ really like? What is the message of the Bible, the Koran, the Talmud, Confucius? There have been many spiritual leaders and teachers. Were their lives expressions of peace, vulnerability and questioning? What can we learn from their teachings and modeling?

We can split the atom, dam the rivers and destroy the rain forests. In the next century, at the rate we are going, we will destroy an estimated 50 percent of all species of life on earth. Of approximately 10 million species of life only half will remain at the end of the next century. Nothing like it has happened in our planetary history. Today 50,000 species of life per year — 120 per day — disappear. Most of these forms of life we haven't even acknowledged or met. They share in life, in creation, with us. Our absence of respect for them reflects our absence of spiritual value.

We did not fall from the Garden, we rose from the Garden, we were given keys to the Garden. With our awareness, the ability to imagine, create, search, question and build we became the guardians of the Garden. Our spirituality is to enjoy, cherish, notice and protect. Our sense of shame, which we discovered in the Garden, is the emotional fuel of our guardianship. We are finding our spiritual mission. Only by developing a healthy sense of shame, that would have us act responsibly and protectively toward all that is vulnerable, will we have the peace that comes with true spirituality.

As the child of an alcoholic and often violent father, Terry had a problem with God. He was taught God was the ultimate authority, the father figure. He believed this and became a lay missionary in the Bahamas in his early twenties. Upon returning after two years in the

islands, he lost his religion for a time. He could no longer believe in a
God who cared, who was personally involved. He still believed in a
creator, for he could see creation. But he couldn't accept a God who was
"involved" with prayers for rain, money or victory. He quit going to
church. His life held less and his problems grew.

Eventually Terry entered Al-Anon, a 12-Step program for family
members of alcoholics. Later he joined an Adult Children's group and
entered therapy. One day Terry was doing therapeutic work on his
family in a men's group. During a role play he was asked to imagine his
father sitting in an empty chair. Terry said, "You just didn't care, you
weren't involved in my life." Suddenly he realized that all of the feelings
he had been having about God were really more about his father.

The teaching of God as a father figure has a devastating effect on
children of low-functioning and abusive parents. We generally have
authority problems anyway, and God is the ultimate authority. Our
defiance toward the parent can become a defiance, disbelief and lost
relationship with our Creator. Every time we try to define God, our
father enters the definition. Instead of trying to work this out with our
father, we need to quit trying to define God and begin defining our own
spirituality. Some people do not think the term God should be in the 12-
Step programs for recovery because many people do not believe in God.
They can accept the term Higher Power because that can be whatever
we make it. We do create our God — what we surrender to becomes our
God. The surrender to creation, love, process, harmony, vulnerability
and guardianship means we have a God of creation and guardianship.

If we have been hurt by authority figures, even though we may have
a problem defining God, we can surrender to what we value, we can
define and find our spirituality or reframe the authority of God to a
being of love and gentleness. Before we can arrive at this, however,
many of us must deal with the hurt and anger that we direct toward
God. Often we must grieve the loss of our child faith to develop an adult
spirituality that can renew the faith of our childhood.

Spirituality Defined

Spirituality is the core of our being. We do not have a shame core, we have
a spiritual core. The spiritual core is the very soul of our existence, we
share in an energy of life and being. What we are is our spirituality, the
birth and song of creation. Our coming to life and living, the becoming
of us is the journey of spirituality. The sharing of life and existence is
being one with creation and the Creator.

MEANING

Spirituality is meaningfulness — life with purpose. The opposite of meaningfulness is despair, the core of addictiveness, our drug problem, the crime rate. The traveling companions for the absence of meaning are loneliness, isolation and emptiness. These are the substances of our co-dependency that addictions and overconsumption feed on.

The absence of meaning in life is a derivation of child use, abuse, neglect and abandonment. One of the key symptoms of PTSD is a loss of meaning about life. The loss of the ability to believe that we can affect our destiny and that what we do matters. This increases insecurity and anxiety, and breeds addiction. Those of us who have experienced trauma and abuse find it difficult to feel safely held in the arms of a life source; we lose our belief in the benevolence of the world. Trauma comes in the form of violence, war, sexual and physical abuse, abandonment, neglect, dislocation, threats, deprivation.

Enmeshment is another form of spiritual abuse. Our primary purpose in life is to become the person we were meant to be by our Creator. We each started out on a path to become who we were meant to be. Many of us were beaten, neglected and abused off the path, but the more subtle enmeshment is the true spiritual abuse. When we get enmeshed onto someone else's journey we lose our own. We become set up and scripted to be like others, extensions of them or what they couldn't be. We become an image of what they want us to be or think we are rather than who we really are. We get enmeshed in acting out denied pathology and modeled behaviors. We get enmeshed by the seduction and abuse, the needs of the family and family members. Enmeshment is the most insidious of all abuse and creates spiritual bankruptcy — the loss of self.

VALUES

Spirituality is a higher-order value system. What we value forms and flows from our spirituality — children, life, earth, truth, love, beauty, gentleness, the future, our history. All aspects of how we live are reflected in our spirituality — recycling, sexual contact, paying bills, serving food, child care, charity, service to others, teaching, how we drive, exercise, interacting with authority figures, the homeless, our mechanics, our neighbors, who we talk to and how we speak to them. All priorities are held in the framework of spiritual recovery.

Spirituality is our relationship with creation and the creative process. It is a sense of the oneness of all things, all life, all people, all nations. It is an acceptance of our place and the importance and uniqueness of our lives and problems as part of the throb of the becoming universe. The expression of our spirituality lies in our interconnectedness, our interdependence with what we touch, learn and see.

Spirituality is relating to creation with noticing and awareness, gratitude and awe, guardianship and care. We must be childlike to achieve the noticing, become like children to enter the kingdom. To walk with the awe and awareness of a child, seeing shapes, colors, the little things. With the noticing we develop an attitude of gratitude. We become thankful for our surroundings, children, life, bodies. We become thankful for the course that directed us to recovery. We become thankful for recovery and all who support our journey.

STEWARDSHIP

Our spiritual journey is one of guardianship: to protect all that is given to us; to be aware and nurturing of vulnerable places, life forms, people. Our strength comes through the embracing of our vulnerability. We cannot have true spirituality until we find our own vulnerability and use it as a stepping stone to protecting others.

Much of what occurs in our culture is based upon misunderstanding the dominion we have been given over all things. Dominion is not the biblical justification to use as we please, it is a stewardship similar to the stewardship of a leader to serve those who are led. Our commission is to serve and protect what we have dominion over, not to use it or abuse it.

Dominion has been the justification for the rape of our planet. It becomes the belief that we can use and abuse our children. It sets up a denial of incest and child abuse. It also causes us to ignore the consequences of abusive behavior toward children and the planet. This is our cultural co-dependent denial, a posture of minimizing or ignoring our impact. Sin is the misuse of this dominion — especially over children.

Parents exercise their parental rights to use and abuse children partly because they interpret dominion as ownership, the right to hurt, the same belief that enables pollution, ignoring our impact on fragile life and ecosystems. The Moral Majority has used dominion as an excuse to eliminate, prevent and undermine child-protection laws, which are often innocuous and unenforceable anyway. Pro-family frequently means anti-woman and anti-child. We don't see the vulnerability of our planet, rain forests, the atmosphere, lakes, rivers, mountains, infants, adolescents, or each other because the vulnerability of our own newness has not been cherished.

Our vulnerability makes us dependent. As we live lives of higher intensity and feel out of control, we fear our children's dependency on us. We deny their dependency, which leaves it unsatisfied and creates the inappropriate dependencies, on substances, insatiable consumption, activity, ownership, sex, food, power and control, drugs and so on. We deny this dependency and vulnerability because of the denial of our own dependency and vulnerability. The denied dependency also creates a pseudo maturity, a toughness and intrusiveness that gets expressed in power, bullying, rape and environmental destruction.

Hurt children lose spirituality, lose stewardship and hurt their space, each other and themselves. Our addictions are a reflection of our human needs and spirit, but expressed in a destructive direction because our guides could not direct our dependency needs toward interdependence, which is based on all things interwoven. The loss of the oneness of spirit creates the "isms" — nationalism, parochialism, racism, sexism. It sets up fear, war, genocide, terror, poverty and addictiveness.

We are one with the derelict, addict and the differently abled, but we cannot nurture and notice who we are one with because we have not been nurtured. We have been neglected, used or indulged, which has created a lack of balance. Cultural misogyny, the fear and hatred of what is vulnerable, is formed from the inability to embrace our lack of vulnerability. Integrity — our integration with the world around us — is lost. Until we address the misogyny and its source, we cannot have the stewardship of dominion, only the abuse of a false dominion.

Our cultural misogyny stems from our basic view of children. We see children as extensions of ourselves, a way to live out our dreams, to continue our journey, to give meaning to our lives. Children are viewed as property to use or abuse. They become the objects of our needs, the source of our affection and companionship, the objects of our rage and frustration and a way to achieve immortality. Children discover spirituality as it is taught: by what we do. We must heed Kahlil Gibran, who said, "Our children are not our children, they are not of us or about us, we do not own or control them. They are a miracle of the gift of life itself." We will not be able to appreciate the miracle of our children until we embrace the miracle of our childness. This embracing of childness will help us flow with creation, not against it, not damming the flow or struggling upstream.

PARTICIPATION IN CREATION

We are called to be saints, to serve creation with grace, awareness, joy and suffering. *Spirituality is our participation in creation.* It is our chance to add a verse to the hymn of the universe. We create through thoughts and imagination, writing, poetry, music, building and art.

Each of us can add something to the enrichment of the human experience. We are called on to create. Our participation in life is a part of spiritual co-creation.

A CURRENT OF LOVE

Spirituality is life that flows with a current of love. To will and do the good of others. To feel the empathic stimulation of appreciation and care of those around us. To be attracted to the energy, the sparkle of the story of those we encounter. These are emanations of our spiritual journey.

Lifestyle

Spirituality is a lifestyle that gives life. Addiction is a process of spiritual bankruptcy. Our life is shattered and shortened through our addictive progression. We no longer notice, we no longer create or love. Addiction is not just a process of spiritual bankruptcy, it is a symptom of it. Who of us will become addicts but those of us who are denied the path of becoming us? The abuse of our childhood that we continue to reenact or react to as adults sets us up for death-style rather than lifestyle. If there is sin in the world it is the neglect, abuse, abandonment and enmeshment of children. This is the set-up for a fall from grace, an obsessive, narcissistic, co-dependent or addictive style of living that prevents our life spark from shining.

Self-Forgetfulness

John Powell once said that *spirituality is self-forgetfulness.* Many of us in recovery have learned that we cannot have what we don't give away. In the giving is the having. This almost sounds like co-dependency. Many people struggling with co-dependency come very close to spirituality, they just miss a step. Many are self-forgetful and give a great deal, but you cannot forget what you never knew, you cannot give what you never had. They keep trying to forget themselves before they know themselves and give of themselves before they name themselves. We cannot have what we have not been given. To continue giving without refueling means we eventually run out of gas.

Kindness and caring are not co-dependency. In the name of confronting these as co-dependency, we are killing spirituality rather than helping people find it. The real purpose in building identity and knowing our self is to forget ourselves. The focus on self is an important part of recovery, but it can become infantile narcissism if we don't move on. Our growth is taking part in the selflessness of love and protectiveness of creation. Humble people do not think less of self, rather they think less often of self. *Interdependence is co-dependence recovery.*

Acceptance

Spirituality is surrender, acceptance and change. What we surrender to we make our God, in the acceptance of the way things are we have reality and maturity, two qualities of spiritual growth. In the willingness to participate and create change, we are being co-creative. This message of spirituality is summed up in the Serenity Prayer:

> God grant me the Serenity
> To accept the things I cannot change
> The courage to change the things I can
> And the wisdom to know the difference.

GROWING UP

Spirituality is childness entering adulthood. We retain the wonder, sparkle, newness and magic of childhood and integrate it with the experiences, strength and wisdom of adulthood. This is called growing up. We don't lose childhood, we gain adulthood. Having a spiritual focus includes learning prayer, not as an activity but as a posture toward life. Prayer is childness woven into adulthood (see Chapter 1).

Spirituality is each of us becoming who we were meant to be.

SPIRITUAL CONVERSION

The process by which we find spirituality is called conversion. To some this is a born-again experience, a cathartic moment or insight that enables one to make an emotional attachment to a spiritual decision. We have had friends who experienced conversion in near-death situations, while driving or listening to the radio, in church meetings and while eating dinner. Many people internalize these experiences and live a life of modeling through spiritual insights. Others join the church of perpetual proselytization and drive us away. They wear their spiritual commitment like a lead prayer cloak, pounding on others with it but keeping well defended.

Conversion does not have to be instantaneous. It can also be an incremental process. The depth of our emotional attachment to spiritual values doesn't appear full-blown, but increases over time. This conversion is the gradual process of making emotional attachment to our spiritual decisions. It will occur as a part of recovery, out of our growth as feeling persons and with the increasing awareness of ourselves and the world.

CULTS

Our society is riddled with spiritual seduction, exploitation, extortion and control. One can find it on TV, college campuses, institutionalized churches, treatment centers, in recovery circles and most other places where people have needs.

In early recovery we need to be very careful about being swayed too much by religious leaders and spiritual guides. There are no gurus, no one has the answer, many who preach don't practice. There is nothing more seductive than a powerful helper, a spiritual evangelist. Cults are common, and those of us who have been victimized as children are vulnerable to recovery and health cults even more than to sick satanic cults.

If you are uncertain whether or not the group you are in is a cult, check your balance. Cults are by nature extreme and will pull you against your better judgment. If the group encourages balanced thinking and independent judgment, it is probably not a cult.

12-STEP PROGRAM

In spiritual recovery one of the most effective guidance systems we know of is the 12-Step program of Alcoholics Anonymous and other similar groups. A wonderful aspect of 12-Step programs is that they are available virtually anywhere. It is a secure feeling to know we can venture into groups and find support wherever we travel or wherever we live.

The 12-Step program was first begun 55 years ago to answer the need of alcoholics to find support from each other and to develop a fellowship that used sound principles of recovery and living to help maintain sobriety. People addicted to other drugs and activities have gradually begun their own programs using the same or similar Steps. Today there are 203 different 12-Step programs, and some of us would feel right at home in any one of them! (See Appendix A for more information on 12-Step programs.)

Some meetings are Topic meetings, others are Step meetings. We prefer the Step meetings. People who attend programs and meetings where the Steps are read but never worked or discussed do not receive what the powerful spiritual healing process can offer. We suggest that these meetings be called 12-Topic meetings rather than 12-Step meetings. Topics are valuable, but many people in recovery, especially newcomers, do not realize what they are missing or where to get it when they attend Topic meetings and not Step meetings.

Some people play alphabet soup, attending several different programs. This may be helpful, but to try to work a different program for every different compulsion and issue in our lives may be overwhelming and prevent a depth of recovery.

Twelve-Step meetings are therapeutic, but they are not a substitute for therapy. The 12-Step meetings generally try to limit or eliminate cross-talk, advice and feedback. Listening, sharing and supporting are the goals. The feedback and process of making the covert explicit are important in therapy and not directly a part of 12-Step programs.

Twelve-Step programs provide us with an environment of support and friendship; beliefs and values such as honesty and surrender; rituals with meaning and tradition; slogans, readings and prayer as daily activities. We develop a sense of trust and interdependence, learning that our needs can be met. It is a grieving process by which we leave the old addictive system and move toward grace, light and community. It is a lifestyle guidance system that heals our dignity and value as people.

It is important not to overidentify with an addiction or group. It is equally important not to be rigid and judgmental of people who choose other courses. There are many paths to recovery.

The 12-Step program is not a religion and has disavowed any formal connection with organized religion, although it is supportive of people using other spiritual support systems. The word religion means "to rebond," and the program provides this, something that many religious organizations fall short of providing. In the program we rebond with a Higher Power, with ourselves and with others.

BACK TO THE STEPS

Each of the 12 Steps is filled with challenge and healing. Following are the steps, and some thoughts about each one.

Step 1: We admitted we were powerless over _____ (alcohol, food, sex, other drugs, etc.), that our lives had become unmanageable.

In accepting we are powerless and that our lives have become unmanageable, we are addressing the key issue of addicts: control. Our disease is a disease of attempting to control the addictions, our feelings, ourselves, other people, relationships and reality. The admission of powerlessness gives us the entry to recovery. To admit the problem is to break the denial that feeds the problem. To admit the unmanageable is to break the denial of the expanded impact of our problem in our lives. To admit our powerlessness is the initial cry for help in this first stage in moving from shame to grace, death to life.

We cannot really see powerlessness without looking at our childhood, the beginning of powerlessness. We often need to find our hopelessness to embrace our powerlessness.

Generally for men there is an immediate relief in acknowledging powerlessness, for men are supposed to appear adequate, powerful and in charge all of the time. The fear and inability to manage their lives that men share in this step is often a great relief — exposing to sunlight and healing what they have hidden so long: their vulnerability.

For women the Step is powerful but may require two stages. Most women are taught powerless roles from the start and learn to exert control and power within those roles. To walk into a First Step and admit, "My life is unmanageable, I am powerless" — well, so what else is new? Women need to embrace the attempts at power set up by powerless roles and then look at the true powerlessness of addictions and co-dependency. Embracing the absence of power gives women empowerment at first from the group and program and then of self. To do a First Step is a written history of women's addictions, the consequences, our denial and self- and other-destructiveness. This is shared and need not be perfect or even well done — just done. Women can always come back through to include what they miss, including the emotional part, the shame, pains and grieving of their addictive history. Admitting powerlessness offers healing. Women now are depending on others in the healing of dependency, in the healing of shame. Step 1 is the embracing of vulnerability, the true beginning of a journey toward guardianship, strength and intimacy.

Step 2: Came to believe that a Power greater than ourselves could restore us to sanity.

This is the beginning of faith. We came to believe. This is the introduction of a new sense of Higher Power. We have given up our addictive substance or behavior and what can fill the vacuum. We believe in something — a new power that can restore us to sanity. Many addicts have a hard time believing in a power greater than themselves, even though this is what an addict lives with all the time. Our addiction is a power greater than us until we find our spiritual empowerment. If there is a power greater than us that can destroy us, it takes only a small leap to accept that there must be a power greater than ourselves that can restore us. This power may be the power of love, the power we find in the group, in nature. It isn't so important that we find a particular right kind of power — just one we can believe in that can help us find meaning and worth.

Step 3: Made a decision to turn our will and our lives over to the care of God as we understood God.

In this Step is the challenge of true spirituality and the conversion process. It addresses our need for control and commits us to the safety of being in the care of whatever Higher Power we have accepted.

This step introduces the word God, which makes it difficult for people who do not believe in God. We supported the people who believed the program should be for everyone and that the word God shouldn't be included, even with the qualification "as we understand Him" (the "Him" was also a bit of a put-off because we believe in a nongender description of deity).

We gave up the campaign to eliminate the word God once we realized the step is not about God but about surrender. What we surrender to we make our God. If our life revolves around alcohol, sex or gambling, if these are the altars we worship at, then these become our gods. In the program we surrender to the power that can heal, to love, to truth, to creator, to beauty — and this becomes our God.

This Step is sometimes used as a cop-out. Many people turn things over as a way of not taking responsibility, not so much trusting God as abrogating their responsibility and stewardship. We must be the instrument of preservation, allowing God as a life force to work through us, doing our best to follow our spiritual values and keep to a decision of moving with the flow of creation instead of trying to create, through our will-power, changes in others or our environment that go against the flow. Leading a life of surrender is the ability to let go, not to give up. To grieve and move forward. Our guide for finding balance between letting go and action is in the Serenity Prayer.

Step 4: Made a searching and fearless moral inventory of ourselves.

This Step is a definite action package. We make an inventory of us. The inventory is a list of qualities and defects. We look at ourselves as objectively and as honestly as possible. As addictive people we can become very deluded and dishonest with self. This Step is our intervention of self, to be honest about our intrusiveness, impatience, short tempers and selfishness as well as our better qualities, our commitment, care and strength.

The inventory must be searching, going back to settings and people in the past, incidents that hide under craggy shelves of shame. To be fearless does not mean to have no fear, but to move through the fear of our dark side to find the light. Using fear as threshold of courage is true fearlessness. The Fourth Step will access our shame along with the honesty. A sense of the shame can be held as part of our powerlessness and vulnerability and help lead us to guardianship and intimacy. Too often we have heard people use the Fourth Step as a way of being hard on themselves, which is what most of us are used to doing. We challenge you to work this Step in a gentle way, doing a *complete* inventory including character flat spots and strengths.

Step 5: Admitted to God, to ourselves and to another human being the exact nature of our wrongs.

When we admit our wrongs to another, we open ourselves up to our Higher Power and a person of our choosing. We continue the path of healing the repressed shame by releasing ourselves from the secrecy of our addictive lives. We open up to true intimacy and courage, for in sharing the exact nature of our wrongs, we use our honesty as an intimate bridge to another and follow our vulnerability toward interdependence. There is no intimacy or strength without vulnerability. Intimacy, strength and honesty are the gifts of Step 5. When we share the exact nature of our wrongs and are still accepted, listened to and loved, we discover the preciousness of our humanity. This Step is best done with a spiritual guide. A nonshaming, caring person experienced in Fifth Step work can facilitate a great deal of healing.

Step 6: We're entirely ready to have God remove all these defects of character.

This Step is not a half measure. "Entirely ready" means we see the pathology of our addictiveness and no longer wish to hang on. We accept the pain and suffering caused by our disease and are ready to let it be removed. This Step is a recognition that we cannot do it alone. We expect perfection of ourselves, and what we do is never good enough for us. Now we can be gentle with ourselves in our surrender that our Higher Power will continue the work of this Step.

The work never seems to be done. We have never met an addict recovering *without* defects of character. When we are entirely ready and they aren't removed, it becomes frustrating — especially for an addict who wants it *now*. The gift of this Step is patience. We strive for improvement and growth, not for instant perfection. Addictiveness generally means impatience. Working this Step is learning patience with us, our program, our Higher Power and each other.

Step 7: Humbly asked God to remove our shortcomings.

Accepting that we can't do it, accepting that we have shortcomings that affect our lives and having to ask affirms our dependency — a healthy dependency on our Higher Power. The gift of this Step is humility. We need help. Our ego's need to do it alone was destructive. Through humility we find honor and pride. Without it, we struggle with despair and humiliation.

Step 8: Made a list of all people we had harmed, and became willing to make amends to them all.

We often want to work on our own victimization, but many of us have hurt others as well. People experienced pain as we self-destructed and they helplessly watched our disease progress, our addictions escalate. Many times we lashed out in our defensiveness and created craziness with our delusion and distortion. The list is a healing, humbling, vulnerable experience in which we take *responsibility* for our actions. The amend is not an apology but a change. To say we are sorry is empty if we continue the behavior; to be willing to change is the healing and spiritual process. To be willing to make the amend is enough for this step; our willingness is learning to not have control, to be open to change, to be flexible, to bend so we don't break.

Step 9: Made direct amends to such people whenever possible, except when to do so would injure them or others.

The direct amends in this Step can be any change that moves us toward honesty and reconciliation. We can acknowledge hurts and apologize. We can make restitution; we can stay out of their lives or recommit to a caring relationship. It isn't always possible to contact people we have hurt, and sometimes the renewed contact would cause more pain than staying away. If someone, including us, is likely to get hurt in the process of making an amend, the possible hurt must be weighed against the possible benefit. We need to look at ourselves as well, how we hurt ourselves, and make amends to ourselves. Change is the one constant in life. In recovery change moves us toward love and intimacy.

Step 10: Continued to take personal inventory, and when we were wrong promptly admitted it.

Our daily inventory needs to be a review of what we said and did and its impact on those around us. Our dishonesty, defensiveness, impatience, absence, projection, denial, unavailability and sarcasm all must be reviewed in a daily inventory. We need to look at our gifts and presence in positive ways as well. It is easy for us to use the Steps to beat ourselves rather than as a way to take a balanced look at our actions and reactions. An emotional inventory is helpful in staying current with our relationships including with self: Who have I hurt? Was I angry? Scared? Did I project worry? Shame? Did I use guilt to control?

When we are wrong, when we make a mistake and admit it, we give the gift of showing our humanity to those around us. The prompt admission prevents festering and setting people up to act out our mistakes and denial.

Step 11: Sought through prayer and meditation to improve our conscious contact with a Power greater than ourselves, praying only for knowledge of God's will for us and the power to carry that out.

We maintain our spirituality through our ongoing awareness of what is meaningful, of creation, of what we value, of our Higher Power. This conscious contact is continued through reading and meditation. The awareness, the noticing is prayer. We stay open to our Higher Power, and in the connecting and awareness we become instruments of the creative process, joining the flow of life. This empowers us to live up to our spiritual mission of co-creation and stewardship. Our life becomes a prayer. Our thoughts become meditations on the wonder, power and beauty of creation and gratitude for the program.

Step 12: Having had a spiritual awakening as a result of these Steps, we tried to carry this message to addicts, and to practice these principles in all areas of our lives.

We are more spiritually aware and gently offer what we have learned, responding to those in trouble with open eyes and hearts. We do this not by forcing a message of what we believe, but by allowing our beliefs to shine through our lives. By living this prayer called the program, we attract interest from others; by talking about it, we drive people away. The principles we practice are gentleness, values, noticing, gratitude, honesty, patience and sharing. What others do with what we model we cannot control; we can only be the channels of a beautiful force of light and life that can be the light in the window for those still lost.

SUGGESTIONS • AFFIRMATIONS • THOUGHTS

SUGGESTIONS

• Try a daily reading from a Health Communications affirmation book such as:
  Time For Joy by Ruth Fishel
  Soothing Moments by Bryan Robinson
  Affirmations For Adult Children by Rokelle Lerner

- Develop an attitude of gratitude — find something to be thankful for each day.
- Find a group of people to discuss, sing, share and pray with.
- Learn prayer as a posture toward life.
- Develop a sense of guardianship toward all life and all things.
- Model, don't preach.
- Accept conversion as a process of emotional attachment to spirtual decision. Accept it as it comes, don't look for it instantly — in the searching there is no finding.
- Work the 12-Steps — use the guides.
- Attend 12-Step meetings that discuss the steps.
- Do a history of your religious/spiritual background.
- What is your image of God? How have your parents or family affected your image and your spirituality?
- Support a cause that gives you a sense of stewardship.
- Avoid religious extortions and exploitations on TV and elsewhere.
- Join a group of people to worship with whom you feel spiritually safe.
- Investigate the business of a religious group before donating money to it.
- Spend a few quiet minutes alone each day, meditating or contemplating.
- Sit in an empty church or synagogue for five minutes. How did you feel? Safe, uncomfortable, sad, connected?
- What did your feelings tell you about your history and church or synagogue, your need for church or synagogue?
- Have an attitude of gratitude.
- Notice and applaud the Creator.

AFFIRMATIONS

- I am spirited and spiritual.
- I notice creation with gratitude.
- My dominion over the earth is guardianship, not use.
- My life flows with a current of love.
- I am a part of all creatures.
- I am the expression of God's love.
- My spirituality lies in my respect and love for others.
- I have a sense of shame that gives me respect.
- My body is the temple I worship in.

THOUGHTS

- Spirituality is forgiveness, which creates the possibility of reconciliation. We cannot forgive what we deny. Forgiveness is not patching up a relationship, but the spiritual healing of a relationship, which opens the possibility of healing. All family-of-origins' work is the spiritual process of forgiveness.
- Whoever inspires us instills spirituality.
- Inspiration is our spirituality in motion.
- Religion is the community support for spirituality.
- We are called to be co-creators.
- Prayer is a posture toward life.

8

PRIORITY 6.

Sexuality:

It's Dirty, Disgusting And Sinful — Save It For The One You Love!

W e cannot *not* be sexual. We are sexual all the time. Our relationships are sexual because we are sexual beings. Many of us are hurt, confused and afraid of our sexuality, which puts us in stress situations with ourselves and requires a process of recovery. Sexual recovery is difficult in a culture that places so much energy and emphasis on sex, sexual attraction and sexual activity. Sex is trivialized, commercialized, mistaken for intimacy and used as power. At the same time it is repressed, secret and shameful. Unless one has recognized sexual abuse in the past or acknowledged sexual addiction as a problem, there is little support available.

Sexuality is a core of our identity. It is our relationship with ourselves as men and women. How we express our relationship is how we express our sexuality. We are gendered beings. How we relate to the gender we are is sexuality.

Sexuality is our immersion in the pool of creation. Through our sexuality — our maleness and femaleness — we experience people, awareness, places, sounds, music. Our enjoyment of ourselves, our pleasure in our surroundings, our relationship with our bodies and our physical reality are all expressions of sexuality.

Sexuality is the physical and emotional response to desires, urges, touch, fantasy, needs, noticing and human survival as well as cultural and family messages. It is our participation in creation and creativity. Creative energy, the poetry of life, is based on our sexuality. Procreation is a function of our sexuality, the need for continuation of ourselves.

SEXUAL ABUSE

Other people do not make us sexual, but they can damage our sexuality. Following is a partial list of sexual abuse and sexual boundary violations:

- lack of information about sex, puberty, our bodies
- inadequate or no physical affirmation
- no right to privacy (no door, no lock on bathroom, etc.)
- absence of values concerning sexuality
- absence of modeling of healthy sexuality
- being given misinformation about our bodies, puberty or sex
- romanticized relationship with adult or parent
- enmeshment in adult sexual relationship or problems
- being sexualized by inappropriate adult sexual behavior
- being belittled, over-controlled or ignored for sexual feelings or dating relationships
- exposed to pornography, excessive joking, sexual innuendo, sexualized rage, jealousy, fighting
- living with parents who repress sexuality and physical affection, overdo affection and physical touch, are involved in affairs, are sexually addicted or acting out
- being a surrogate spouse to a parent
- living with an adult who fantasizes or obsesses inappropriately
- exposed to inappropriate nudity
- living with voyeurism
- lack of sexual boundaries in family
- being set up to act out a parent's fantasy or image (dress seductively, be a little girl for Daddy, or a lady killer for Mom)
- sexual orientation, identity confusion or denial
- stripping and sexual punishment
- watching others have sex or be abused

- being pushed into sexual situations too early
- not being taught choices, the right to say no, the right to change your mind at any time, the right to ask for what you need
- not being taught safe sex
- being touched or massaged in a sexual manner
- given wet or lingering kisses
- seductive dancing
- genital touching or fondling
- breasts rubbed or fondled
- sexual games
- oral sex, anal sex or intercourse
- mutual masturbation or being used for masturbation
- penetration with finger or objects
- sexual torture
- rape by stranger, friend, acquaintance, date or spouse (marital rape)
- emotional rape

All abuse is sexual abuse because all abuse affects our relationships with ourselves as men and women in a negative way. Abuse, be it physical, emotional, intellectual or spiritual, damages our response to our bodies. It affects our trust and spontaneity, our fantasy and desire. It sets us up to reenact the abuse in inappropriate sexual behaviors and relationships.

Abuse creates a shame response that is difficult to label, expose, express, embrace and deal with, so it becomes internalized. All internalized shame becomes sexual shame because it affects how we feel about our bodies and about being men and women.

Sexuality and spirituality are interwoven. A tear in the fabric of one always requires the mending of the other. *Spirituality is the core of our being, the soul of existence. Sexuality is a core of identity, the soul of who we are.* Sexuality is integrated with spirituality. Being is *what* we are. Identity is *who* we are. Who we are comes from what we are. This is the essence of integration and interdependence living. The spiritual realm of the nonphysical, our life force, values and thoughts, are integrated with the feelings, expressions, beliefs and physical sensation of sexuality beliefs.

We suffer from a spiritual and sexual bankruptcy. Our sexual bankruptcy includes:

- inadequacy
- confusion
- shame
- fears
- excess jealousy

- physical shame
- sexualized anger
- inabilities to risk and explore
- fears of rejection
- unrealized passion
- ignorance
- naivete
- absence of choices and boundaries
- addiction
- obsession
- repression
- guilt
- pain/pleasure fusion
- sexual identity confusion
- gender orientation confusion
- sex-role rigidity
- apathy
- pain and excess risk

It all comes from being sexually used and abused.

RAPE AND SEXUAL MOLESTATION

Rape and incest are common in our culture. About one out of a thousand rapists gets prosecuted, the average sentence is six months and the offender is sent to a rape system for rehabilitation. The victim often gets raped several times by the system while going through the legal process.

The most common form of rape is friend, date or acquaintance rape. A related form of rape that is nearly always overlooked is marital rape. Rape always involves a power differential. The rapist may be an acquaintance, friend, stranger or spouse. Whenever a person says no at any point in time, and the no is not respected or listened to, it is sexual molestation: rape. This includes situations when a person is unable to say no due to confusion, naivete, ignorance, vulnerability, impairment, special learning problems, being sick, drunk, passed out or in a one-down position. In light of this, how many of us have had a no not listened to, and how many of us have not listened to or respected the no?

Men commit most but not all rape. Because of our society's obsession with penetration as the criteria, molestation and much sexual abuse — especially rape of males by females — goes unnoticed or is minimized. Molestation is a form of rape without penetration. Some people say it should not be called rape because it reduces the impact of the term. We believe penetration should not be the criteria, and to not call it rape enables sexual molestation and rape. Men are not born rapists, they are learned rapists. Men are taught conquest in sports, politics, business, sex and love. Men back away from the original bonding with Mom, often with child anger, so they can bond with Dad and develop male identity. Men can't find Dad and still yearn for Mom, but are stuck in the child anger, the anger of the yearning and the absence of identity greatly affects sexuality.

Men are also abused through objectification. They become power objects and depersonalized by becoming economic symbols. Men are expendable warriors doing the dirty job of the culture. Men are taught to play war as the ultimate game, with rape and dishonesty as war games. Men get killed, maimed and lose their friends in war all in the name of good causes, and become high at the prospect and traumatized by the reality. Men are taught to kill animals and each other, and when they can't access killing in war and hunting and no longer feel like men they can form gangs and kill anyway.

What many men are taught about sex is sexual abuse. They are not taught intimacy, nor is it modeled. Sex is intimacy, sex is power, sex is seduction, sex is having sex. They are taught that no doesn't mean no, and that women like force and rough treatment. Men who offend are often victims of the same offenses. Almost all offenders are victims who have bonded with their offenders. The offender in rape is a culture that doesn't protect and affirm, that worships power and denies vulnerability — of men and women.

Women in our society live in fear, adjust their schedules, adjust where they work, park, live and exercise because of society's acceptance of rape. The reason so little is done is that most of us have experienced sexual molestation at some time. Our denial of the experience as a rape sets up an altered baseline tolerance level, a collusive, co-dependent, enabling posture toward sexual abuse. We teach and accept that no doesn't mean no.

In our culture we have pretended to have a taboo on incest and other forms of abuse for generations. There has never been a taboo on incest. There has been a taboo on *talking* about incest. There has been a taboo on prosecuting parents who have been involved in incest. Incest is not about family nor is incest about sex. Incest is about power, rage, addiction, partriarchal systems, religion, psychopathology and compensatory masculinity. Incest is the form of rape that involves a power differential and authority: Anyone who uses authority for sexual gratification commits incest. There is always a power differential with sexual abuse and rape. Incest is rape and involves both a power differential *and* an authority figure. The authority figure may be a teacher, therapist, minister, employer, doctor and so on. Child sexual abuse is incest when it involves an authority figure. Adults always have authority over children.

One of our problems with intimacy is the absence of sexual recovery. Intimacy comes with the convergence of spiritual, sexual and emotional healing; we must find the path to becoming the person we were meant to be by our Creator. Along the path we must practice emotional congruence and enjoy ourselves as men and women. Our relationships with others flows out of self-relationship. Sexual damage produces intimacy dysfunction.

Many of us who have experienced sexual abuse are still able to find intimacy and can still function sexually. Our primary difficulty is in having sexuality and intimacy together in the same relationship.

Sexual damage sets up pseudo-maturity. We act sexually sophisticated but feel fearful, small and inadequate. We fear what is inside, our vulnerability. We often are unable to express our needs or even notice them. We find it difficult to cry or grieve because that makes us more vulnerable, susceptible to more hurt. It also makes people notice us, which is another avenue to abuse. We practice being inconspicuous as an art form, believing if we are not noticed we will not be abused. We feel different, damaged and responsible for what happened. We feel dirty in a way that won't wash off. We dissociate, triangulate, repress, suffer memory loss and fear the anger within. Our fear and shame become the controllers of our lives.

We don't recognize our fear because we feel it all the time. We live in fear — recreating terror to attach the fear to. Our tendency is to reenact the abuse in some form so we can attach the regressed feelings to what is current rather than the terror-ridden denied past. We may also be excessively phobic about avoiding any situations that remind us of the abuse.

KEEPING THE SECRET

We know how to keep the secret. The reason we *learned* to keep the secret of the abuse becomes the basic theme, posture or fear in our lives and relationships. If we were sexually abused we know not to talk about it. The secret must be kept.

We are told or led to believe that:

- If we tell, we will be sent away.
- We won't be believed.
- It will hurt someone else (for example, "It'll kill Mom").
- It will destroy the family.

- People will think we're crazy.
- People will believe it's our own fault.
- The abuse will get worse.
- We'll be beaten or murdered.
- A parent will leave.

The reasons we learn to keep the secret control our lives as much as the abuse. If we believe in telling others what happened to us, that we will be sent away or won't be believed, our entire lives will be controlled by the fear of getting too close to people for fear of being sent away or not believed. If we believe it will hurt someone else, our lives and relationships find us constantly caretaking and worried about our impact on others. If we are taught that telling will hurt someone else, our lives are marked by secrecy and distance for fear that what we say or do may hurt others. Or if we were threatened with harm, our lives are marked by the fear of being physically harmed if we get too close or share too much. This can even lead us to live with battering or physical violence as a form of obsessive fulfillment, or we move from the threat or reality of overt violence to that of covert violence or vice versa.

In recovery it is important to talk about the abuse. It is equally important to free ourselves from the secret and the dynamics of the secret keeping.

OFFENDERS AND VICTIMS

Many of us have been sexually abused by religious leaders and teachers. The undermining of much religion is sexual shame, often resting on rafters of woman hate. People from Fundamentalist, Evangelistic, Protestant, Catholic, Jewish or other families with a great deal of sexual shame, denial and repression often act out. *What is repressed becomes obsessed. What is obsessed gets acted out.*

Not all sex abusers are full of rage and violence. Many are gentle and violent. It is more difficult to deal with a seemingly gentle, loving offender in therapy. Often the offender will romanticize the relationship with the victim, but that does not justify or explain it. It is not romance, it is abuse, and a few offenders only abuse the person they have romanticized.

Sexual and physical abuse victims generally feel responsible for the abuse. "It must be about me, something I do or did, what I wear or look like, something that is wrong with me." It even feels less crazy if we can make it about us. There is a chance that we can change or do something to make it stop. Otherwise we are truly faced with powerlessness and a fear for our lives.

The abuse creates more guilt if we respond to the touch or attention with physical or emotional pleasure. When the victim experiences orgasm or has suffered from touch deprivation, the responses may create greater self-blame. The victims may be convinced they wanted or liked the abuse, thus the shame and denial increase.

Offenders and our culture blame the victim. As victims we take on the blame of the offender. Victims also take on the overwhelming emotional package that offenders cannot deal with and are trying to unload. The unloading, the getting rid of the disgust, fear, rage, shame, pain, take place in the abuse. The offender leaves with a temporary fix, a relief; but the victim is left with the emotional garbage, feeling fearful, disgusted, shameful and isolated.

We tend to see the victim as "asking for it" rather than filling out a victim's role they learned before they had choice. The saying, "There are no victims, only volunteers," is absurd. Three-years-olds don't volunteer to be hurt, nor do thirty-year-olds.

The abuse makes us feel unique. In recovery our uniqueness must be affirmed — but not too much uniqueness should be affirmed. Sexual abuse does not make us gay, lesbian, bisexual or heterosexual. It can damage our ability to discover our individual sexual orientation, according to who we were meant to be by our Creator.

Often sexual shame, anger or impotence in parents is projected as anxieties, financial issues, physical abuse, jealousy, helplessness or rage. These may not look sexual and the abuse caused may not overtly seem sexual, but when the source is sexual the results are sexual damage, fear and acting out.

SURVIVORS

The term "survivor" should not reflect the term "victim." Both are roles we played or were forced to play. We were victims *and* survivors. We can still fall into either or both categories.

Violence and rage that are sexualized covertly or overtly must be dealt with as sexual abuse or the self-destruction, dissociation and fears will continue.

Judy was in her tenth week of a five-week treatment program and obviously stuck. Terry was doing training and heard her debrief for the fifth time her background of physical violence. She really seemed stuck, so he began asking very specific questions about time, place, color of room, what she was wearing. The story that unfolded revealed that the most violent incidents occurred right after school and just before bed, and she was wearing her school uniform or her pajamas when it started.

With further questioning she remembered her father rippng her clothes off as she was beaten. Judy had been working hard to heal from the physical violence, but the therapists had missed the sexual abuse and trauma. More incidents gradually came up. But even as she remembered and dealt with the shock and trauma of being molested by her father, she felt a sense of relief and was able to leave the treatment program and continue outpatient therapy.

When children are physically abused and sexualized at the same time, or when parents take pleasure from inflicting pain, the child may develop a pain/pleasure fusion, the mixing of painful experiences with sexual activities. Many people involved with sadomasochism or bondage and discipline suffer from pain/pleasure fusion as a result of being abused and eroticized at the same time.

Society tells us that it's OK to fight about money, but it's not OK to fight about sex. This can lead to real confusion.

Jose told how his parents fought about money every day, which must be why he felt so financially insecure. He couldn't quite figure out why he felt sexually inadequate, compulsive, jealous and insecure until he realized his parents were not really fighting about money, but sex — sexual rage, inadequacy, jealousy, fear of impotence, seduction. The core issue was sex, but fighting about sex made them feel vulnerable. So money became the focus, and the real issue was never addressed.

SEXUAL DYSFUNCTION

"Disorder of desire" is one of the more common sexual dysfunctions. Often this is a result of emotional denial and repression, since sex is also a feeling. Much of it comes from the absence of communication in a relationship, but a big part of it is the result of trauma. It is often a PTSD issue. Sexual trauma can produce sexual fears, inhibition and loss of desire. When victims begin sharing their fears, anger and other feelings, the sexual feelings are usually awakened.

All relationships inevitably have a sexual component because we are sexual beings. When we are sexually attracted to another person we need to acknowledge but not necessarily with the other person and not at length. Simple, brief acknowledgment can lessen our need to act out.

We often misinterpret data and signals from others. One way men can seduce is by learning to share feelings, yet be dishonest about sex. Men often see nuances in women as permission to "come on."

Sexual affairs outside the marriage are a common recovery issue. The affair often involves betrayal and dishonesty, but these are less often the cause of a relationship break-up than a symptom of deteriorating intimacy. Affairs are hurtful and require a grieving process — dealing with the loss of trust, uniqueness and honesty. Emotional affairs sometimes do more damage than sexual affairs. Friends and family often focus on the affair and miss the other issues. Many of us feel inadequate, hurt and shameful around our sexuality, but we cover it with a veneer of "OKness." When we are betrayed, the veneer is ripped off and all of our past hurts and shame attach to the affair. We must sort out what it is about the affair and what it is about our past, make a realistic assessment of responsibility, a commitment to change and support for ourselves. Expect strange reactions to the affair, including increase of sexual fantasy and stimulation, waves of anger and feeling hopelessness and guilt for both partners. These waves can continue for months, even years.

An affair is not a reflection of either party's adequacy but may be a symptom of relationship problems or a compulsion problem for the one having the affair. Affairs are a red flag for addiction, but also signify a need for change. Some affairs can be a desperate calling out for help, some may be random and even a noncataclysmic occurrence. An affair can be an attempted equalizer in a relationship where other affairs have occurred in the past, an angry act or a last resort. We do not believe affairs are a way of taking care of oneself, but we do believe healing is possible. There is usually an important message for both partners in the affair.

Symbolic work helps in letting go of sexual abuse or affairs, but we must do the deep feeling work first. The rage or pain, the shame and fears must be expressed. Forgiveness and reconciliation are possible, but the most important aspect is self-protectiveness. We will continue to be abused and used or to hang around abusive people until we develop healthy reality and boundaries.

In recovery learning to choose is important. We are not free to say yes to a relationship, a touch, a sexual exchange until we are free to say no. We're not free to be in a relationship until we are free to leave. Freedom is the ability to choose. Our ability to choose rests on our information, boundaries, identity and support systems.

Sexual recovery is

- understanding the relationship between sexuality and spirituality.
- having information and affirmation about our bodies, our maleness and femaleness and sexual functioning.
- liking who we are as people.
- deciding to like our bodies as they are.
- liking ourselves as men and women.

- having same-sex and other-sex friends, acquaintances, nurturing and parenting.
- learning to enjoy appropriate sexual contact with ourselves and others to the extent of our desires.
- learning to enjoy sexual feelings in the context of our values.
- developing boundaries, rights and choices.
- being able to initiate, defend and enjoy ourselves sexually.
- learning that we have the right to say no.
- learning we can change our minds about anything at anytime.
- understanding the difference between safe sex, addictive sex, abusive sex, trivial sex and healthy sex.

In addition we can

- understand and enjoy the healthy part of seduction, flirting and sexual expression.
- learn how to talk about sex.
- remember that others don't make us sexual, but others can damage our sexuality.

Right now we are unaware of any nationwide program offering this type of recovery. Ideally we would find it in the program called "our families," but since most of us didn't receive it there, we need to look elsewhere. We already have excellent spiritual recovery programs, so our suggestion to the recovering community is to integrate sexual recovery into 12-Step programs. First though, the 12-Step programs need to be discussing and working the Steps rather than topic whims. One possible solution would be to work three Steps for three meetings and devote the fourth meeting to the topic of sexuality as it relates to the previous three Steps. In addition the program could develop and promote information on sexuality as it already does with spirituality.

SUGGESTIONS • AFFIRMATIONS • THOUGHTS

SUGGESTIONS

- Read about sexuality. Carol Cassell, Sol Gordon and Pat Carnes have written some wonderful books and pamphlets on it.
- Read — everything you want to know about sex.
- Ask questions of confidants, therapists, recovery groups — talk.
- Develop a language of sex and ask for what you need and like in a relationship.
- Learn about safe sex and sexually transmitted diseases.
- Do an inventory on sexual compulsions or co-dependency.

- Practice flirting in safe settings.
- Ask for help if you are having trouble on your own.
- Take risks with socializing and small talk and be cautious when you meet people. Share about yourself slowly as you build trust with another.
- List some things you can do to take better care of your body so it feels more attractive to you such as . . .

    paint your toenails
    fix your teeth
    redo your hair
    be physically active
    get a therapeutic massage.

- List some things you can do to feel more attractive on the inside, such as . . .

    being honest
    sharing openly
    affirming and loving yourself
    clearing out old baggage
    dealing with how you were abused and used.

- Dance or learn to dance with confidence.
- Dance for joy.
- Be physically active and be attrACTIVE!
- Do a sexual history.
- Debrief abuse.
- Talk about sex to same-sex and other-sex friends.
- Don't go anywhere private with someone you don't know well.
- If you use a dating service, meet and remain in a public place, bring a friend, don't give your phone number or address.

AFFIRMATIONS

- I am sexually alive and attractive.
- My sexuality comes from within me and no one else.
- I am a good lover.
- I can express passion in a safe way.
- My sexual boundaries come from my identity.
- My identity is within me.
- I am sexually free.
- My body is full of compartments of pleasure.
- I make love all the time with the world.
- I please myself alone and with others.
- My sexuality is a freedom not a burden.

- My genitals are mine to cherish and share as I choose.
- I have the right to change my mind.
- I know how to defend myself.
- I can ask for what I need.
- My greatest pleasure is in giving and receiving pleasure.
- I don't need pornography to be turned on.
- My sexual partners reflect my healthy sexuality.
- My passion for life enhances my sexual pleasures.
- My sexual passion comes from my passion for life.
- My sexuality is self-repairing, given support and love.

THOUGHTS

- Others don't make us sexual, but can damage our sexuality.
- Sexual abstinence should be a choice not an assignment.
- Sexual abstinence is overrated and does not mean we stop being sexual.
- Our sexuality is not about genitals or having sex.
- Intimacy does not come from sex, but sex may come from intimacy.
- All shame becomes sexual shame. It always makes us feel worse about being men and women, about our bodies.

9

PRIORITY 7.

Play and Recreation:
The Play Must Go On!

We started this chapter time and time again. Every time we began, we decided to go out and do something playful. Fortunately we were able to achieve some balance in this area by having fun *with* our work!

Many of us were not affirmed and noticed as children, we did not get a chance to play, to be spontaneous. In recovery we are told to be spontaneous. Going out purposely to be "spontaneous" is rather an absurd idea. We can't suddenly "be spontaneous." When we have to practice being spontaneous, it is hardly spontaneous! We can make an intellectual decision to play, laugh, be silly and not take life so seriously. At first it might feel a little stiff, awkward and "put on." When play doesn't come naturally we have to decide to participate and allow ourselves to experience the feelings that come from taking the risk to play; feelings that come out of the play. With time the feelings will reinforce the risk taking and play.

139

Play is not an activity, game or contest. It is not **building** or creating
Play is a posture toward ourselves, others, creation and activity that
enhances all of what we do and creates joy and pleasure, serenity and
excitement. A playful posture toward life is an offshoot of a prayerful
posture in which we maintain a childlike noticing of the world, forms,
colors, movement, size, texture and possibilities. It is an adult awareness
of newness, nuances, anomalies, idiosyncrasies and complexities that
create endless games of fascination and humor.

LEARNING TO PLAY

Play is the work of children. We do not lose this need for play, even as
adults. In play we embrace the newness, imagination and creativity of
childhood integrated with the ability, experience and wisdom of adulthood. Play does not lie so much in what we do as in our approach to
what we do. Some people participate in sports and games, but have no
sense of play in their participation. Others seem to participate little, but
are filled with such spontaneous playfulness and childlike magic they
really play most of the time.

Some of our play must be physical and involve our bodies. All of our
play must be responsible. We play with a sense of care, the ability not to
hurt other people with our play and humor. If our play, teasing and
humor are at the cost of someone else's feelings, it is no longer play or
fun. Play needs to be affirming in its nature. It must affirm our spirituality — our relationship with creation, the people around us, and us.
Play must be safe. The essence of safe play is that it will not cause harm
to ourselves, the environment and others.

When we can't play well we get stuck in the same roles and we don't
create new parameters for our lives, new risk, new roles, experiences,
learnings and laughter. We might say it just isn't fun anymore. This
happens when we lose our playfulness around recovery work, sex,
sports, kids or life. When it's not fun anymore, we begin to replace the
playfulness with obsessing ritual.

We need to be careful that our playfulness doesn't get mixed in with
our anger, for it can become cruel. We also need to watch when it
interfaces with someone else's anger or stress and we get shut down. In
play mode we are childlike. And the slam that others can give us when
we are in play mode can send us scooting away feeling little and shameful. The best thing to do is to scoot back, lick our wounds and go into
play mode again.

A playful spirit is built from within. Terry once went on a ski trip with
a friend and was really excited about all the playful possibilities of skiing

in the mountains. But his friend was working so hard at doing it right, learning the techniques, taking lessons and getting upset whenever he didn't do it the way he was told, there was no playful attitude left. Recently the friend began a recovery journey and is developing a whole new attitude toward his work, recreation and life. He is learning play!

Marvel has many outdoor recreational friends who talk about having lots of toys and playing, but sometimes the play turns into a competitive drive. Once she was on a canoeing expedition from the Rocky Mountains to Hudson Bay — not exactly everyone's idea of a good time, but she expected to be both challenged and enjoy herself. The participants were not noticing the beauty of the surroundings or taking in God's playground; they were too busy trying to conquer it. After the first 700 miles Marvel and her friend decided to leave because the entire focus was on the end product of getting there rather than the process of the journey.

Early on in our recovery our play can be stilted. Sometimes we will try too hard; sometimes it will seem uncomfortable, tense or even a little silly and weird. All of that is OK. Recovery conferences often have playrooms. These playrooms may not create spontaneous play, but the people in the recovery room are learning and risking. We believe all rooms are playrooms. This includes living rooms, bedrooms, kitchens, conference rooms, bathrooms, factory rooms, board rooms and meeting rooms.

Most adult children of alcoholics and dysfunctional families worry too much and take life too seriously, but many of us still have the ability to be funny, to be outrageous, to have fun and to see things in a playful manner. Some of us, though, have that ability stifled, criticized, made fun of or abused out of us. Part of recovery is rediscovering the playful spirit within.

Much of what we do can become playful if we adopt a different view of what we do — it's called *reframing*. When we reframe things, they can become more enjoyable. *In childhood we learn whether parenthood is a playground or prison; we learn free expression of our child within as adults.* When parents view parenthood as a prison, they tend to sentence their children to early adulthood without a sense of childhood. But parents can teach a playful approach to responsibility, they can teach the playfulness of family and they can use humor in their parenting.

Here's an example of how Terry reframed our workday: "I have a tablet in front of me in which I can scribble thoughts to share. Since my scribbling is illegible I get to go to a tape recorder and read my thoughts and make up new ones. Marvel has a portable computer in front of her.

She types away, taking phone calls from around the country, while faxes
are being sent around the world.

"Next we drive a self-propelled big toy car to an airport with real
planes. We get inside one and it takes off into the sky. As we peek
between the cotton, billowy clouds we get glimpses of the earth and its
ant residents and more toy cars and tiny trees.

"Then we land and get to tell jokes and talk with several hundred
pairs of eyes watching us. If this isn't play, what is?"

When we complain about writing, traveling and lecturing, we realize
we've left our childlike sense of wonder behind. Recovery must be
playful or our child within remains hidden and if we can't find our child
within we can never grow up, since growing up is the integration of
child and adult. Without a sense of fun our recovery is dull, empty and
incomplete. If we view our life through the lenses of our child within
there unfolds a mosaic of wonder and play.

PLAY IN EVERY WAY!

Play comes in many packages and settings: shopping play, mental
play, physical play, creative play, team play, competitive play, cooperative
play, meaningless play, productive play, expensive play, rewarding play,
dance play, giving play, cooking play, teasing play (always gentle), laugh
play, joke play, sex play, puppy-wrestle play, travel play, visual play or
kaleidoscope play.

Want some more? Other play is mimic play, acting play, noisy play,
pretending play, career play, complex play, adventure play, play on words,
played out, foreplay, five or six play, as many as want to can play.

The potential and possibilities of childlike play are limitless, yet by
trying to imagine the potential and possibility we can reach toward it.
Parenting is play, recovery is play, learning is play, prayer is play, life is
play, and all the world is a stage for us to play our part. And play we
will, for the play must go on!

PLAY IN RECOVERY

We are all children. The earth is a large, space-bound playground.
The average time people in many native tribes spend working for food
and shelter is a little over a couple of hours a day. The rest of the time
is for play and relaxation and learning. A playful spirit is part of a sense
of humor and comes from a light heart. A light heart comes from not
taking oneself too seriously. This recovery is heavy stuff — violence,
incest, addiction, neglect and so on. This shame and fear can control our

lives, but nothing unlocks the grip on these feelings faster than laughter and a playful posture with ourselves.

In recovery a time comes when we are ready to play. For some of us this comes easily because we never really stopped playing. But for others it is very new and much more difficult. Often those of us who grew up too fast and too serious have a difficult time imagining what real play is like. Recovery is painful, difficult work, But any recovery program that isn't fun, that doesn't contain levity, playfulness and laughter isn't a recovery program but a misery program. Some of us act out with play and humor, so in recovery we need to continue the play and humor but stop the acting out.

If we watch porpoises, sea gulls or butterflies, we need to learn to play as they do, soaring around in the naturalness of their creation and environment. Play is the goal of recovery — not just the ability to play, but finding people to play with, and having the time and physical energy for that play. People who play together, pray together and stay together.

MUSIC, MUSIC, MUSIC

Music is the universal language. We can listen to music, we can feel music, we can move to the music. Music offers us a time of calm and relaxation, an opportunity for dancing and celebration, a point of community and orchestration together.

Keep some notes of goodness in your life. Whether it is a guitar, harmonica, piano, flute, harp, violin, xylophone, trombone, oboe, kazoo, spoons or tissue and comb — play it! If nothing else play the stereo. Whistle and sing — in the shower, in the car, by yourself, with others — just belt it out! We take ourselves so seriously when it comes to music and are so self-conscious that we end up with a music void in our lives. If you don't "do music" yourself, hang around people who do and hum along.

LOVE TO LAUGH!

Terry once worked with a group of kids who had all been to half-way houses and were *very serious*. He took them up to the wilderness during the coldest part of the year. They met in a big wigwam the first night, before sleeping out under the stars. The kids were way out of their element. Everyone was a little nervous and uptight. Then one of the members of the group started talking and he was very funny. Then the person next to him started giggling, and then the first kid started giggling, and then Terry started giggling, and then the rest of the group started giggling. Their entire group meeting that night consisted of

about 120 minutes of giggling! The weather during that group wilderness experience was foul. They were dog sledding, and the dogs were
unmanageable. In some respects, Terry recalls, it was a disastrous
group, but at the same time one of the best groups he ever had. Why?
Because the kids bonded through the laughter, the giggling and the
childlike qualities of that first meeting which stayed with the group.
That group still meets after almost twelve years.

Laughter is the cement that bonds the group or family or friendships
together. The healing power of laughter is legendary. Norman Cousins
talked about using laughter as a form of therapy for cancer patients.
Some question whether laughter has a healing power or not, but even
if it turns out to be just a placebo and even if the medicine really isn't
that strong in changing the illness, it is one of the most enjoyable cures
we know.

Humor is a posture toward life that makes possible our playful attitude. Humor shortcuts shame, heals the body, lifts the spirit, facilitates
change, dissolves grief, diffuses hopelessness and destroys secrecy. A
sense of humor is not the ability to tell jokes or be funny, but rather the
ability to laugh at jokes and notice what is funny (which is most things
that don't hurt people, other creatures or our planet). Occasionally we
find a little humor in some of the things that do hurt — if they don't
hurt too much.

TERRY'S QUESTIONS (THIS IS HUMOR!)

S ometimes what isn't funny is the funniest of all, and what is really funny can be really sad. This may seem contradictory, but much of life is. All co-dependents are contradictory. Even the smallest particle known to humans behaves in contradictory ways. This contradictory stuff works its way up to children, automobiles, governments, football teams and (in this case) the airline industry. Remember, the opposite of everything is true — and usually funnier!

Life is a quest and on a quest we end up with a lot of questions. Some of my questions are about the airline industry.

- Why do they call some flights nonstop?
- Why do they call that place you land a terminal?
- Why, when I'm five miles up in the air, do they tell me what my final destination will be?
- Why, when an airplane is getting in trouble, do they give everybody peanuts and free booze? We all know what a calming effect peanuts and free booze have on a crowd.
- Do I really want an oxygen mask on a burning jet?
- Does it matter in a plane crash if my seat back is straight or not? I can see them going through the wreckage and saying, "Oh! here's the problem."
- Why have nuns and flight attendants switched dispositions in the last 20 years?
- Why is it when I went to the United Airlines desk and I said, "I want this bag to go to New York, this bag to Seattle and this one to Chicago," they said, "We can't do that, you must think we're United Parcel Service." And I replied, "Well, you did it last time."
- How can they find that little black box after a plane crashes in a billion pieces and they can't find my luggage after a safe landing?
- My final question, do endorphins look as good as they feel?

PLAY-TIME NOTES

Some people say they have fun playing slot machines. Most gambling really isn't play because the excitement comes from the money, not the game. Playing poker or Black Jack without wagering is boring to many people. Golf is often a gambling game. Certainly playing the horses has little to do with horseback riding or polo, which sound more like play to us. Gambling is addictive.

Professional sports are more like gambling than playing because the money is more important than the game. We watch but don't play, and our egos get involved in picking the winners. We call the team *our* team, but it has almost nothing to do with us since it could be sold or moved to another city and only one or two players are from where we are and they usually don't like it there. Watching can be play, but we can't take it so seriously. We focus so much on winning that it isn't playful anymore. Watch the performers, the play, not the score so much. Better yet, go home and do it.

If you feel worse at the end of play, it probably wasn't play. Play is refreshing and enlivening even though it may be tiring. Select playmates carefully. If you find a good one, get married or at least go steady!

Television, movies, video games and computers can be types of play, but more than a little can give one an electronic lobotomy. We lose our drive, creativity, initiative and emotional and physical capabilities. All electronic devices should carry a warning level, "Danger, use of this device in excessive amounts may damage your health, anger your family and be addictive!"

Play, in the form of intensity and risk, can be addictive because our brain gets excited too and produces substances that make us feel good all over. We keep escalating the risk to continue to feel good and can no longer feel good without the intensity. Just like drugs. Eventually we crash, and don't feel so good anymore. Addictions aren't playful.

Creative stuff is play until we invest our ego into everyone approving it and liking it. Our self-worth gets tied into their art appreciation skills and we usually fare better if they don't have any.

Dancing is play, especially when it's fun and spontaneous.

Traveling is play, except when it's for work. Play is harder to maintain when we are doing something for money or career. Not impossible, just more difficult.

Jim Ballard, a runner, ran almost every day for 30 years. When asked how far, he said, "I don't know." When asked how long he runs for, he said, "I don't know. I just start, and then end. That's how I enter my day."

A half-hour of play time can provide us with great balance in our life. It can mean the difference between a positive, wonderful day and an ordinary or down day.

SUGGESTIONS • AFFIRMATIONS • THOUGHTS

SUGGESTIONS

- List five playful activities you enjoy in your life now. List five playful activities you used to enjoy but no longer do. After each activity write down when, why or how you stopped the activity. Write what it would take to pick it up, if you'd like to pick it up again. List five activities that seem playful to you that you would like to learn or try or do. On second thought forget all the writing and go out and play!
- Write down the names of three to five friends who you think are playful. Try to spend time with these friends. How many couples do you know who play well together? Try to spend time with these couples.
- Plan a playful event and invite those of your *family of creation* whom you would trust and want to be at this event.
- Give an example of mental play that you enjoy — chess, checkers, trivia games, word games. Continue on this with physical play, creative play, team play, competitive play, pretend play, rewarding or productive play.
- Play dress-up!
- Join a team or club that combines play and community.
- Please yourself with your funny thoughts and jokes.
- Go to a comedy club instead of a movie.
- Don't watch more sports than you play.
- Play music and play dance. A serious dance is choreographed and supposed to produce income. The rest is fun and playful, and full of mistakes, which is the most fun, even though hard on the toes.

AFFIRMATIONS

- My recreation is the re-creation of my spirit.
- I pray through my play.
- I am childlike and playful.
- My joy nourishes my gratitude.
- My childness tickles adulthood.
- I take play seriously and seriousness playfully.

- I am a good friend and a great playmate.
- My humor is my humanity.

THOUGHTS

- Balance is easier when we're in motion.
- It is too late for many of us to have a happy childhood, but it is never too late to have childness integrated into a happy adulthood.
- Carol Burnett once said that humor is often something that in the past was a crisis, but in the present is funny. We often debrief tragedy with humor, but some tragedies are never humorous.
- Let the play begin!
- If all the world's a stage, I want better lighting.
- The earth is my playground.
- The family who plays together stays together.
- Laugh lines are life lines.
- Laughter is the release of the hidden child.
- Humor and human are synonymous.

10

PRIORITY 8.

Nutrition And Food:
Gentle Eating

R ecovery involves self-care. Self-care involves nourishing ourselves with food
and fueling our bodies with life-giving
energy in a gentle way. It is common to be hard on
ourselves about our bodies and what we eat. Food and
eating are basic to all people and most work and social
situations. We can use food as an ever-ready means of
repressing feelings and avoiding real issues. We can
medicate with food — with the food itself and the process of eating.

WHAT'S EATING YOU?

We are *how* we eat, not *what* we eat. Food and eating
are ongoing experiences in our lives. Unfortunately few
of us are comfortable with what and how we eat because food is what we focus on when we are uncomfortable with our bodies.

Food can be used to distract us from the physical aspects of emotions. People commonly use food to avoid anger. For some of us an angry jaw becomes a munching jaw. For others the constriction in our throat is loosened when we swallow, the tightness in our chest is relaxed and sedated with food. Sometimes the knot in my gut yields and is soothed when I have a full gut.

IT'S ALL IN THE FAMILY

Many of us have painful memories of family food fights — the supper table and the explosiveness or the deafening silence of everyone being together. Often food was easier to fight about than the other issues. Some of us seldom sat down together at all. Everyone was so caught up in their own lives or it seemed better to avoid the pain and fighting by not sharing mealtime.

In families food can be love, punishment, power, medication, control, seduction, guilt or even the focus of life — everything but nutrition! Through food we may have been shamed, abused, deprived or manipulated. With food we could find isolation, insulation, medication or elation.

DISORDERED EATING

The two major categories of disordered eating problems are *lifestyle related* and *responsive*. The former has to do with sedentary living, stressful lives, boredom eating, lots of television watching, a limited "dieting" history and frequent consumption of high-fat, low-nutrient foods. Responsive eating is emotional eating. It is eating in reaction to many things other than physical hunger — "I only eat when I am mad, glad, bad, sad or have been had!"

Responsive eating includes the problems of anorexia nervosa, bulimia nervosa, compulsive/obsessive eating and chronic dieting. People struggling with these problems may be male or female, come from all socioeconomic groups; usually have poor self-image or body image; are emotional eaters; rely heavily on the scale for messages of self worth; are *hard* on themselves for what they did or did not eat (they *should* on themselves regularly!); and have been on diets repeatedly. The common link in the symptoms of all these life-threatening or life-impinging states is "dieting" or restrictive eating.

The common precursor to disordered eating is co-dependency — the absence of a healthy relationship with self. It stems from abuse, neglect, trauma and enmeshment.

DIETING ROLLER-COASTER

Diets do not work. Nonetheless intelligent people continue to buy the powders, creams, food packages, pills, potions, books and magazines with weight-loss gimmicks. The diet industry is the only industry that survives on its own failures!

We want a quick fix — just pop one more pill and everything will be OK. If any one diet worked, wouldn't everyone be on it and satisfied with their bodies and their lives? As we all know, it isn't quite that simple. More commonly we go on a diet and the first thing we lose is our sense of humor. We do lose weight — water, fat and muscle — and then we no longer follow the diet, mainly because it is unreasonable, unreal-isitic and unhealthy. And then, of course, we blame ourselves.

The very concept of "going on" a diet seems to mean we will go *off* the diet. We can then say, "The diet worked but I blew it." Now we can beat ourselves up about how we didn't do it right and can feel terrible all over again. We gain weight again, this time mostly water and fat, and since our metabolic rate has dropped, we don't need to eat as much to gain. Dieting is a no-win situation — the *rhythm method of girth control!*

FOOD, GLORIOUS FOOD!

Often people with eating problems are harshly confronted and shamed. The biggest eating disorder in our culture is how we treat eating disorders. We need to learn to enjoy food without being over-whelmed by guilt and worries about weight gain. Dieting and restrictive eating is about deprivation and punishment for something we supposedly have done wrong. We must be gentle with ourselves and give ourselves permission to eat.

There is little or no point in calling foods "junk" or "bad." When we eat them, then *we* feel like junk and bad — is eating potato chips worth beating ourselves up over? Suppress equals Obsess. We need to give ourselves permission to eat a fun food or treat once in a while, so we won't be so likely to binge and overdo. We call it the two-cookie syn-drome: "Well, I blew it and ate two cookies, so I might as well eat the whole bag!" We need to learn the art of gentle eating.

Give up the scale. So far it probably hasn't improved the quality of many of our lives. What messages do we get from getting on the scale? "Oh, I am so terrible, I should have never eaten that ice cream last night." Or "Whew, I finally lost enough so I can start eating again." The scale doesn't tell us whether we are fit or healthy, but some of us let it tell us whether we are good or bad people.

Here are some simple steps toward healthy eating:

- Give up dieting. If this feels overwhelming, attend an Overeaters Anonymous or other 12-Step meeting and join a support group.
- Get aerobically active, not for weight loss but for emotional and spiritual well-being. We make better food choices when we are physically active.
- Give up the scale and other deprivation and punitive activities.
- Give yourself permission to eat.
- Follow the Guide To Healthy Eating on the next two pages. This is the *minimum* of what we need and then we can make additional choices.

Following are some basic guidelines and ideas about food issues and concerns to consider for healthy living. Above all else, we need to be gentle and caring with ourselves.

Abstinence

Our definition of abstinence in regard to emotional eating problems is guilt-free eating. Abstinence is what each one of us needs concerning our particular issues. It may be abstaining from using the scale, not snacking, refraining from dieting, not being hard on ourselves about what we eat or how we look. Abstinence is not about eliminating white flour, sugar, additives or food groups, unless something is a specific health concern for us individually. In the past the concept of abstinence actually created more rigidity and a focus on food and eating, which those of us with eating disorders already did. We do not need to spend our life energy thinking and worrying about food. We need to let go of the symptom with which we have learned to medicate our pain and emptiness.

Artificial Sweeteners

Fructose, sorbitol, manitol and xylitol have all been used as substitutes for sugar in foods for people with diabetes, and all of these sweeteners provide as many or more calories as sucrose (table sugar). Some people have reported problems with diarrhea when using these products. Saccharin is a noncaloric sweetener used to sweeten beverages and foods. There has been some concern from animal studies about a correlation with cancer, which has resulted in a ban of its use in some countries. Most people complain about its aftertaste. Aspartame (Nutrasweet), a synthetic combination of two protein components, is available for use as a sweetener in breakfast cereals, powdered beverages, gelatins, puddings, fillings, whipped toppings and chewing gum. It can be purchased as a

GUIDE TO HEALTHY EATING

Minimum Daily	ANYTIME Low in fat, salt, or sugar. Vegetables, fruits and grains in this column are high in fiber.	IN MODERATION Medium amounts of fat, salt, or sugar.	NOW AND THEN High in fat, salt, or sugar.
VEGETABLE/FRUIT 4 or more servings 1 vitamin C rich 1 dark green leafy 2 others 1 serving = ½ cup, 1 piece, or 4 oz. juice	All vegetables and fruits except those listed at right. Applesauce, unsweetened Fruit juices, unsweetened Potatoes, white or sweet Vegetable juices, unsalted	Avocado Guacamole Vegetables, canned with salt Vegetable juice, salted	Fruits, canned in syrup Fruit juices, sweetened
GRAIN 6 or more servings 1 serving = 1 slice bread, 1 ounce cereal, or ½ cup cooked pasta or rice	Barley Bread, whole grain Cereal, whole grain Oatmeal Pasta, whole wheat, spinach Popcorn, plain Rice, brown Tortillas, corn Tortillas, whole wheat	Biscuits Bread, white Cereals, granola Cereals, refined Corn bread Muffins Pancakes Pasta Popcorn, small amount of fat and salt Rice, white Tortillas, white flour Waffles	Pretzels
MILK PRODUCTS 2 servings 1 serving = 1 cup milk, 1 cup yogurt, or 1½ ounces cheese	Buttermilk Cheese, farmer or pot Cottage cheese, low-fat Milk, low-fat (1%) non-fat dry skim	Cheese, low-fat or part skim Cocoa, made with skim milk Cottage cheese, reg. Ice milk Milk, low-fat (2%) Yogurt, low-fat, frozen Yogurt, low-fat, plain	Cheese, hard or processed Eggnog Ice cream Milk, whole Yogurt, fruit flavored

Minimum Daily	ANYTIME	IN MODERATION	NOW AND THEN

MEAT/ALTERNATES
2 servings
1 meat, fish or
  poultry
1 vegetable protein
1 serving = 2 ounces
  meat, fish,
  poultry or
1 cup cooked
  beans or
¼ cup nuts
	Vegetable: dried
	  beans, peas, lentils
	Fish: cod, flounder,
	  haddock, perch,
	  sole, water-
	  packed tuna
	Poultry: chicken or
	  turkey (no skin)
	Meats: cuts or
	  ground meat
	  labelled very lean
		Eggs
		Fish: herring,
		  mackerel, salmon,
		  sardines, oil-
		  packed tuna,
		  shellfish
		Meat: flank, leg,
		  loin, round, rump,
		  tenderloin, most
		  veal
		Vegetable: nuts
		  (including pinon)
		  refried beans,
		  soy beans,
		  peanut butter
			Fish and poultry:
			  deep fried
			Meat: brisket, chuck,
			  chorizo, cold
			  cuts, corned beef,
			  frankfurters,
			  ground beef or
			  pork, hamburger,
			  jerky, liver, rib
			  roasts, rib steaks,
			  sausage, spare ribs,
			  untrimmed meats

**COMBINATION
FOODS**
	Mixtures of
	  "Anytime" foods.
	Salad: mixed fruit,
	  tossed greens
	Soup: vegetable
		Beef and vegetable
		  stew
		Burrito
		Chile con carne with
		  beans
		Chile, green or red
		Enchiladas
		Lasagna
		Pizza
		Posole
		Salad, three bean
		Spaghetti
		*Prepare these items
		with lean meats,
		low-fat cheese, and
		minimal fat and salt.*
			Chicken a la king
			Chile relleno
			Fast food:
			  hamburgers,
			  sandwiches, main
			  dishes
			Macaroni and cheese
			Meat loaf
			Pot pies
			Soup, canned and
			  dried
			Stroganoff
			Tacos
			Tamales
			Tostadas

OTHERS *Provide few nutrients. Many are high in calories. Eat as needed for more energy and enjoyment.*	*Bacon, butter, cake, candy, chocolate*, coffee*, cookies, cream, cream cheese, French fries, gravies, jams, jellies, lard, margarine, mayonnaise, olives, pickles, pies, potato chips, presweetened cereals, sauerkraut, salad oils, soda pop, sopaipillas, sour cream, stuffing, sugar, syrups, tea*, tortilla chips.* **May be high in caffeine*		

Source: Adapted from *attrACTIVE WOMAN, A Physical Fitness Approach To Emotional & Spiritual Well-Being.* Harrison, M. & Stewart-Roache, C. Parkside Publishing, Parkridge, IL, 1989.

tablet or powder and is very sweet and low in calories. Some people report experiencing dizziness, blurred vision and other side effects, but there is no definite conclusion that these are caused by aspartame.

We are not in a position to argue pro or con about the safety of artifical sweeteners. Clearly not all the data are in. If you choose to use them, do so with moderation, maybe once or twice a day. The more important issue is that large-scale studies have shown that *such sweeteners do not prevent weight gain*. Indeed, they may stimulate appetite and actually promote weight gain. A study of weight gain over a six-year period of time in more than 78,000 women found that those who used sugar substitutes were more likely to gain weight faster regardless of their beginning weights. Another study found that aspartame increased feelings of hunger and decreased feelings of fullness. It is possible that when you use the sweeteners, it leads you to overindulge in high-calorie foods you might otherwise pass up.

Caffeine

Caffeine is naturally found in some plants, such as cocoa and coffee bean. Food or drinks that are derived from these plants contain caffeine. The most common places caffeine is found in our diet are coffee, tea, some soft drinks and chocolate. Caffeine is also found in some over-the-counter drugs, such as diet pills and certain pain relievers and allergy medications.

Caffeine is a stimulant. It can be addictive and related to increased or irregular heartbeats, headaches, trembling, nervousness and irritability. It can increase urine output, which increases the risk of dehydration. Studies have indicated that moderate amounts of caffeine (four cups of coffee) can trigger panic attacks in people who are prone to them. There is an association between caffeine ingestion and certain cancers. As caffeine consumption increases, so does the need for more calcium.

Because caffeine is a stimulant, if you use it at all, use it in moderation. When we insist chemical dependency treatment centers become places to treat nicotine addiction, people always respond with "When do you stop? What about caffeine and sugar?" The death statistics do not reflect that caffeine and sugar are terminal chemical dependencies — nicotine is.

Calcium

Calcium is a necessary mineral for building strong bones and teeth, transmission of nerve impulses, muscle contraction and relaxation, and blood clotting. Women commonly do not get enough calcium unless they pay special attention to their food choices. Without enough dietary calcium, women are particularly at risk for osteoporosis (bone thinning) (Other risk factors for osteoporosis include being Caucasian or Oriental, thin, sedentary, smoking cigarettes, drinking excessive alcohol, living to an old age and having a family history of osteoporosis.) There are some risk factors over which we have no control and several about which we can make lifestyle choices.

Being active and exercising as opposed to being sedentary will help thicken and strengthen bones if we are getting enough calcium in our food intake. It is recommended that women get 800 to 1,000 milligrams of calcium each day. Following menopause women require about 1,200 to 1,500 milligrams daily. In order to do this they will need to include dairy products in their food choices, since they are calcium-rich foods. Women who are unable to consume dairy products will need to carefully choose other high-calcium foods and possibly take a calcium supplement. Estimate about how much calcium you are getting from food (one glass of milk has about 300 milligrams) and then supplement what you need. Read the label carefully on the supplement package for the calcium content so you don't "over supplement," since you are likely getting some calcium in your diet. A key here is understanding the term "supplement," which means *in addition* to food intake, not *instead* of food. Some calcium tablets do not digest in our system. A simple test to check this is to place a pill in a cup of vinegar for an hour. If it hasn't dissolved, it is probably not being absorbed in your system. Return them and ask for your money back. If you had kidney stones composed of calcium, you should not take calcium pills and you need to ask your doctor for advice.

Some people are lactose intolerant — they lack the enzyme necessary to digest fluid milk, get indigestion and feel bloated when they drink milk. They can usually drink milk labeled "acidophillus" (available in most grocery stores) or purchase lactose tablets from a pharmacy to add to regular milk, which will usually alleviate the problem. Often these people can enjoy buttermilk, yogurt and cheese without discomfort.

Carbohydrates

Many people still believe that carbohydrates and starches are "fatten-ing!" They are not. In fact they have less than half the calories of fats. Complex carbohydrates like bread, cereal, pasta, rice, potatoes, beans, and vegetables are the basis of an active person's energy stores. The more active we are, the more of these vitamin- and mineral-loaded foods we need. Now if the baked potato is merely a boat to float the butter, sour cream and bacon bits, there is a slight problem! Enjoy bread, spaghetti, potatoes without frying or adding extra fats.

Cholesterol

Increased amounts of cholesterol in our blood is associated with heart disease. The cholesterol in blood comes from within the body (some of us produce more than others) and from the food we eat. Since we can't control what our body is producing, we will talk about the food sources. For people with cholesterol problems, eating fewer high-cholesterol foods may help. Cholesterol is found in animal products only (fatty meats, egg yolks, whole milk products); plant products contain no cholesterol.

Other dietary factors affect the amount of cholesterol in our blood. More fat, oil or grease of any kind will probably increase it. Saturated fats — those that are solid at room temperature like animal fats, butter, lard or hard margarine, whether from plants or animals — and coconut and palm oils can add to the problem. Try polyunsaturated oils like safflower, soy or corn oil, or monounsaturates like olive oil or canola whenever necessary. Increasing the amount of fish we eat may help. Eating certain high-fiber foods like oatmeal (or oat bran), lentils and legumes, carrots and apples may be helpful; choose some of these foods regularly.

Other factors affect our blood cholesterol level: smoking increases it; a high body-fat content increases it; and regular aerobic activity decreases body-fat and can increase the "good" HDL cholesterol, which carries cholesterol away from our blood vessels.

It is not possible to know whether blood cholesterol is high or low by how we feel. A simple blood test called a blood lipid profile can detect cholesterol problems. Some of the finger prick, blood droplet tests are not accurate. Check with your physician, local public health department or Registered Dietitian.

Cravings

Many of us struggle with a craving for particular foods. We feel "weak" because we crave something and are not "strong" enough to overcome it. Cravings are very real. Rather than spending a lot of energy fighting the craving, which generally makes it worse, give yourself permission to have the food you crave and enjoy it.

Often cravings are due to restrictive eating (dieting). *When we suppress, we obsess.* Choosing poor quality food or not having enough complex carbohydrates can also lead to cravings. Follow the Guide to Healthy Eating on pages 153-154. Cravings rarely occur due to nutrient deficiency. A craving for a non-food item like chalk or starch may require medical attention. If you feel out of control with sweets and binge on large amounts frequently seek out professional help for compulsive eating.

Fat

A fatty diet is high in calories, has few nutrients and increases your risk of heart disease, cancer and other serious problems. Choose lean meats, fish, poultry and dried beans for protein. Select low-fat cheeses, yogurts and milk. Cut down on bacon, fatty sausage, butter, margarine, shortening, pastry products, mayonnaise, sauces, gravies and salad dressings. Retire the frying pan . . . bake, broil, boil or roast instead. Limit "fast foods," which are usually high in fat. This doesn't mean you can never have a French fry again — just enjoy them occasionally.

If you are going to make one single change in your eating, eat less fat. Simply cutting back on all fats eliminates the hassles of figuring out how many milligrams of cholesterol, monounsaturated, polyunsaturated or saturated fat to eat. Just because a food product is labeled "no cholesterol" does not mean it is not high in fat — vegetable shortenings have no cholesterol but are 100 percent fat.

Fiber

Try nature's "broom" by including fiber in your diet. Fiber absorbs water, aids digestion and helps prevent constipation. Increased fiber is associated with lowered risk of some cancers and certain fiber may help lower blood cholesterol levels. Choose fresh vegetables, fruits, dried beans and whole grain and cereals.

Iron

Iron is a trace mineral that builds red blood cells and carries oxygen. Women's regular menstrual flow makes them prone to iron-deficiency anemia (iron-poor blood), which means feeling tired or weak, experiencing shortness of breath or maybe a loss of appetite. Living at higher altitudes puts greater demands on the blood supply to have more iron. Tests for anemia are simple and inexpensive and can be done by your physician or local health office personnel. Sometimes women need to take iron supplements. To prevent iron-deficiency anemia, choose foods rich in iron.

Processed Foods

Select foods that are close to the way Mother Nature gives them to us. Many nutrients are lost during food processing and when they are cooked. So choose orange juice instead of orange drink; a baked potato instead of potato chips; whole grain breads and cereals instead of white bread and processed cereals; and instead of canned vegetables, enjoy raw or lightly steamed ones.

Salt

Go easy on salt. Most people eat more salt than they need. It is a learned taste to like more salt, so by slowing down on the salt shaker we can "unlearn" it too. Cutting down may help lower your blood pressure if it is high. Use more unprocessed foods as suggested above and use less salty foods (such as ham, pickles, processed lunch and breakfast meats). Try seasoning with fresh herbs and spices or powders (such as garlic or onion powders, celery seeds).

When exercising you will lose some salt (sodium) through perspiration. This is a normal response. It is not necessary to take in more salt, because our body reacts immediately by not losing as much sodium in the urine. Over time, as we become fitter, our muscles will lose less sodium and other important electrolytes when we are active. Aren't we amazing?

Sugar

Too many sweets may promote dental decay and mean calories with little or no nutritive value. Sugar comes in many forms: white sugar, brown sugar, raw sugar, cane sugar, molasses, honey, corn syrup and fructose. Sugar is used extensively in processing foods. Many foods that don't taste sweet contain sugar (check out a ketchup label). When you cook or bake, try cutting the sugar in the recipes by one-fourth.

Don't give up sugar altogether. Enjoy your sweets, treats and fun foods, and choose the mainstay of your foods from the eating guide outlined earlier. Sugar is made into a much bigger culprit than it is. Some people react to sugar, especially excess amounts. Few people are "addicted" — anyone can consume so much they will experience emotional vacations — but quitting sugar is a choice to cut out a product, it is not recovery from disordered eating. For some of us rigidity and an all-or-nothing approach is a bigger problem than using sugar.

Snacks

Just about everybody snacks . . . and why not? Snacks give us a lift when we need it, particularly with the kind of hectic lifestyles many of us lead. You have probably heard that "snacking makes you fat." On the contrary: Frequent small meals eaten throughout the day are much less fattening than infrequent large ones. Enjoying a snack is not the same as compulsive eating or "grazing" continually.

Sometimes hunger and thirst signals get confused and we may snack on something to eat when we are actually thirsty and not hungry. It would be better to have a thirst-quenching snack. This happens particulary to active people, so before you snack, think about whether you are hungry or thirsty. There are lots of foods and drinks to snack on that have the bonus of energy plus nutrients for action! See "What's Your Snacking Mood?" below for over 50 suggestions that will suit your snacking mood whether thirsty, smooth, crunchy, juicy, fun, or really hungry. So, "nosh" away!

WHAT'S YOUR SNACKING MOOD?

Thirsty!	Smooth!	Crunchy!	Juicy!
cold milk	yogurt	raw vegetables	fresh fruit
mineral water	banana	asparagus	berries
with lime	papaya	bell pepper	cantaloupe
fruit juice:	mango	broccoli	grapes
apple	custard	cabbage	grapefruit
grape	cottage cheese	carrots	kiwi
grapefruit	Fruit Smoothie*	cauliflower	nectarine
orange		cucumber	orange
pineapple		zucchini	peach
raspberry		apple	plum
chilled vegetable juice		corn on the cob	watermelon
		popcorn	frozen juice pops
		puffed rice cakes	tomato
		wheat crackers	pear

Fun!	Really Hungry!	
fruit	hard cooked egg	pizza
frozen grapes	granola	peanut butter on crackers
frozen bananas	sandwich	or bread
	cereal with milk	nuts
	bran muffin	cheese

Source: Adapted from NM Nutrition Bureau publication.

*Fruit Smoothie Recipe: Blend one cup of skim milk, 3 ice cubes, your favorite fresh fruit, a dash of vanilla, cinnamon, and nutmeg in blender. Presto! A refreshing, everpleasing sensation!

Stopping Smoking, Eating And Weight Gain

One of the most common concerns about stopping smoking is the issue of weight gain. Janna said in exasperation, "I want to quit, I really do. And I even know how. I just have to work my 12-Step program for smoking like I do for alcohol. They are both drugs so I know I can do it. But every time I quit, I freak out when I gain weight so I light up again." Janna, like millions of others, battles the issues of the *quit-and-gain game.*

About half of the people who quit smoking gain weight. In the past it was assumed to happen because a person replaced smoking with food — to get their "oral fix." Now research supports what many ex-smokers have suspected all along: that people gain weight when they quit smoking regardless of food intake or physical activity levels. Metabolic changes occur when we stop smoking, and the body's adjustment period often results in weight gain. What is the immediate reaction to the weight gain? You got it — to jump on the dieting roller-coaster (and what a wild ride that turns into) or to light up.

What Can You Do If You're In This Situation?

First off, smoking is a life-threatening chemical dependency and needs to be treated seriously. Get help from people or treatment centers who consider smoking a primary chemical dependency and attend nonsmoking 12-Step meetings. Next, follow the guidelines we have outlined for body recovery and stopping dieting. Chances are you may gain some weight when you quit. If you are still allowing the scale to tell you whether you are a *good* or *bad* person, you will likely gain even more weight when you stop smoking. You will need to accept the possibility that your body will change in response to the choices you make. Take a gentle approach to reclaiming your body, in essence yourself. Your body will adjust in time to being smoke free and will stop compensating. You will not continue to gain weight due to quitting smoking if you don't get caught in the dieting craziness. Body acceptance is critical here, and getting out and moving is a key — not as a means of preventing weight gain, but for gaining energy. You are worth taking care of! Go back and revisit priority three on physical balance if you are struggling with this.

Scott was doing great cutting down on cigarettes during the day. He had gone from two packs a day to a couple of cigarettes and he felt proud about it. In the evenings he attended AA meetings; he had four years of sobriety and knew AA had saved his life, but during the meetings, Scott would inhale a pack or more of cigarettes. This is not surprising, since meetings are a time when many emotions surface and cigarettes are a powerful way to suck those feelings out of sight. After we talked, he decided to switch to nonsmoking meetings, since his chemical dependency program was going to kill him of a chemical dependency! Does anyone remember what Bill W. died of? That's right: lung cancer.

Supplements

The vitamin and mineral industry is booming in America, and it's no surprise. We are a people who believe if a little is good, more must be better, and popping a pill will fix almost anything! Most of us don't need to supplement our food with pills or powders. If we eat a variety of foods we will seldom need to add a pill. Unfortunately many of us are more apt to try a quick fix, to use pills rather than take responsibility for the choices we make.

Frequently the person who advises us on what to take is also the person selling the product. Do you have any idea what the mark-up is on vitamins? Would you be a little wary of buying pills directly from a physician who just prescribed them to you?

Very little is understood about the effects of large doses of supplements. Some can cause numbness, headaches or irritability; others can be toxic, resulting in lasting damage. We do know that a large dose of any supplement acts as a drug and needs to be respected and treated as such. Isn't a goal of recovery to be drug free? Just because you can buy it over the counter or from a neighbor doesn't mean it is harmless. Every vitamin or mineral that we digest affects the metabolism of something else and we have only scratched the surface of knowing the intricacies of this highly integrated, interdependent system.

If you decide to use a supplement, choose a multiple vitamin/mineral supplement that doesn't exceed the Recommended Dietary Allowance (RDA). When you want specific and personal nutrition advice, call your public health department or local hospital and seek out a Registered Dietitian (RD) who is well trained in the science of food and nutrition.

Vegetarian Eating

Eating in a vegetarian style can be very healthy and rewarding. The Food Guide on pages 153-154 provides information for lacto-vegetarians (vegetarians who consume milk products). If you follow a diet that has no milk products, be sure to get information on eating complementary proteins. The Thoughts section at the end of this chapter contains information on the environmental benefits of vegetarian dining.

If you are following a vegetarian diet as a way of restricting your eating, being manipulative with food and manifesting disordered eating problems, consider what you are doing. This same concern applies to food allergies, which can be a way of being rigid about food and eating patterns. Both can take over your life in a similar way to overeating or dieting. If you choose vegetarian eating in concern for the planet, bravo! You are on your way to interdependence living!

Water

Last, but by far not the least, is the nutrient water, probably the most forgotten nutrient of all. Ignoring water has the most potential for harm. We can live much longer without food than we can without water.

It is important to drink *before* we are thirsty, since the receptors in our brain don't let us know immediately when we need water. When we are losing water and are even mildly dehydrated, we might experience fatigue and irritability. Dry lips are the first physical sign of needing water. Many people seldom drink just water. If the thought of plain, old tap water doesn't sound very appealing, add a drop or two of lemon juice to liven it up or burst into some fizzy mineral water. We need at least six to eight cups of clear liquid each day and more when active — add two cups for every hour of aerobic exercise. Be sure a portion of this liquid is water. Make water one of your everyday health kicks!

FOOD AND CHEMICAL DEPENDENCY RECOVERY

Eating well never "cured" anyone from dependency on drugs, but making choices that are nourishing and respectful certainly is a way to demonstrate to yourself that you are worth taking care of. Many people end up switching addictions. The most common recovery for addiction is another addiction — we just choose one that doesn't make people so mad! Food fits the bill: It is readily available for most people, medicates pain and is an easy substitute.

People who are in treatment for chemical dependency are very susceptible to fads and gimmicks and quick fixes. False notions about food and chemical dependency recovery abound. For example:

- When you stop drinking alcohol you will crave sugar, and so you need to suck on hard candies for the first several years of your sobriety. False!
- Many alcoholics and other addicts are hypoglycemics and need the sugar. False!
- Replacing alcohol use with overeating is okay for acceptable recovery. False!

Alcohol and other drugs affect nutrients in five major ways:

1. **Substitution.** Alcoholic beverages and other chemicals often substitute, or replace, nutritious foods and beverages in the diet. People sometimes abuse crack and cocaine to decrease appetite in an attempt to lose weight.
2. **Malabsorption.** Drugs can cause changes in the digestive system so nutrients are not absorbed and thus can not be used by the body.
3. **Alteration of organ functioning.** Alcohol alters liver and other organ cells so they are not able to function properly and have limited ability to utilize nutrients. Nicotine affects triglyceride metabolism. Other drugs interrupt much of normal functioning.
4. **Blocking.** Drugs block the normal interaction between nutrients.
5. **Hyperexcretion.** Alcohol increases the loss of nutrients, both in the urine and feces.

Nutrition Therapy For Chemical Dependency

Here are some simple nutrition guidelines for people participating in chemical dependency recovery programs (adapted from the Indian Health Service Nutrition Training program).

- Enjoy a varied, balanced, moderate-fat diet in a tolerable form.
- Eat frequent small meals when first abstaining.
- Stop smoking in order to repair gastrointestinal damage and let go of a life-threatening chemical dependency.
- Consider your activity level and lifestyle. Eat enough to allow weight gain if you are underweight, but not enough to gain weight if you are overweight (see the Food Guide on pages 153-154).
- Protein intake should be the recommended daily amount (see the Food Guide).
- Restrict sodium (salt) intake if fluid retention is a problem.
- Eat nonirritating foods for esophageal varices.
- Use supplements moderately. Do not rely on meganutrient therapy as the backbone of long-term rehabilitation.
- Get regular aerobic activity, as outlined in Chapter 5.

For inpatients in chemical dependency treatment programs, the following considerations should be made by the treatment facilities or hospital's Registered Dietitian, physicians and therapists.

1. Individualize strategies, but develop and use reliable assessment and therapy protocols.
2. Use oral feeding as soon as possible, limiting milk if lactose intolerant.

3. Dietary supplements: Drug addicts are at high risk for multiple nutritional deficiencies. Dietary prescription for certain nutrients must be greater than the Recommended Dietary Allowance (RDA), since goals are to combat malnutrition and metabolic disorders related to alcohol and other drug abuse and related disorders. Biochemical assessment of the nutritional status of addicts during detoxification is highly recommended, because multiple nutritional deficiencies may be present. If biochemical assessment is not available, the following guidelines are recommended under the supervision of Registered Dietitians and physicians:

- On admission give a single i.m. dose of 100 mg thiamin (Thiamine hydrochloride USP solution, 100 mg/ml)
- If macrocytic (megaloblastic) anemia is present, check vitamin B-12 status before prescribing folic acid greater than RDA.
- Give daily water and fat-soluble vitamins in hospital oral mixture based on approximately the following dosages: Thiamin Mononitrate 15 mg; Riboflavin 15 mg; Pyridoxine Hydrochloride 25 mg; niacinamide 100 mg; cyanocobalamin 5 g; Folic acid 1.5 mg; Ascorbic acid 200 mg; Vitamin A 5000 IU; Vitamin D 400 IU; and Vitamin E 30 IU.
- Correct electrolyte imbalance and magnesium deficiency by i.v. mineral solutions.
- If zinc deficiency is clearly present or suspected, give zinc sulfate 300 mg daily.

Most standard (commercial) vitamin preparations do not conform with the composition of the recommended mixture for rehabilitating chemical dependents.

SUGGESTIONS • AFFIRMATIONS • THOUGHTS

SUGGESTIONS

- Do lunch!
- Quench your thirst — enjoy sparkling water with a twist.
- Enjoy your fun foods and treats.
- If you don't cook, do the dishes.
- Make eating fun.
- Venture toward vegetarian dining out of respect for our planet.
- Learn food etiquette — rituals can enrich.
- During the holidays, eat at the children's table — you usually get served first and it is a lot more fun!

- Grow something edible — anything from a tomato plant to a fruit tree to a corn field.
- Add a little spice to your life! Try an indoor herb garden for looks and cooks.
- Tickle your taste buds.
- Eat something wild (that isn't poisonous) — find a field guide to wilderness edibles.
- Go berry picking.
- Pack a snack — it saves time, money and health.

AFFIRMATIONS

- I eat for nourishment and pleasure.
- I know the joy of gentle eating.
- I am worth taking care of.
- I fuel my body for energy and well-being.
- I enjoy treats and fun foods.

THOUGHTS

- Is it food that makes the holidays or is it people? Which do we spend the most time on?
- Alcohol is a drug, not a food group.
- The adolescent diet includes the four food groups — salt, grease, sugar and a beverage!
- It's not what we're eating, it's what's eating us.
- Buffets are all you *want* to eat, not all you *can* eat.
- Diet is a four-letter word.
- We are *how* we eat, not *what* we eat.
- Food is fuel for physical healings, not a tool to medicate feelings.
- Vegetarian choices are good for the entire planet:*
- Estimated rate of worldwide tropical rain forest deforestation per minute: 150 acres per day: 216,000 acres (roughly the size of Rocky Mountain National Park).
- Percentage of tropical rain forest deforestation directly linked with livestock raising: more than 50 percent.
- Amount of forest lost for every hamburger produced from livestock raised on what was Central American forest: 55 square feet (size of a small kitchen).

- Estimated weight of trees, saplings, seedlings, insects, birds, reptiles, mammals, mosses, fungi and microorganisms killed or displaced for every hamburger produced from Central American forest: 1/2 ton.
- Year in which Central and South America will be stripped of tropical rain forest if present rate of deforestation continues: 2010.
- How often an acre of U.S. trees disappears: every 8 seconds.
- Number of U.S. forest converted into land for grazing livestock and/or growing livestock feed for every acre cleared for urban development: 7 acres.
- Amount of trees spared per year by each individual who switches to a vegan diet: 1 acre.
- Percentage of U.S. water used for some phase of livestock production: more than 50 percent.
- Water needed to produce 1 pound of wheat: 25 gallons. Water needed to produce 1 pound of meat: 2,500 gallons.
- Main source of water for High Plains region of the United States: Ogallala Aquifer. Percentage of water drawn from Ogallala that is used to produce beef: 75 percent.
- Estimated cost of subsidizing the meat industry in California with water per year: $24 billion. 1991 budget for child welfare services in California: $4,425 million.
- Average amount of water required daily to feed a person following the standard U.S. meat-based diet: 4,200 gallons.
- Average amount of water required daily to feed a person following an ovo-lacto-vegetarian diet: 1,200 gallons.

---

*Excerpt from *Vegetarian Times*, April 1990.

11

PRIORITY 9.

Intellect And Creativity:

*Everyone Is A Genius,
Some Are Just Less
Damaged Than Others*

T he integration of wisdom from various
sources and times leads to intellectual
congruence and a creative passion for
life and learning. Unfortunately this creative passion is
not nurtured enough by our society or our schools.

Our societal messages tell us to think rather than
feel. We say that we believe in schools and education,
but our priorities for education are skewed toward production not education. The goal is knowledge for its
own sake, not integration, warmth, success, balance or
stability. We dedicate this chapter to all teachers who
create a safe place for children to learn.

A WEALTH OF INFORMATION

Thought and the ability to imagine seem uniquely
human. This gives us the ability to anticipate and analyze, which can be a problem that often creates anxiety

169

and mischief. Much of our anxiety comes in the form of obsessional thinking and worry. Much of our mischief comes in the form of building things that spring from our imagination, without also imagining the destructive consequences of what we build and create. We have a gift. When we operate only on instinct and impulse we are prevented from fully implementing our gift of thought and imagination.

One problem is the sheer quantity of information. No one can keep up with the advancement in ideas and discoveries, even in minor fields of study. Our intellectual output is staggering: The sum of our information doubles every fifteen years. On the same day that seven thousand scientific studies and reports are published, one hundred and twenty species of life are wiped out. Can we survive our intellectual growth and planetary destruction?

Along with this problem is our increasing specialization. We cannot understand each other if we each work in a different discipline. No one is able to be aware of everything and no one person can integrate or implement the information needed to change what we need to change.

Finally, we have no long-term goals. Our leadership success is based on short-term success in putting out fires. Our leaders depend on election and reelection from a misinformed public. They become so removed from the reality of most people that they cannot address real needs. If change is going to occur it will have to be a gradual movement of people committed to learning and self-discovery, willing to find information and integrate what is found in teaching others and taking action.

INTELLECTUAL ABUSE

Intellectual growth occurs through affirmation of awareness, thought, learning and imagination. It is taught through the modeling of intellectual curiosity and the appreciation of ideas. Einstein once said that everyone is a genius, some are just less damaged than others. We all have the capacity to learn and create, and many of us have not discovered our potential. Some of us have been talked out of it. Others of us have never been taught in a style that matches our learning. Many of us have been intellectually abused.

Intellectual violence is difficult to identify. The very process by which we are able to label and identify this often covert form of abuse is damaged by the abuse itself. Many of us grow up feeling stupid, lacking the ability to trust our own imagination or creativity, lacking the ability to trust our thought processes.

When our intellectual boundaries have been violated, we have a difficult time seeking educational advancement and we are vulnerable to other people's ideas. This sets us up to be used, to get involved in enmeshed relationships, to be underemployed, to underachieve. It is often the basis of our internalized shame and poor self-image. The following is a partial list of intellectual boundary violations and intellectual abuse:

- being denied information
- given misinformation
- being told what to think
- told what we really mean when we say what we mean
- being spoken for
- being made fun of
- being ignored, not listened to
- always having ideas altered or improved upon
- being treated with cruel mind games
- being called names like stupid or dummy
- not being recognized for special learning problems
- being tested in nonsupportive ways
- having excess pressure to perform for grades
- being failed in classes where the teacher has not taught in the style in which we can learn
- not being allowed to make mistakes, being belittled for asking questions
- being overly focused on for intelligence and being smart
- having our curiosity stifled
- not being taught in the paths of our interests
- not being supported for continuing education
- having no right to privacy of thoughts
- being raised in a limited environment with the absence of people who provide stimulation and show us how to find information.

INTELLECTUAL RECOVERY

In recovery we need to seek and share information; do a realistic evaluation of our learning process; develop our own ideas and beliefs; read things that interest us; provide ourselves with intellectual, educational and vocational challenges; speak out about what we believe; ask questions; make mistakes; and become knowledgeable about what is going on in the world. Through self-affirmation, support and surrounding ourselves with people who stimulate us, we can repair the damage.

It is more important to know how to find information than to have information. Ken Blanchard tells the story of a lecturer who holds up a one hundred dollar bill and says anyone who can name the capitals of

North and South Dakota, Florida, Maine, Vermont, Arizona and Nevada can have the hundred dollars. He has never given one away. We have all "memorized" those capitals. Why were we not allowed during a geography test to look at an atlas? Which is more important: to have information, to know the capitals of states, to memorize them or to know how to use an atlas? We will forget the capitals, but we will never forget how to use an atlas.

The reason we require memorization and regurgitate back a teacher's words is, according to Blanchard, so we can fail people. Our entire social system is built on failure. Any teacher who gave out all A's would be fired. We must divide students according to their ability to retain information in their heads until the test and then they can forget it. Temporary retention makes them successful students. The others may be above average, average, below average or failures, but by whose criteria? What learning format?

It is a system suited to poor teachers — they really do not have to teach the way people learn. They can do what they want as teachers, and students will pay and pass or fail depending on their adaptability, not based on their reality or learning ability. Why shouldn't we all get A's and have the answers to the tests? Why do we not research teaching methodology and learning styles to find out what works? Why do we have illiterate adults when Japan has a one hundred percent literacy rate?

Einstein was once asked his phone number: He looked it up in the phone book. Is a genius one who knows the number or how to find it? Is a genius the one who can regurgitate information or think critically? Is a genius one who can copy the model or create an original model? Memory does get lost; the knowledge of how to find information doesn't. To be affirmed in our curiosity and creativity and our ability to imagine and learn doesn't get lost. How to think critically, to create something out of a plethora of information, to find meaning in confusion — this is what is important. To look at the consequences of the impact of thoughts, ideas and movements is what is important, and these can be taught.

LEARNING STYLES

We each experience learning in different ways and process learning differently. Right-brain learners deal in concepts and logic. They are more rational, concrete and systematic in their learning and processing. Left-brain dominated people tend toward an emotional, intuitive and free-form thinking and learning style. The goal in education should be to balance the two. Learning also varies according to personality types. One of the common tools for assessing personality type is the Myers-

Briggs Personality Inventory. Some characteristics reviewed in this inventory include our style of being extroverted-introverted; thinking-feeling. This inventory is not an answer to who we are but can be helpful in indicating our orientation and style of relating to others.

Ordinal positioning — your birth order may also affect learning. Firstborn children tend to learn in pieces, perhaps because they are taught that way. They like to know the rules, and they operate better when structure is clear, overt and explained. They perform well and handle responsibility naturally in a safe and healthy environment. Secondborn children search more to learn the covert system and rules. If things feel all right and feelings are dealt with appropriately, and if the covert rules are nonconflicting and nonabusive, secondborn kids do well. Thirdborn children respond more to relationship issues: relationships with teachers, fellow learners and subject-matter relatedness. Fourthborn children need to know why they are there and the goal of the learning. They do well with clear and effective leadership and when the pieces fit into a logical whole.

Another learning format involves four groups of learning styles:

1. *Social/Creative Learners.* This group searches for reasons and learns best in social and group situations through listening and sharing. They focus more on the human element and tend to view reality from different perspectives. They can be innovative and imaginative. They do poorly in pressure situations on big tests or surprise quizzes. They prefer more teacher interaction and more frequent and smaller tests and peaceful settings for reflections.

2. *Factual/Analytical Learners.* They do well in traditional classrooms, seek facts, look to the experts, are research oriented and prefer the world of ideas. They can create models of thoughts and concepts of reality based on data more than people. They don't do as well in open, flexible learning systems, essay tests or unclear teaching.

3. *Practical Learners.* They learn by doing and like to learn what they can use. They like to know how things work and tend to test theories in practical applications. They like the challenge of problem solving and detest ambiguity. They don't do so well with lots of reading, lecturing or discussion, memorization, group work or feelings talk. This is the group many people in recovery are married to! They need movement, lab work, field trips and experimentation, they tend toward common sense and street smarts.

4. *Teaching/Experimental Learners.* This group is similar to the Practical in that they learn by experiencing and teaching. They also learn well on their own. They look for what can be done with ideas or

things and like to make things happen. They enjoy knowing what can be done with it more than how it works. They don't do well in lecture and teacher-dominated learning situations. They avoid formality, silence, rigid structures and repetition and like to manage and set things in motion.

Effective education needs to include each style of learning. Each learner will have to stretch and work harder some of the time, while having time in their own learning style. Learning in various settings and with different approaches enables us to respect our style and the unique learning process of others.

There is no correct style of learning. The different styles have many strengths — and thank goodness we are all not the same! Each of us needs to consider and be aware of what learning style we are most comfortable in. We must do what we can to create environments for our learning and the learning of those around us.

LEARNING AS PLAY

Curiosity, experience and awareness are the keys to learning. The child is the natural student for whom learning is not work. Learning is play, utilizing the childlike capacity for fascination, creativity and curiosity. Biology is a natural wonder. Children are fascinated by math principles. History is a story and everyone loves stories. English, the language of our culture, contains more stories, words and imagination. Poetry is creative play and art in words. Art is the greatest of play. Geography is vacation travel without motion sickness or long lines! Reading opens the door to infinite possibilities and adventures. Theology and philosophy are the ultimate play, *how we view the play.* Psychology is the behind-the-scenes of play and "the play." A sense of industry built on our initiative is the ability to learn the difficult stuff and not lose the playfulness of the journey of learning. Intellectual games such as chess, checkers, cards, Jeopardy, trivia, Pictionary, Scrabble and hangman, all stimulate learning. Toys can teach, they can help us with organization, coordination, help us learn chemistry, science, biology, building, designing and geography. They can help us understand history and they can help us learn about and appreciate nature. We believe that when a toy is bought for a child it should be playful. When there is a learning part of the toy it increases the benefit of the gift beyond measure. As parents and teachers, our personal continuing interests and learning become the gift of interests and learning we offer our children.

IMAGINE THAT!

Imagination is one of the most powerful of our intellectual capacities. We become what we imagine. The use of imagery in therapy has a very powerful impact on helping people change. The ability to imagine gives us the power to achieve. Our image creates a picture that is planted in the mind. Even if we lose the image for a time, the picture remains planted and the life decisions of the subconscious mind move us toward the realization of the picture.

The imagining can be a visual creation, a sense of something that will happen, a feeling of a process, event or a relationship. For it to occur it must be within the realm of possibility and the overriding or sabotaging messages and images must be dealt with. Many of those are the messages on "old tapes" and pictures that we received in childhood of life and ourselves. Until we deal with those messages of childhood, it is hard to use the power of our images to create change.

When we stay overly focused on the image, we try too hard. We second guess ourselves to try to achieve it, or give up when it gets too tough. We must let the process of our image evolve. This is done by following our instincts, accepting setbacks and not having narrow or singular goals. Our ability to expend energy is an important aspect of achieving our fantasies.

DON'T IMAGINE THAT!

When our fantasies are destructive, our energy goes in the direction of achieving destructive fantasies. When there is a picture placed in our mind of failure, our decision-making process can help us realize the failure. If we envision that all relationships are abusive, won't work out and end in abandonment, if we see ourselves used and hurt in relationships we greatly increase the likelihood of it happening. If we keep fantasizing acting out, being addicted, getting hurt, losing jobs, our reality will follow these paths.

Creating positive images may mean first dissolving the destructive images that were created for us by nonaffirming or abusive caregivers. Sometimes we get enmeshed in the realities of those around us who felt like failures, who were angry, hostile, self-destructive or addictive. This enmeshment produces the image.

To repeat positive imagining is a reinforcement of the image. Imagery is used with varying effectiveness in sports, weight loss, business as well as therapy. We can become who we imagine ourselves to be. Affirmations can be a mechanism for positive images. Imagery can help us realize our goals, and it can also give us insights into our pasts. Imagery can give us awareness in making decisions and finding directions for our life.

Our culture does so little in supporting the use of signs, visions or dreams as life guides. Even when the sign is from the outside, from nature, events or words, the meaning of and direction of the sign come from the inside. Jungian therapists that utilize dream work find it very powerful in self-discovery and motivating toward healthy change. Our dreams are the love letters and hate mail of the subconscious. Dream repression is in fact one of the dissociative responses from trauma and abuse.

I DECIDED NOT TO DECIDE!

Another important aspect of intellectual recovery is decision making. Many of us get frozen when it comes to decisions. We experience an intense fear of making mistakes or having been criticized for all the decisions that we have made. We have had such disastrous implications of having made decisions in the past that we have a difficult time making decisions, or committing to an action, so we stay stuck, frozen and immobile. Recovery is a process of constant decision making about meetings, about acknowledging, about making amends, what to hear, who to go to, who to see, what groups to belong to, who to listen to.

Many of us believe that we are making decisions, but our life still doesn't change. That's because the decision wasn't a real decision. We may say, "Ah, I wish I wasn't plagued by all these cravings," but we haven't done anything about the cravings, about finding support for filling the obsessions with positive imagery, people, joy or risk. A wish is not a decision. It is a very early stage of making a decision; it is part of the process. We need to look at what we wish; what we want in our lives has a way of filling out the decision.

For some of us the next stage is, "I *will* get this done. I *will* go there. I *will* find friends." This is still not a decision. The decision comes not in making up our minds to do it but in beginning the process of doing it. Many of us have tried to make changes in our lives. But if you tell a friend that you "tried" to get downtown, does that mean you made it or does that mean you didn't make it? A decision leads to action and so many of us are so hung up on looking at all sides of the issues, that we have a hard time making the decision and taking the action.

THE INFORMATION EXPLOSION

The recovery movement for addiction, co-dependency and adult children has brought about an information explosion. The amount of motivational tapes, recovery books, videos, articles, lectures, talks and workshops filled with information and suggestions for recovery and mental health have increased a thousand-fold in a few years. Most of it is prepared for the layperson, not the professional. Much of it is not researched. This doesn't mean it's unhelpful, however. Research material is not always helpful and much nonresearched material is helpful. Some of it lacks bibliography, but each part of it contributes something to the truth and the direction of the movement. Even psychiatrists, psychologists, social workers, clinics and hospitals are offering lectures, opening book stores, using tapes and videos. They teach as a part of therapy.

When families of alcoholics were first brought in to treatment for the so-called "family disease," the alcoholic was given a treatment program and the family members and the co-dependents were given information. The family fooled those who were "pretending" to treat co-dependency by taking the information and making important changes in their lives! Information does help us change. It helps us make the valid decisions that lead to the actions that move us toward the realization of us.

SUGGESTIONS • AFFIRMATIONS • THOUGHTS

SUGGESTIONS

- Don't accept everything you read — including this.
- Learn critical thinking and question.
- Attend cultural events that enrich noticing and appreciation.
- Read for fun, learning, sharing and just because you feel like it!
- Become computer literate or form a relationship with someone who is.
- Find hobbies that support your continued learning.
- Be open to teachable moments.
- Add a little class to your life — try your local community education.
- Get lost in the stacks of your local library.
- To travel is to learn, to travel with a tutor is to become learned.
- Imagery can help realize our goals.
- Curiosity and awareness are the keys to learning — the child is a natural student. We must let children teach us how to learn.
- Visit your local museum or art center — for a few minutes or for a few hours.
- If you have always wanted to learn to play an instrument, give it a try. If you don't like it, keep playing your stereo anyway.

AFFIRMATIONS

- I am educable.
- I am music, my gift is my song.
- I am open to new ideas.
- I am willing to ask questions.
- My opinions are important.
- I imagine my possibilities.
- I create a loving reality.
- My imagination enriches.

THOUGHTS

- Common sense and street smarts are more important for many of us than a graduate degree.
- "Our imagination is more important than knowledge" — Einstein.
- If you can read this book, thank a teacher!
- Intelligence is knowing where to find information, not having information.
- Trivial pursuit is just that.
- Memory is just memory, not intellect — and don't forget it!
- It's not that elephants never forget, but it's that no one confronts them about not remembering.
- Selective memory is manipulation.
- Most of us have forgotten more than the rest of us know.
- In our imagination is the creation of reality.
- We become who we imagine ourselves to be.
- Failure in school is more a reflection of a failed educational system than a failed student.

12

PRIORITY 10.

Career:

Play Is The Work
Of Children

R emember God's words to Adam and Eve in Genesis? "By the sweat of your brow, you shall eat bread till you return to dust." Sounds as though we have a command to work to death and work is our punishment! We have many reasons for why we work: We can work to survive, to discharge guilt, to avoid pain, to get sympathy, for meaning, pride or retirement. Many of us work for the sake of work. Others work because we believe in our work. Still others work for accumulation. Most of us have a combination of motivations for our work. We have a cultural work ethic. Work structures our time, provides us with a regular social interaction or a way to avoid it, provides identity, self-esteem, respect of others, community positions, survival and income.

Childhood work postures, habits, ethics, limits and boundaries affect how we work in adulthood. Many of us who are consumed by work as adults were consumed with work in childhood. Some of us were raised by parents who were extremely work-oriented. Work can be an overcompensation for poverty or for some aspect of our life that we feel shameful about.

Obsession with work is expected for some careers, such as religion, writing, art and helping professions. Homemaking and parenting are jobs that many of us become obsessed with, but we very seldom get seen or labeled as work addicts in these positions. Some of us work overly hard because we fear laziness. Many of us are Type A personalities: "Whatever we do, whatever is worth doing, is worth doing fanatically." We operate on overdrive and supercharge.

ROLES, ROLES, ROLES

We tend to carry unresolved and hidden childhood and family issues into the workplace. In fact we reenact the roles of our family in our work settings. Let's take a look at some of these roles:

1. **The hero role.** If we were the hero in our family, always looking good and doing good to make the family look better, we will continue to act as a hero in our workplace, continuing to do good and look good, making the work place look better, but usually not feeling so good about ourselves. We either have the good we do ripped off by the system, or we feel as though it's being ripped off.
2. **The martyr role.** We tend to offer and sacrifice ourselves for the sake of those around us. We "die" for the cause and very often get crucified or we become the savior of the system.
3. **The pleaser role.** We try to do whatever people want us to do. We try to make everybody happy — even if it means we are unhappy, or we have to sacrifice our integrity and honesty to do it. Oftentimes we get into trouble trying to please too many people with too many different things and we get caught — usually with dishonesty.
4. **The parent role.** Many of us parented our parents, parented our younger or even older siblings, and we continue to act as parents in our work settings. We try to instruct, guide and model for too many people who really don't want us as parents, and who refuse to see us as parents. This rejection makes us feel like real parents!
5. **The good-guy or gal role.** We always try to be good, look good and have everybody like us. We never take a firm stand on anything so we can be viewed as good. Being a good person can set up tremendous anxiety about doing the right thing. This is very similar to the pleaser.

6. **The rebel role.** We react, defy and rebel against the system. We pick at and sabotage the structure. We defy authority. Few rebels move up the ladder very quickly, but many have a strong following and a big impact on the system. The rebel suffers in actually being controlled by what is rebelled against.

7. **The lost child role.** We do our job — unrecognized and undercompensated. We feel lost within and we look lost without. We isolate or feel unwanted and not belonging. Our real life is in fantasy.

8. **The extension of parent role.** We make our boss our mentor, our new parent. We model ourselves after our boss — in words, neighborhood, family, clubs or clothes. We take on the boss's affect and identity. We don't lose our own, because we were the extension of our parents and never had our own identity.

9. **The mediator role.** We muck around in other people's business. We try to fix everything. Anytime there is a problem, we are there to solve it. We are good at solving problems, but those we help with their problems end up resenting our meddling after a time. We then feel used and unappreciated.

10. **The clown, mascot or entertainer role.** We distract everybody from their pain, from the seriousness of their projects. We joke around, clown around, sometimes acting the fool, sometimes acting the comic, but usually minimizing our own needs, our own pain, our own feelings and sometimes, our own work. The office clown is not taken seriously and does not take self seriously and that's serious!

11. **The charmer role.** We seduce people. We don't have to be productive, we just make sure that people are well fooled by our insincerity. We charm our way through tests, contracts and the workday with our supervisors. If we are charming enough, we can become the surrogate spouse to the supervisor, administrator, boss or owner — maybe even become the boss.

12. **The victim role.** We feel buffeted around by the winds of chance, unable to make choices. It feels as though other people are doing it to us and we frequently blame others or the system. We know the "art of fine whine." Our anger goes inward and we perfect helplessness.

13. **The offender role.** We also feel buffeted around by the winds of chance and think that other people are doing it to us — except we are doing it to them with our intrusiveness, bullying, aggression, arousal, irritability and impatience. We hurt other people and offend them. We blame and fire others, still assuming they were doing it to us.

14. **The enabling role.** We seem to have an altered baseline tolerance level for dishonesty, violence, anger, pollution and chaos that goes on around us. We are able to enable by wearing blinders, being or acting naive, or simply not knowing what to do about it. We may not participate in what we don't approve of, but we have the co-dependent posture of enabling.

15. **The addict role.** Nothing is ever enough. We keep doing things that alter our feelings and our consciousness. We keep doing things for the high, the excitement and distraction, whether work, sex, sexualizing relationships in the workplace with people, drug use, three-martini lunches, wining and dining. We seem to lack boundaries in several areas of our life, have little impulse control, become preoccupied and obsessed with those things that might distract or make us feel better. We try to sell our addictions to those we work with, especially our work addiction.

16. **The scapegoat role.** We are similar to the victim, but we actively get blamed and set up to take the dive for a system gone awry. We carry the burden and very often do the acting out to insure that the burden will be placed on us.

17. **The organizer role.** We are constantly organizing — our desk, their desk, the office, the company picnics, the volleyball matches, the teams — we organize until we lose our sense of direction. We become disorganized!

18. **The healer role.** We listen and placate — always fixing, giving advice, caring for others, until we burn out. Usually we are not too great at caring for those immediately and intimately around us. The closer people are, the less we are able to give because they can see through our role. They can see that real intimacy isn't there. We never allow ourselves to be cared for or be vulnerable with others.

19. **The Jeremiah or prophet role.** We prophesy the doom of the company and the system. We are always foretelling what will happen and are constantly obsessed with the future and negativity.

20. **The queen bee role.** We have everybody covering for us, doing our work and running around for us. We are bossy, demanding, distant and unable to offer support for people around us. We send the workers and warriors out so we can lay eggs.

21. **The gadfly role.** We are always buzzing around, noticing and prodding. We work toward change — sometimes positively, sometimes destructively — but always buzzing.

22. **The odd-duck role.** Whatever is happening, we do it differently. We dress, act and do our work in an unusual way. It gets to be

a repetition in sameness of how different we are always trying to be.

These roles overlap and change, and there are many more. They are residuals of all the different roles we played in our families. We must go back and look at our families to rework our work roles.

WORK IN RECOVERY

The concept of work pervades our recovery: doing our work, workshops, working on our stuff, working it out, getting a work-up done on who we are, even physically working out. Career concerns include: the impact on our home life, whether we have a sense of autonomy within our profession, enjoy a variety of action and interaction, can maintain balance in our life, have job suitability, whether the work affects our health, if we have possibilities or opportunities for advancement, creativity and fair compensation.

Compensation can come in many different forms — not just money. There can be compensation through opportunities, benefits, time off, doing something meaningful or being able to contribute with creativity. Some of us tie so much into our work that retirement can kill us. If we do overwork, we need to go back to adolescence and look at the values we thought were important. At one time, most of us believed in family, intimacy, recreation and health.

GENDER POLITICS

There are many gender issues connected with work. For men, bankruptcy and job loss generally involve more shame because men are seen in our culture as providers and economic symbols. Women usually have more shame regarding relationship issues, more shame about family and children problems. Women frequently don't have as much of their egos tied up in their careers, how much they earn or their advancement opportunities. This also means women will have a more difficult time finding appropriate compensation and advancement because people expect it to be less important to them. This is not true for all men and all women, and is less true now than 20 years ago. However, many of these assumptions still stand.

GETTING HELP THROUGH WORK

Many Employee Assistance Programs (EAP) and Worksite Health Promotion Programs don't work because they overlook how people have been traumatized, abused, neglected and struggle with codepen-

dency issues. They miss dealing with people's family and family of
origin problems and they miss addiction, except for alcoholism, and
even that is frequently not identified. We're not likely to follow up on
a dental health program or an exercise program if we've been violently
abused, suffer from post-trauma effects or are struggling with dependency issues and compulsion.

WHO IS IT?

Many of us feel like imposters in our work. Many professionals who
are seen as highly competent feel as though they are fooling people. We
wear the adult work clothing and habits, but many of us don't feel like
adults. We haven't quite grown up.

Why? Most of us don't feel like adults because we had to grow up too
early and never experienced childhood. We have never gone through the
developmental stages of childhood to reach adulthood. In recovery we
can use the 12 Priorities to help us move through our developmental
stages and use our survival skills.

PUTTING OUR SURVIVAL SKILLS TO WORK

If we came from low-functioning families, our family survival skills
can, in recovery, become tremendous talents in our work and career.
Here are some examples:

- We can act well in chaos and can organize to avoid heavy fallout.
- Our overachieving can keep things from going to hell in a hand
  basket.
- Our ability to intuit the emotional state or needs of others can keep
  things flowing smoothly.
- Our ability to mediate differences can help the organization. We
  are usually great at cleaning up messes.
- In recovery we begin to see through the false issues and the lies
  around us.
- We frequently see and understand the shaming postures and unre-
  alistic expectations in work settings.
- In recovery we no longer accept abusive authority because we can
  smell it out and stand up to it.
- We learn to stand up and protect others and we despise injustice.
- We can sniff out addiction.
- We are capable of intense loyalty.
- We notice the needs of others to be noticed.

- We are sensitive and can turn our feelings into energy — our anger and fear into strength and action.
- We won't shy away from a fight if there needs to be a fight.
- We don't run away from a tough project, even when it looks impossible.
- For many of us responsibilities come naturally.
- After losing a "big one," we can get up again.
- We are good at creative ways of getting things done.

Now each of these can be pathological and have its opposite pole show up. In other words, instead of standing up to protect others, we might either shy away or be the one that others need to be protected from. Instead of smelling out addiction, we might be falling into our own addictiveness. Instead of mediating differences, we might be causing the differences or the messes that we clean up. If we are working a recovery program, the list of survival skills can be our strength in what we bring to our work settings. In recovery we don't lose the survival talents that we had in our families, we learn to put them to use in better ways.

Healthy work comes from being believed in. Then we can believe in ourselves. Productivity is a human need; it is linked to survival, yet is separate. It is possible for some of us to survive without being productive. Most of us rely on productivity for lifestyle, as well as shelter and sustenance. Work that we do not see as intrinsically productive may still produce essentials for us or our families. Not all work produces — some work may be counterproductive. Sloppy work may get us fired or ruin our reputation. Some work may just kill time. To a work addict, killing time is murder. Some of this killing time results in little or nothing gained. Many of us who don't play well use work to pass the time. If we can see our work as honing skills, producing, contributing something or facilitating others to produce, it gives us a sense of pride.

Our value as people must come from who we are, not what we do. When we do something which has meaning, we are supporting and feeding our self-esteem. Some of us are human doings rather than human beings. Human doings derive value from actions. Human beings can use their actions to support their values.

JOB SUITABILITY

When we are well-matched with our careers or jobs, our lives hum along like a well-tuned engine. When it is a mismatch, when we are scripted or enmeshed in someone else's idea of who we are or what we should do, we clunk along, in need of a tune-up. Our stress level and arousal responses escalate. Finding a job or career that matches our interests and personality may not be immediately possible, but we can find ways to do work that matches who we are. We can volunteer, use skills part-time, as a hobby, and train in or teach it. Our careers move along better in the direction we wish them to go when our job matches our reality. Success is about the match as much as it is about hard work and skill. Testing, career counseling, risk in trying new things, internships — all help us find that match.

CAREER DEVELOPMENT

Career development is a different experience now from what it once was. In the past people chose a career or a company, went to work and that was it. They would climb the corporate ladder, if possible, and would receive a pin and certificate at five-year intervals and a company watch when they retired. Much of that has changed. Both of us, for example, have already explored numerous career opportunities in our lives and fallen off more ladders than our parents ever tried to climb!

Today people often change careers several times in a lifetime, or return to school for different training. Switching employment locations is commonplace. It is now a world of headhunters, aptitude testing, self-employment and a long, varied resume. It seems as though students now can take courses in resume development and formating, specialize in application writing and receive a degree in interviewing!

Career development is certainly more sophisticated. Resources for assistance include guidance counselors, career-development specialists and college career-placement programs. Career development is a career in and of itself. If you seek help you will probably be given a battery of tests (there may be lots of forms to fill out or computerized evaluations to do) including various interest inventories and aptitude tests to help identify your strengths, needs and goals. You will be given numerous categories of careers to think about and will probably be surprised at how many opportunities there are to pursue that you never thought about before. We have had many clients and friends who have received excellent assistance from seeking out career-development specialists.

There are also government and private employment agencies to specifically assist you in finding a particular position of employment. Some of these services will offer assistance in a variety of fields, while others are highly specialized and focus on positions in particular industries or fields such as medicine or computers. The service is one of *matchmaking* —a person to a position — and hopefully it becomes a mutually satisfying relationship! Sometimes the employer pays for the service and other times the employee is charged. Be sure you understand the terms fully when you enter into an agreement. We have a good friend who is a "headhunter" for the computer industry. In his own recovery he has learned ways to help clients that go way beyond "finding a job."

A FEW NOTES OF CAREER CAUTION

Whenever you seek private or public employment assistance, be sure you clearly understand your financial obligations in the agreement — they can be very expensive. Doug had been out of college for two years, had done some traveling and worked a variety of different jobs but had never struck on any steady work in his field. Finally he headed for an employment agency, which got him an interview almost immediately. He had a good interview and a new position soon after. Even though it was a starting position and the financial compensation was relatively low, he was thrilled. A week later Doug received an unexpected bill for $1,700 for the services of finding him a position that paid $12,000 per year. Needless to say he was in shock for some time and had to make a quick trip to the bank for a loan.

You also need to be sure you are getting constructive advice. As Marvel was finishing high school, she was given the regular aptitude tests and her school counselor told her that all the tests showed that she should be a florist. It would be a waste of her time and money to attend college and clearly she was cut out to cut out flowers! That was several degrees and a couple of books ago. Fortunately her mother saw it differently and encouraged her to attend the university. If advice doesn't feel right to you, get a second opinion.

For many people the days of the nine-to-five job are gone. People work shifts, weekends, six days on and three off — there are endless combinations. Explore opportunities for part-time work, job sharing, "as needed," flex time and per diem alternatives. You don't have to limit your options.

Most of us will spend a great portion of our life resources on careers — our time, energy, creativity and human potential will go toward some form of work. It is worth investing some time and energy by sorting out what will be satisfying. Every job, position or career is going to have its stresses, and there will be days regardless of what we presently are doing that we will want to *bag* it! There are times when manuscripts are due, planes are late, books are not available and schedules are clashing that Marvel wonders what it would be like to be a florist and Terry thinks about returning to UPS and shipping packages. Sometimes we both have to take time out simply to think about the wonderful opportunities we have and to be grateful for the challenges — amidst the occasional chaos.

COMPENSATION

Compensation should be commensurate with the input or we end up feeling used. When we give more than we have and more than we receive, we run out of gas. Compensation comes in many ways: lifestyle, money, prestige, power, social, benefits, recreation, physical opportunities or service to others. The compensation should be based on our production, our contribution and the profitability of the enterprise we're involved with, as well as our particular needs in a given area. It does make sense to choose work based on financial considerations. But when these are the only considerations, we may get into miserable situations that feed our greed.

Most people overidentify with work as their source of value. When we get fired and change jobs, our self-esteem gets all tied up with the change or loss. Those of us from low-functioning families have all the family insecurity placed on financial and job security. When it cracks we tend to get very anxious, often panicky, making mistakes along the way. This results in taking on inappropriate jobs, allowing the stress to ruin our health and often get involved in dishonesty. Those of us with money addiction can lose all sense of balance in its pursuit.

OTHER WORK CONCERNS

Dishonesty In The Workplace

Sales, industry, advertising, marketing, research, government — the dishonesty of many businesses can make recovery difficult. Since this is a program of "rigorous honesty," we must maintain it without risking our lives or family. Of course not all businesses and business people are dishonest. If we look we can find people with integrity in the business field. We need to be real, but we also need to cover ourselves, knowing that we are doing our best in searching for a way to live with integrity.

Business With Friends

Who wants to work with strangers and enemies? It is great to do business with friends and make friends with business partners. But sometimes we get too casual. When business is involved and contracts are not, the friendships can deteriorate whenever there is a problem. The contract is not just business insurance, it helps maintain the friendship. Many people use others and befriend them to use them. Protecting oneself in all business areas is impossible and contracts aren't the solution, but they may help.

Working With Our Significant Others

Working with spouses or partners can deepen the sharing and connecting. There will be times of tension and distance because of work problems and deadlines. The worst scenario is grandiosity and overcommitment. A friend recently said, "I could not maintain an intimate relationship with someone who could not or would not share my work." Some people leave their work at work; others work where they are, whenever they are. Having people in our lives who notice, support and cherish our work is more important than their ability to share our work.

There are many paths to intimacy. Work is a possible path. Given how important our work is to each of us it can be a very powerful bond. It is no coincidence that many affairs and relationships begin in work settings. Work is where many of us show our best stuff, the top of our form and derive the most pleasure from who we are and what we have learned. Some of us, though, are very different in personal and home settings than we are at work. One of our favorite quotations is a Maori saying that goes, "Never judge a man by how he behaves outside of his own hut."

Family Familiarity With Our Work

Family members should be aware of our work and when possible be involved. Children should see their parents in work environments. The environment of our work should be structured to accommodate children. In Fiji parents bring children to work; it is the expected way.

Home Office, Home Work

Some of us don't go to work. Terry was recently asked if Marvel had an office in her home. He responded, "It depends on how you look at it. Does she have a home in her office, or an office in her home?" Occasionally, Marvel has to take inventory of how much of the office is oozing throughout the rest of her home. If you choose to work at home, be careful that you keep your work life from impinging on your home life.

Men's And Women's Jobs In Our Culture Are Changing

Fifty percent of medical doctors in training are women. More psychiatrists are women and more men are becoming nurses, social workers, daycare workers, kindergarten and elementary school teachers. Women are getting into coaching and are more involved in the military. In the past men have done a better job of networking in work settings, while women networked better in other settings. We believe if people will risk

interdependence, women will be able to learn from men about network
ing at work and women would teach men about integrating effect and
fairness into the workplace.

Choice

Work should be a choice. Unfortunately many of us have not chosen
to be doing what we do; we just ended up doing it. Sometimes the two
of us sit around and simply wonder what we will do when we grow up.
We are still waiting to see — we see no point in rushing into anything!

SUGGESTIONS • AFFIRMATIONS • THOUGHTS

SUGGESTIONS

- Continue to pursue education and training, in present career or a
  new direction.
- Find a mentor or become one.
- Start following your dream.
- If stuck, seek outside help.
- The one thing most of us can change in our work setting is us.
- Volunteer services you enjoy providing, but not so much you feel
  used.
- Take the following Work Addicts inventory from Workaholics Anon-
  ymous:

1. Do you get more excited about your work than about your family
   or anything else?
2. Are there times when you can charge through work and other
   times when you can't get anything done?
3. Do you take work with you to bed? On weekends? On vacation?
4. Is work the activity you like to do best and talk about most?
5. Do you work more than 40 hours a week?
6. Do you turn your hobbies into money-making ventures?
7. Do you take complete responsibility for the outcome of your
   work efforts?
8. Have your family or friends given up expecting you on time?
9. Do you take on extra work because you are concerned that it
   won't otherwise get done?
10. Do you underestimate how long a project will take and then rush
    to complete it?
11. Do you believe that it is okay to work long hours if you love what
    you are doing?

12. Do you get impatient with people who have other priorities besides work?
13. Are you afraid if you don't work hard you will lose your job or be a failure?
14. Do you do things energetically and competitively including play?
15. Do you get irritated when people ask you to stop doing your work to do something else?
16. Have your long work hours hurt your family or other relationships?
17. Do you think about work while driving, falling asleep or when others are talking?
18. Do you work or read during meals?
19. Do you believe that more money will solve the other problems in your life?

If you answered yes to several of the questions above, we recommend you seek out a Workaholics Anonymous program. (See Appendix A for more information.)

AFFIRMATIONS

- My work is a reflection of my spirit.
- Work is a prayer done not said.
- I am a human being, not a human doing.
- I can say no and I can change my mind.

THOUGHTS

- Many of us work to play.
- A few of us play to work.
- A machine can answer our telephone, but not a loved one.
- Our children will only be children once — what a shame to miss it.
- Industry is an earlier developmental stage than identity.
- Providing for someone may or may not be loving them.
- Give a person a fish and you feed them for a day. Teach a person to fish and you feed them for life.

13

PRIORITY 11.

Community:
The Planet —
Love It Or
Leave It!

C ommunity involvement is the expression and combination of all the previous priorities. It rests on our identity and spiritual development. It involves work, play and learning. We participate with emotional and intellectual boundaries, and it is through community that we may express our passions. Human survival is based on community — the family, clan, tribe, village or state. Individuals rely on community for protection, production and belonging. We are community beings. The interaction provided in community can stimulate our interests and potentials.

Two community-based processes are learning and survival. As children, human beings are dependent longer than any other species. This allows us time to do the amount of learning of the ways, history, science and technology of the community. The community is a source of information and the process by which we pass it on.

We were born into the community of family, although many of us missed the sense of support or the chance to participate in family. The family is the place in which we learn to function in community, to give and take, learn and teach, support or destroy. Our early family experiences affect how we relate to other communities. Our style of operating, the roles we played, and the overt and covert experiences of family are reenacted in each subsequent and overlapping community we participate in. As we grow our involvement with groups other than family deepens.

We don't recover alone, we recover in settings with people: We have a recovering community. This community has its own language and style. It is very invested in reaching out. We recognize the uniqueness of our recovery community as well as the wholeness of the human community.

Recovery involves several subgroups, and many of us are involved with different programs. We can be a part of a recovering community that focuses on chemical or other addiction, co-dependency, gambling, sexual issues, family problems or participation in particular therapy styles. Yet, with all of these differences, we still have the sense of connectedness within the overall recovering community.

COMMUNITY INVOLVEMENT

As children and adolescents most of us were involved in a religious community and had social, recreational and school structures. A few of us may have been politically involved. As we enter adulthood our community participation broadens. We can involve ourselves at local, state and federal levels through voting rights and political participation. We find work and career settings, develop an expanding social sense, and some of us find a recovering community while building a new family, either nuclear or of creation. All of this can occur while moving toward recognition of our involvement with a global community.

Religious

There are many positive religious communities that are important for providing a support system for our worship. They give us a place to express and get feedback for our spiritual thoughts, a setting in which to enrich ritual and continued learning. Religion can be a very powerful support system for our spirituality. Community worship can support the emotional attachment to our decision about our spirituality. Organized with bylaws, canon law, tradition and ritual or a few people who that show and support our personal, spiritual journey, this is community. It allows us to continue our journey without isolation.

Political

Political communities involve laws, legislation, lobbying, spending priorities, zoning, policing, protecting, and politicking. A tremendous number of people work hard and long hours in government and politics, doing research, campaigning and legislation. The politics of local, state, federal and international arenas affect our lives in powerful ways, and we need to be knowledgeable and involved.

We often feel powerless to effect change, but this is just not true. A local politician recently told us that fifteen active people can do or prevent almost anything in most communities. Most letters to elected officials are read, especially during an election year! Lobbyists and special interest groups *do* have an impact. Political and government leaders can be convinced within the parameters of their own interests and backgrounds.

The recovery movement could become a political force if we begin to accept how our politics and our recovery are interwoven. Being political is often interpreted as being manipulative and underhanded. It can mean having a well-founded network of people and resources which takes time and energy to create. It can mean that our concepts of honesty, preciousness and vulnerability and guardianship could show up in legislation and spending priorities.

Social

Social community is partially discussed under Friends and Family in Chapter 5. We need to have our own particular support group. An acceptance of the oneness we have with all people is an important stage of recovery. We are our brothers' keepers — and sisters, cousins, aunts and uncles. We belong to a social class and a social economic strata, and to limit the social community to friends of our class limits our recovery to narcissism. We only care about reflections of us or our lifestyle. An acceptance of our common humanity and sibling relationships to the homeless, mentally ill, desperate, crime-addicted, differently abled, as well as our religions, races and ethnic backgrounds is and must be a part of the embracing of our humanity and vulnerability. Our social recovery cannot occur without our involvement and belief in social action and justice.

A social community is like single-lane traffic. It only goes as far or as fast as the slowest vehicle. We can only travel as far spiritually as our neediest member. We can have social pride when we all treat each other with dignity and guardianship. To recognize how each of us has participated in violence and oppression in our culture, actively or passively, offending or colluding, is a part of community recovery.

Recreational

Recreational community is a concept that is covered in more detail in Chapter 9. The sense of community comes from our contact with others who share our recreational interest — a club, team, organization, committee or a group of people. With these people we can chat and compare notes. Subscribing to magazines, joining clubs, participating and sponsoring events, volunteering to help host events, attending clinics, camps, workshops in our sport or activity all help us maintain a sense of belonging to a recreational community. Lessons also help; finding mentors, teachers and coaches is very important. Group lessons are another way of feeling the communal aspects of our activity. Sports can provide us a chance to learn sportsmanship, which we can bring as a posture to other communities in our lives.

Since there are so many sports and activities we cannot do alone, being involved is an automatic way of creating community. Marvel is an avid whitewater canoeist, a sport that demands depending on other people for safety. Her boating community has been an integral part of finding support for her journey. Activities become a place for us to learn about team spirit, leadership, camaraderie and interdependent living. Terry played rugby for fourteen years, traveling with a group of athletes who are still friends, integrating into other cultures. Marvel sang and traveled with a choral group. The rugby and choral community allowed both of us to enter people's lives, homes and areas in a way vacation travel could not have done.

Career

Our occupations can be a source of community involvement. The workplace is a community. People with similar careers have a felt sense of commonality, often belonging to the same professional organizations or unions. A balance of involvement with our work peers offers us a chance to find growth and support in occupational settings. Some of us try to meet all of our social and community needs in work institutions. This is an indicator of work addiction.

Neighborhood

Our neighborhood, geographic area or physical region also provides a community sense. Part of recovering is having an awareness of the uniqueness, the people and the history of the area where we live. To feel as though we belong in our area and know our neighbors can provide us a source of meaning and pleasure in our lives. When we have an involvement with shops, improvements, parks and neighborhoods we find a feeling of belonging, a sense of well-being and a positive self-image.

Many of us came from families who were disconnected because of shame, rigidity, alcoholism or secrets. Our tendency to reenact this posture in our local communities is strong. By doing so we reinforce our shame and isolation and set up the possibility of more acting out.

Not all neighbors or community members will be open to involvement. Not everyone will like us or understand what we stand for or are about. If we are in recovery, we can bring some of the elements of the recovering lifestyle into the communities where we live and have a profound impact on the people we touch and the place we live.

Country

Our country is a community. A country's style reflects its population, and our country has its unique problems. Violence, fiscal irresponsibilities, boundary problems, aggression, dishonesty, greed, obsession with power, disdain for vulnerability, arrogance, perfectionism, detached leadership, illiteracy, high infant mortality rates and poverty are all brought to our government by us. When we change other things in our lives, religions, work, social and local communities, our country will change as well. When we change ourselves our country will change. When we embrace our own vulnerability, develop our own boundaries, look at our own aggressiveness and detachment, our leadership will change as well.

The strengths of our country also reflect us — the valuing of freedom, still striving for cooperation, the feelings of protectiveness, advanced technology and scientific capabilities, a giving spirit, and a tremendous diversity of our people and geography. National pride is a positive feeling, but blended with too much denial, a sense of being better than, it can become a very dangerous thing. Much harm has been done in the name of nationalism and patriotism.

WHEN COMMUNITIES GO SOUR — CULTS

Some communities become cults. Those of us who lacked healthy family sense, haven't developed identity or don't have involvement with communities and people elsewhere are most vulnerable. Cults are a substitute for what we missed. The cult may be religious in nature, health oriented, recovery groups, new age, environmentally directed — the list is endless. Significant traits of cults are:

- a powerful and controlling leader, sometimes hidden, often seductive
- living together with a false sense of reality and separate from outside influences

- belief in having the answer or something unique that others don't have
- enticing members into turning over property to the community
- some method of extracting money or property, often escalating spending for materials
- gradual brainwashing through positive reinforcement, play, a family sense
- little respect for individuals, families and other communities
- beliefs and practices often are elaborate and often logical, but are based on false and unproven assumptions, usually the assumptions of the cult leader
- subtle and covert, usually unnoticed coercion is provided to protect the cult and to engage members to follow its beliefs and practices.

Cults do not usually pressure people in overt ways but maintain a false pretense of the freedom to come and go. The coercion is underlying and subtle, so people are left with the illusion that it was their choice to participate. Seldom do cults respect boundaries of members, which means that their families or people involved tend to be boundary-less in both victim and offending postures. Much child and spouse abuse in cult families is because of the eroding sense of boundary — even in nonsatanic cults.

THINK GLOBALLY, ACT LOCALLY

The most important community of all is our global community. The concept of a shrinking world, faster travel and communication, makes it important to look at the impact of our behavior on other people and places throughout the world. Recognition of the needs of all people, the brotherhood and sisterhood of all cultures is the ultimate in community awareness.

Following is an excerpt from *Broken Toys Broken Dreams* which summarizes how broken children can grow up breaking the planet. We believe in it so firmly, we wanted to take this opportunity to share it with you again:

> On this planet Earth life is common and abundant, but in the immensity of the universe and the limits of our awareness of creation, we are told that life may well be a rare occurrence. The likelihood of other planets orbiting in the billions of galaxies is high. There is a good likelihood that some have conditions present to nurture life, and a real possibility that life has developed on a number of these planets in orbit around their nuclear furnaces. It is even possible that on a few of these other planets, life has achieved an awareness, a consciousness of conscious-

ness, the ability to wonder and dream, the ability and the desire to search for more of its own, to pray, to notice, to be filled with gratitude for and awareness of, this gift of life itself.

We may not be alone in the universe, but we are rare. Life is not cheap; it is precious. The human mind, the human soul, the life spark of our being, are unique. With its possibilities, curiosities, noticing, wondering and craving, human life is one of the most precious and rare items in the entire universe. To stifle it, confuse it, threaten it, deprive it — of nutrition, information, freedom, a chance to achieve its potential — may be the most heinous, insidious crime in our universe.

Each child is the culmination of the potential of this universe. To provide the child with safety, gentleness and awareness of that uniqueness and preciousness, to provide all of the encouragement and information they can handle, is the prime responsibility of adulthood. This guardianship of children, of our own potential, includes the nurturing of our own childness, our newness in our expanding universe.

Children learn cruelty, self-destructiveness, apathy, anger, fears, shame, anxieties that not only prevent the continuation of learning and seeking, the enjoying of the adventure of life, but it begins a legacy of cruelty, greed, narcissism, judgments, parochial defensiveness, covert manipulation, violence, abuse, neglect and carelessness. This spreads like a fire, burning and destroying the potential and the gratitude, the chance for more awareness, to achieve new heights of conscious being.

The real parent of this precious, aware, unique form of life is the beautiful blue planet we inhabit. We spring from the waters and are nurtured in the soil of the Earth itself. All of life on Earth are our cousins and siblings. The Earth is a parent without consciousness, without a conscience. We are the eyes, ears, voice, awareness, sentience and conscience of our planet — our parent, the Earth. Our primary responsibility and goal should be as guardians, not only for our children who we participate in the creation of, but of our parent, the earth itself, the vehicle of our creation. The first priority in our own awareness must be to protect the basis for and of our existence, to look at the consequences of our behavior, to be gentle and supportive of all life itself and to insure the survival and balance of our planet. Earth is the source of the continuing nurturing of life. It is the life giving vehicle of the Creator and our continuing quest must be to ensure its protection. Accepting the challenge of guiding and loving children, the lives that we produce, involves a teaching and modeling of love and respect for life itself and for the place of life spring, Earth.

We live in a garden. We did not fall from the garden. With our growing awareness we became more than "of the garden." We became the keepers of the garden, the guardians of all that grows there. Our survival now depends upon taking the message of this guardianship seriously.

Recently, with our growing awareness of the need for personal healing because of past hurts, addictions, relationship problems or poor self-esteem, there is awareness of the processes of recovery. From this awareness, a recognition of the impact and concepts of co-dependency is also developing. Most of co-dependency has been described in the

context of its symptoms — relationship with alcoholics, painful patterns
of living, dependency problems and other definitions. We hope we've
gone beyond the symptoms and immediate consequences and opened up
some of the core issues of family and culture that create co-dependency.
We hope we have helped expose the continuing impact of co-dependency
in our lives and on our planet.

The concept must move beyond the enabling spouse of an alcoholic
and must be seen as a basis for intimacy problems, our addictive and
self-destructive behaviors, including the crimes against each other and
our planet. Co-dependency is an issue of planetary existence, survival
and health. Co-dependency becomes a destructive force because it involves an absence of self-respect, a lack of respect for life, manipulation
and denial of consequences. It involves the absence of boundaries that
enables and creates violence. Co-dependency involves collusion and the
enabling of inappropriate activities, the violations of environment and of
people. Co-dependency brings with it a sense of helplessness and unwill-
ingness to make the changes we need to make. In healing our co-dependency we may be taking the most important step in the healing of our
planet. We have become the collusive enablers and participants in the
destruction of our planet, in the ignoring of vulnerable life on our planet
and in the neglect of self. This is co-dependency.

This co-dependence prevents us from accepting the interdependence
of all of life, and of life with the planet that gave life. Recovery is the
healing of relationship, first with self, then others and then our environment. Co-dependency goes beyond the lack of identity. It goes beyond child abuse. It goes beyond family systems. It goes beyond lost
intimacy. Co-dependence threatens the survival of all of us. It is the
basis of the victim/offender relationship, the need for control and power
to destroy and hurt. Co-dependency is the inability to stand up for what
we believe and feel. In the face of crazy, destructive courses, it is the
feeling of helplessness to effect change and bring about peace.

Co-dependency affects our lives, organizations, government and culture. It is born in dysfunction, in not recognizing the preciousness of
children and not teaching gentleness and respect for life, of not modeling
healthy boundaries and in giving up the ability to impact toward sanity,
peace, care and spirituality.

Co-dependency occurs in dysfunctional families, families with addiction, neglect, abandonment, abuse, victimization, dishonesty, unpredic-
ability and denial and it affects all levels of our society. Children who
are abused, hurt, neglected, tend to continue this pattern, not just
toward themselves, their relationships and their children, but toward

their physical environment as well. Children who have been hurt will hurt their surroundings.

Pollution comes naturally to someone who has been boundary-violated because pollution is essentially a violation of our physical boundaries, the boundaries of our life source, the boundaries of our planet. The ozone layer disappearing, the greenhouse effect, oil spills, acid rain, air pollution, our garbage crisis, nuclear waste, exhaust poisons, the disappearing wilderness, the destruction of our planet's lungs, the burning of the rain forests, the killing of the dolphins and whales, the cutting of the redwoods, threats to rare plant and animal life — these come from people who have not been taught to respect life, cherish vulnerability, or take the time to look at consequences. This is the result of careless families, of child abuse, neglect and denial, of not teaching limits, impulse control, of the need for immediate gratification and insatiability of addictive systems. A dysfunctional family creates this lack of respect for life and creates in its members, in children, the co-dependency that continues the dysfunction through our adult lives. Co-dependency is a by-product of how we treat our children. How we deal with children is a result of cultural misogyny, the fear and hatred of vulnerability. In our culture, vulnerable people do not fare well — infants, children, adolescents, disabled, mentally ill, immigrants, minorities, poor, Native Americans, homeless, women — any group with vulnerability, with differences. The worship of power is the flip side of misogyny. Cultural and family co-dependency is the result.

Recovery from co-dependency is the development of identity, the ability to have intimacy and a respect for life, an acceptance and cherishing of vulnerability and fragility, the ability to find strength through vulnerability. *Recovery is interdependence and integration.* Flowing out of these is a respect for creation, a way of seeing behavior in terms of its long-term impact. We learn we can make a difference. We can stand up in the strength of our outrage. We can move ahead with the wisdom of our fear. We can nurture life with the healing of our sadness and pain. We can protect life with a sense of guardianship from our shame and the voice of conscience from our guilt. We can heal ourselves, our families, relationships and communities. Most important we can heal the planet we live on.

As residents of our global community, we need to reinvest in the Earth. We have been making withdrawals and expecting it to find its own deposits. We need to cut down and give back. Consumptive economics is the primary pollutant. The tremendous energy involved in keeping up with our cultural consumption is destroying our planet. It is a system of destruction we have exported to other countries. Responsible global

community means we recycle, avoid overconsumption of products and
energy and natural resources; we do our best to keep local air space
clean, water pure and wilderness intact. To enrich the quality of life
through cleanliness, promotion of national park areas, we need to teach
and learn the intricacies, beauty and balance of the natural world as well
as its tremendous recreational and spiritual possibilities. It involves:

- not abusing or offending by pushing an inappropriate lifestyle on
  others
- insisting on elimination of all weapons that can destroy the planet
- accepting a maxim that if it is not a biodegradable container, don't
  use it
- if its by-products are toxic, don't create it
- if the pollution is endemic to its manufacture, don't produce it.

ROLES IN COMMUNITY

Cherishing the vulnerability of all aspects of our global community
and measuring the consequences of each of our actions before acting is
recovery. Our role in any subset of community is greatly determined by
the roles we played and the roles modeled for us in family. Community
roles are based on family roles. Roles support the function or dysfunc-
tioning of a system and give us a style of operation. Healthy systems
require healthy roles, dysfunctional systems encourage dysfunctional
roles. Individual roles are based on many things:

- gender
- personality
- cultural messages
- body type
- bonding issues
- needs of a particular system we are operating in
- responses to abuse
- needs of others
- how we learn
- modeling we have had.

Healthy roles are chosen. Healthy roles help us become the person we
are meant to be by our Creator. Healthy roles provide feedback about
how we are doing in the role and we are free not to be in the role.
Unhealthy roles are not chosen, are usually assigned and may be based
on a particular physical characteristic or a need of the system we are in.
They are not based on our uniqueness or who we are and they don't help
us become who we were meant to be. We are usually not free to be out

of the role, and we only receive negative feedback about how we are doing in the role. Roles are multiple, dynamic and changing. The role affects our life and our involvement with our community long after we have left the roles that we learned in family. We reenact the roles when we get into stressful settings, attempt to live up the expectations of others and when we start to operate with other people in new systems.

For example, if in the family our role was to be defiant, rebellious or destructive, we tend to act out the role in our work settings and in our *family of creation*. If we were an overachiever, a hero in our family, we often did good things, looked good, but didn't feel very good on the inside. The hero role does good things to make the family look good and the family essentially rips off the good feelings from the person. Many of us are trying to do good things, continue overachieving and being the hero, but we are the ones who burn out and get limited good feelings out of the good we do.

If we were a victim in our families, we will continue to feel like a victim at work, a victim in our communities and maybe continue to get victimized. If we were offending, if we bonded with the aggressors who were victimizing us, then we will probably continue to be intrusive, boundary violating, dishonest, greedy and offending in the community.

If we always had to be there for others, take care of members in our family, the caretaker, guardian or parent role, we may find ourselves in other institutions and settings, giving too much, taking care of others, trying to be the guardians of the systems or the individuals within the system — always listening and always giving — but not receiving and not sharing much of ourselves. The enabling role, the collusive role, is one most of us have learned. It creates an altered baseline tolerance level for addiction, offending, irresponsibility and dishonesty. The collusive role is the co-dependent enabling posture of our population toward all the ills of our culture that could be changed, but we don't because we barely notice them. If we lived with those things in our family of origin, we will probably tolerate it in the community.

In each system that we enter we fall back on familiar roles. In families we all played more than one role depending on the time and circumstances and so we do the same in our roles in our other communities. We become extensions of other people, not living our own lives. We are co-dependent reactors, believing that life is a popularity contest. We get into the role of the addict, overconsuming, overusing, distracting from our pain with intensity or substances. We become the martyr and sacrifice ourselves for the causes of others and often muck around in other people's business or become the nice guy, the good girl, the rabblerouser. We might even feel on the "outside," be the lost child we grew up as, or

feel like the orphan that we always felt we were as children, the feeling
of not belonging in the community.

MAKING CHOICES

To know the roles we played in our family is to know what it felt like
to be in the role. This can allow us to make choices about setting up new
roles. We can make choices based on the particular community that we
are involved in. The role of giving out of our fullness can and must be
chosen and protected in our new recovery of community belonging. It
takes more than just a decision, however. We must grieve and feel the
loss of our dysfunctional family roles. We need to recognize these roles
often acted as addictions, for they will likely come back to us when we
are not taking care of ourselves. Our workaholism, our giving too much,
overperforming or intensity can be role-based addictions. We maintain
an ongoing process of recovery for our roles just as we do for addiction.

Our communities can become what we envision and advertise them
to be and say they are. Our communities will maintain themselves as
reflections of how we maintain ourselves in balance, care and openness.

Dr. Robert Kegan tells wonderful stories of how our perceptions and
beliefs are an aspect of our developmental stages. Our favorite story is
about a little boy who has an imaginary farm — not just an imaginary
friend, but an entire farm! One day he was telling his parents about
how he was going to order up some baby calves from the stork for his
farm. Being progressive and contemporary parents they decided to engage in conversation with their son and explain how calves are born
into this world. So they talked about the mother cows and the fathers
and how they get together. Their son stared in amazement, shook his
head and adamantly exclaimed, "Not on my farm!"

Many of us have not accepted certain realities of life and the needs of
our communities. We respond with "Not on my farm!" If we farm
together and grow honesty, spontaneity and joy we can reap the harvest
of a healthy community.

Community is built through sharing and honesty. In recovery we
discover community through sharing our losses, hurts, and self destructiveness. We build on community by sharing the joy and insights of the
recovery process. Community is built on acceptance. Too many communities have destroyed community sense by becoming self-protective,
defensive, parochial, narcissistic and self-serving. *Communities must also
learn interdependence, no community exists alone or on its own.*

GIVING FOR COMMUNITY

Social action flows out of interdependence and integrity. When we give of ourselves, not out of guilt but out of our priorities and values, the giving has meaning. It is living a prosocial life. Public figures who try to give privately often miss the impact of public giving as modeling and leverage for change. *We need to give of what we have from who we are.* Our talents vary. One person might give in time, maybe money or act as a catalyst by giving their name to a cause or group. There isn't a right or wrong in giving, but there is a meaningful and effective giving as opposed to empty gestures and wasted resources or giving because it means getting something in return. Giving need not produce a particular result. It is about building a spiritual community and the healing of self. The intent and action work together, each having its own value and importance. Sanctity lies between intention and action and we are all called to be saints — we are called people.

Our parochialism and nationalism is our sense of community gone awry. We must be involved with electing responsible leaders, with local zoning, recycling, parks, playgrounds, quiet areas, billboards, industrializing of our neighborhoods, waste dumps, land fills, traffic and freeways, housing for low income, old age, halfway housing for those who need it, community treatment facilities, pornography, liquor sales, blue laws, pet control, water use, school issues, building issues, money issues, use of fertilizers for lawns, air pollution. We need to be aware of county, state, federal and community politics, the campaigning, the voting, the awareness of platforms and issues. We have to be aware of our religious communities, their leadership, and responsibilty, our ability to switch churches, and the need for rituals, prayer, song, the messages of hope and brotherhood that the religious community must spill out into the community.

The modeling of charity is part of our spiritual connection to community. We must also be aware of the vulnerable groups within our community and how we treat them. *The least of our brethren is a reflection of our spiritual sense of community.* We need to support and enjoy what our community offers in terms of sports, culture, arts, music, expositions, fairs, celebrations. Embracing the responsibilities of community can enable us to participate in the celebration that community is. We can stand up against the double messages of community about voting, choices, freedom, gambling and pollution. We form the guidelines, the laws, and the rules that our community and community leaders operate by. Our leadership detachment reflects our detachment, our leadership dishonesty reflects our dishonesty, our leadership aggression reflects our tolerance

level and history of aggression and violence. As we heal ourselves our
leadership will be healed. It must come from us, not from above. We are
the community; leadership only reflects community.

A healthy community moves us toward self- and other-acceptance
with honesty, risk and gentleness. Prejudice is the absence of identity
and self-acceptance projected outward. Community is the integration of
self-projected outward. It is our extended *family of creation.*

SUGGESTIONS • AFFIRMATIONS • THOUGHTS

SUGGESTIONS

- Support recycling—demand it in your community and set up recycling in your home and office, if you cannot recycle plastic contain-
  ers in your community return them to the store where you purchased the products.
- Limit consumption — we're not talking about dieting — we mean
  "stuff."
- Register to vote — and then vote!
- Support a cause — not just any cause for the sake of being chari-
  table but a cause that you can believe in and grow with. Your
  Better Business Bureau can offer you valuable information on what
  organizations do with your donations. Donate responsibly. If you
  don't have money, give time and encouragement.
- Comment — verbally and in writing to stores, restaurants, hotels
  and other businesses on how they rate in terms of recycling and
  environmental issues. Airlines don't always recycle aluminum!
- Write — to your senator, member of congress, state or provincial
  legislative member, local government official regarding a social issue
  that concerns you. You will almost always receive an answer. A
  post card takes only a minute to write.
- Reflect — on a group of people you may hold some prejudice against
  — an oppressed group such as another race, religious group, gays
  or lesbians, differently abled, women, people of different shapes
  and sizes. Spend some time and energy reading, asking questions,
  finding out more about them — as individuals, their culture and the
  obstacles they face from the dominant culture. Take a risk and
  expend some energy finding out about an oppressed group's uniqueness, strengths and the problems they face.
- Share your resources — your creativity, talents, energy, physical
  and fiscal abilities.
- Notice creation — demand respect for creation.

- Learn fiscal responsibility and balance — we are all part of the national debt.
- Don't spend what you don't have, don't spend just because you have.

AFFIRMATIONS

- My community is a reflection of me.
- I am a recycler and a bicycler!
- I enrich my community with my presence.
- I am a responsible participant in community.
- I cherish and protect the vulnerable of my community.
- My community is life, my community is Earth.
- I take pride in my community contributions.

THOUGHTS

- Our overextended landfills are a reflection of our family garbage.
- Recovering people are going to make the difference — we can't depend on others who have not been able to embrace the fragility and preciousness of life to protect our blue planet.
- Did you know that tobacco companies are still subsidized by the government?
- The USA has one of the higher infant mortality rates of industrialized nations.
- Americans produce three to four times more pounds of garbage per capita than Japan.
- Thousands of people each year are murdered with hand guns.
- Two of the most powerful and wealthy lobbyists in the USA are the National Rifle Association and the tobacco industry.

"From the standpoint of daily life . . .
there is one thing we do know:
that man is here for the sake of other men —
above all, for those upon whose smile
and well-being our own happiness depends,
and also for the countless unknown souls
with whose fate we are connected
by a bond of sympathy.
Many times a day I realize how much
my own outer and inner life is built upon
the labors of my fellow men,
both living and dead,
and how earnestly I must exert myself

in order to give in return as much
as I have received.

— Albert Einstein

14

PRIORITY 12.

Passion:
Recovery Rocket Fuel

L ast, but not least, is passion. Passion is the confluence of many streams: non-constricted emotional energy, the challenge of physical energy, the direction of spiritual energy mingled with our imagination, creativity and integrated into our love relationships and value systems. This is passion.

INTENSITY

Passion is last on our list for a very good reason. Just as spirituality can become religiosity, passion, too early in recovery, becomes obsession. Many of our addictions are passions gone awry. Healthy passion is the integration of physical, emotional, intellectual, sexual and spiritual energy, placed on a course or path. The energy created by a congruent balance of these aspects of self is filled in by beliefs, values and commitments.

Given a direction, our goal becomes our passion. Before we seek passion we need the balance or congruence, the clarification of beliefs and values. With an absence of direction or goals, our passions can spin us around like the mixing bowl with no firm foundation. We get in a whirl, and our passion places everything in our lives out of balance. Passion gone awry is the core of the intensity junkie who seeks the high that passion can arouse, usually having to change the object sought as it loses its ability to maintain the transient arousal, to alter our brain chemistry.

Passion without integration is a mark of the obsessed. People may starve themselves fighting for world hunger; lose their families for their work; kill for peace; die for the right to life; become insatiable; and become obsessed with activity and eliminate balance in life. We can do it with sports, writing, art, music, dieting, cooking, analyzing, politics, work, money, volunteering, power or gambling. We may be consumed by a relationship, romance, a person, children or sex. We can be eaten by our own passion. The passion for a state of achievement or immortality can prevent a state of realism.

In our passion we can become perfectionistic, obsessed with goals, purity or saintliness. We may be constantly trying to analyze or figure everything out. We worry about "giving enough," "doing enough" or being the perfect spouse or parent. We can use passion to avoid past wounds or trauma. It can distract us from our loneliness, channel our anger and alleviate anxiety, although covertly increasing it. Passion can assuage our guilt, maintain the repression of our shame, and give us a sense of meaning and belonging, as well as excitement and intensity. When based on a value or strong belief, passion can even provide religious spiritual direction.

Passion can stem from an unresolved childhood hurt or loss. Passion, like drugs, has a very addictive nature. Our brain chemistry responds quickly to our passionate involvement, but we begin to rely on the involvement for good feeling. With a lack of identity formation, it is easy to over-identify with the cause, person or need. We can find the value in it, rather than us.

- Jane, while working for world hunger, heading a national organization, stopped eating for days at a time. She struggled with anorexia nervosa and eventually was hospitalized. She came into therapy and realized the passion for world hunger came out of the deprivation of attention from her upper-middle-class family. She continued to work for the cause, but began to focus more on friends and support outside of her passion.

- John, a physician, began to volunteer his services at a teen clinic while maintaining a full practice. Volunteering became an obsession with the issues of adolescent pregnancy, and he began to fight for pro-choice rights, setting up free clinics. His practice, his family and his health began to suffer. After a workshop John told us that his younger sister, whom he had taken care of most of his life, had gotten pregnant by a man who had abandoned her. She secretly went to an alley abortionist. Due to the conditions and resulting infection, she subsequently had to have a hysterectomy. His sister's resulting depression and infertility affected John deeply.
- Carmen had spent most of her adulthood volunteering at a center for children with special learning problems. She had skills and experience, but refused a paying job, even though she needed the income. Discussing her family of origin, she told of her younger brother who was severely retarded. She was responsible for his care. She resented the demands on her time and was very mean to him when they were alone. Out of her guilt, she became obsessed with making up for her meanness and refused compensation. She still utilized her talents during her recovery, but out of love, not guilt. She is also being paid for directing a center, after having gone back to school for a graduate degree in health care management.

Many of our passions have a family of origins basis that keeps us from finding balance and making choice. We are not free to be doing something until we are free not to do it. Jane's and John's passions were not bad things. The inability to maintain life balance came from the repression of the motivation for the passion. They couldn't ever satisfy the passion until they identified the basic need underlying it. They were driven by the repressed hurt. Carmen was driven by guilt and could not choose. Once she saw the unfairness of being forced to give up her own child-hood and how natural the anger was, once she accepted that her treat-ment of her brother came from her own being used and neglected, she was free to make changes in her own life. That she chose to be in the same field was a sign of her new approach to life, that she was making choices, not reacting, and she maintained her passionate love for the children she worked with and added a love for herself and her talents.

PASSION, LOVE, SEX

We must be careful that our passions don't become proselytization, constantly pushing our passionate interests onto others. With identity we can allow other people to be neutral about our passions. We can also avoid driving them away with our intensity. Passion shared with others can be enjoyable in measured amounts. When we are obsessed we cannot measure the amount. We can either swallow people in our passion or drive them away.

Randy developed a passion for cycling and spent the next year obsessively talking about trips and equipment to anyone who slowed down around him. Even bicycle enthusiasts began avoiding him. He shared that he had always done this. He found an interest and needed the world to listen and share it. As the baby in his family, everyone gave him a great deal of attention and he was still demanding it. Everyone encouraged his focused obsessions of childhood, but as he entered adolescence, even the family tired of his need for continuing attention and his singular focus. The absence of friends drove him further into his passions. He went from Dungeons and Dragons to NFL football to rock music to biology. All became a cover for his real need to be noticed, including his bicycling. He is finding that interests can be a way of making good social connections, but the sharing of interests needs to be done with an equality of listening and talking, teaching and learning, but mostly, by community experiencing. When Randy is sold on something now, he no longer feels that he must sell everybody. He can enjoy it with others who have chosen it. His childlike neediness is reclaimed as childlike enjoyment. Rather than a cry for everyone to enjoy me, Randy is enjoying himself. Passion is now a part of the enjoyment.

Passion, commitment and intimacy are the three ingredients in love relationships. Passion is often the first to be noticed, and the least stable. Relationships built on passion tend to be volatile and temporary. In our culture, we are taught that intimacy comes from sexual passion. This is a dominant theme of most movies. "What takes longer often takes better" may apply to intimacy and passion. Growing passion builds a relationship. Early passion, that comes from two congruent people, can be maintained, but early passion can be a substitute for the building of intimacy or avoidance. Sexual passion may come from a lustful and addictive posture, or a congruent or romantic one. Sometimes only time will tell which is which. Indications of the lust and addictive posture involve a history of the same scenes, of not being able to get enough, of being me-centered, insatiable, or searching for stimulus on the outside rather than the inside. Love comes from within and creates passion. Lust usually has an external focus and need.

Two congruent people with energy and creativity can find early intimacy and passion. A new relationship requires not just maintaining passion, but dealing with the time when it is not there. No one can maintain great passion all the time. Even as it grows there are down times, distractions and cycles that must be met and shared. Passion isn't something that happens to us. We do it. We create it out of our integration and identity. Sexual passion, based not just on lust, comes from a passionate person — the ability to channel intense energy, love and care into what we value: learning, oneness, the planet, vulnerable groups, space exploration, mathematics or whatever. When not obsessive, this passion enables us to make the choices that channel the energy in directions we choose. We can be passionate about several things, including our relationships.

RELIGIOUS ZEAL

Many people turn their passion toward religion. When the religion espoused involves heavy emotionalism, the state of arousal is maintained. We can get high on the music, prayer, message and rituals. Religious passion is what some call conversion, the intense emotional attachment to a decision about religion or spiritual commitment. To be born again into this religious zeal can be a powerful turning in one's life. Like other passion the passion for religion can become addictive: religiosity. Our religious practices and needs become insatiable, bottomless, because the spiritual foundation is absent. When identity is a void whatever is poured in, flows through, becoming insatiable. We can't get enough. We use our zeal as an escape from reality. Religion becomes our new drug and we try to drug others into our system.

Spiritual passion can be a holistic and holy commitment to a lifestyle of spiritual values. A spiritually passionate person may express this in a meaningful commitment to a guardianship of creation, of noticing and enjoying the gift of life in all forms that share it, in speaking and working for the vulnerable. A worship of action and social responsibility can come from spiritual passion. Our religious support system can be others who share our spiritual passion, but who model balance and enthusiasm as well as belief and tolerance.

So many hypocritical religious zealots use and abuse the planet and its inhabitants that many shy away from a passionate posture toward creation and the Creator. We need the passion in our spirituality, but we need to let it evolve over time. Allowing our emotional connections to our spiritual decision to grow as we grow keeps us as a part of creation, rather than the power God-replacement for the Creator. We need to search for and create a group of spiritual people to bond with who help us emotionally attach through song, prayer, meditation and celebration to the unfolding of creation. This group must be open, tolerant and affirming — not just of the immediate bonded group, but teaching the oneness of all groups and individuals who share in the gift of life.

COMPASSION FATIGUE

When passion comes too early in our process, it can be a powerful distraction, overtake us and easily lead to burnout. One form of passion we might reflect is the passion with and for people and causes. This passion "with and for" we call compassion. When we become compassionate before we understand the meaning and beauty of balance we fall off our course, get lost, are mystified and become exhausted. Compassion fatigue is a serious and debilitating syndrome. It is when we give of ourselves before we have of ourselves — and we can't give away what we don't have. Compassion fatigue is commonly experienced, especially by people in the helping professions. We see so much pain and grief in the world, our vision can be blurred in the storm of neediness; we get fogged in, lose our direction and stumble and fall. We need a firm grasp on the realities of the lifelines of the earlier priorities in order to weather life's inevitable storms.

When we have a beginning grasp of the first eleven priorities we can safely explore and venture into the thrilling world of passion.

1. *Priority One. Feelings.* We need to recognize our feelings so we don't let them overpower us, so the channeling of emotional energy can become our passion.
2. *Priority Two. Identity.* We need to know ourselves so we can identify the focus of our passions, so we don't lose ourselves to other people or causes.
3. *Priority Three. Family and Friends.* We need to use our support systems of family and friends because "When the going gets tough, the tough seek help from others!" We can draw on the energy from others to continue our passionate drives.
4. *Priority Four. Body/Physical.* We need to accept and care for us, embodied in our physical beings. We are energized to give to others; the tool of passion is our body.
5. *Priority Five. Spirituality.* We need to travel the path we were meant to by our Creator so we are not lost, our passions wandering aimlessly. We need to be filled with strength that comes from knowing we are loved and protected.
6. *Priority Six. Sexuality.* We need to reclaim our sexuality. With sexual identity our passion is not lost in lust and our passionate energy emerges from within in healthy sexual expression.
7. *Priority Seven. Food and Nutrition.* We need to nourish ourselves in a gentle way to fuel our drives of goodness and passion.
8. *Priority Eight. Play.* We need laughter and play in order to keep a perspective and prevent our passions from becoming obsessions. Play is the re-creation of vitality, and all passion is play.

9. *Priority Nine. Intellect and Creativity.* We need to tickle our brains to spring the creative juices that spawn our passions.
10. *Priority Ten. Career.* We need a career that is a good match for our inner selves. Then we can enjoy a passion within our work.
11. *Priority Eleven. Community.* We need community awareness, the recognition of our passionate targets, to work for interdependence.

When we enjoy aspects of these first priorities, our passion for life, each other and the world can flow—as the trickle of a babbling brook, a splash of a valley stream, a roar of a canyon river or the still of a mountain lake — and we will navigate with sense and wisdom. We will know when the current dictates to stroke at an even, steady pace to endure the distance or float by dreamily, to absorb the breathtaking view of God's art. We will know when to backpaddle with finesse to maneuver around obstructions and realize when it is time to get out and portage. We will be able to plunge through waves and holes, anticipate rapids and eddy into calm water. Paddling down the river of life requires integrating a sense of adventure with the art of balance.

Passion is a unique human quality that is built by our ability to imagine and create. At its peak it is a soaring out of human spirit, creating a world that reflects our possibilities. Passion is the vibrancy of our dance around the Maypole of interdependence. With it we find the deepest of love and joy; with it, we bond and serve; with it, we grow into ourselves. *Passion is the blossoming of imagination, the fruit of creativity, the nourishment of our soul.* Our Maypole of interdependence living towers high and the ribbons flutter freely when we dance in balance. This is *not* a dress rehearsal. This is the dance of life!

SUGGESTIONS • AFFIRMATIONS • THOUGHTS

SUGGESTIONS

- Go fly a kite!
- Get prosocial!
- Find it, play it and feel it!
- Go see a passionate movie.
- Read a passion-filled novel.
- Choose a cause that you can become passionate about.
- Rediscover an interest, hobby, sport or adventure that at one time you wanted to try or learn — check it out.
- Play a piece of music that moves you.
- If you are in a sexual relationship, make a decision to express your passion with your partner without depending on their response.

Sometimes it is helpful to talk about your passionate desires first. Remember, passion is from the inside out.

AFFIRMATIONS

- My passion is the life source of love.
- My heart soars.
- My passion does not require having a partner.
- I have arrived!
- I am full of passion.
- My passion is energy, directed toward goodness.
- I am passionate toward what and who I love.
- My sexual passion comes from within.
- I affirm the passion in others without enabling the obsession.
- My passion is within and the glow that warms those around me.
- My passion is expressed in my physical activity and body movement.

THOUGHTS

- What our minds can imagine our passion can achieve.
- Passion is the vehicle to realizing our dreams.
- Passion is the fruit of imagination — can you imagine passion fruit?
- A life without passion is like flying a kite on a still day.
- Passion is expressed from the inside out.
- Passion is in fashion.
- I don't have to ration my passion!

RECOMMENDED:
Reading, Viewing And Listening List

We recommend the following books, audio tapes and video tapes for your further learning pleasure.

Bass, E. and Davis, L. (1988). **The Courage to Heal: A Guide for Women Survivors of Child Sexual Abuse.** New York: Harper & Row.

*Belenky, M. (1986). **Women's Way of Knowing.** New York: Basic Books.

• Brownell, K.D. and Foreyt, J.P. (1986). **Handbook of Eating Disorders.** New York: Simon & Shuster.

Cassell, C. (1984). **Swept Away: Why Women Fear Their Own Sexuality.** New York: Simon & Shuster.

• Chaplin, J. (1988). **Feminist Counseling in Action.** London: Sage.

Chernin, K. (1986). **The Hungry Self: Women, Eating and Identity.** New York: Harper & Row.

George, D. (1974). **My Heart Soars.** Saanichton, British Columbia, Canada: Hancock House.

*Gilligan, C. (1982). **In a Different Voice.** Cambridge: Harvard University Press.

Goldberg, N. (1986). **Writing Down the Bones.** Boston: Shambhala.

Gordon, S. and Brecher, H. (1990). **Life Is Uncertain . . . Eat Dessert First.** New York: Delacorte Press.

Gordon, S. (1988). **Why Love Is Not Enough.** Holbrook, MA: Bob Adams, Inc.

Harrison, M., Kellogg, T. and Michaels, G. (1990). **Butterfly Kisses: Little Intimacies for Sharing!** Amherst, MA: BRAT Publishing.

Harrison, M., Kellogg, T. and Michaels, G. (in press). **Hummingbird Words: Self Affirmations and Notes to Nurture By.** Amherst, MA: BRAT Publishing.

Harrison, M., Kellogg, T. and Michaels, G. (in press). **Roots and Wings: Words for Growing A Family.** Amherst, MA: BRAT Publishing.

Harrison, M. and Stewart-Roache, C. (1989). **AttrACTIVE Woman: A Physical Fitness Approach to Emotional and Spiritual Well-Being.** Park Ridge, IL: Parkside Publishing.

Harrison-Davis, M. and Swarth, J. (1989). **The Wellness Workbook for Correctional Officers: A Step-by-Step Guide to Reaching Your Health Potential.** New Mexico: Corrections Academy.

- Ivey, A.E., Ivey, M.B. and Simek-Downing, L. (1990). **Counseling and Psycho-therapy. Integrating Skills, Theory, and Practice**. Englewood Cliffs, NJ: Prentice Hall.

- Kegan, R. (1982). **The Evolving Self.** Cambridge: Harvard University Press.

* Kellogg, T. (1990). **Broken Toys, Broken Dreams: Understanding and Healing Co-dependency, Compulsive Behaviors and Family.** Amherst, MA: BRAT Publishing.

* Kellogg, T. **My Mother, My Father, My Self — Dysfunctional Family Systems.** (6 audiotape set)

* Kellogg, T. **Know Thyself — Boundaries, Bonding and Sexuality.** (6 audiotape set)

* Kellogg, T. **Co-dependency — The Absence of Relationship with Self.** (6 audiotape set)

* Kellogg, T. **Return to Intimacy — Relationships, Spirituality, Sexuality and Workaholism.** (6 audiotape set)

* Kellogg, T. **A Never Ending Story . . . Recovery.** (6 audiotape set)

* Kellogg, T. **Processes of Recovery — Including Feelings, Grieving and Anger.** (6 audiotape set)

* Kellogg, T. **Broken Toys — Adult Children of Alcoholics and Dysfunctional Families.** (6 audiotape set)

* Kellogg, T. **Family Roles.** (Videotape)

* Kellogg, T. **Intimacy in Recovering Relationships.** (Videotape)

* Kellogg, T. **Victimization, Roles and Recovery.** (Videotape)

* Kellogg, T. **My Mother, My Father, My Self/Dysfunctinal Family Systems.** (Videotape)

* Kellogg, T. **Shame and Recovery.** (Videotape)

* Kellogg, T. **Broken Toys/The Inner Child Responds to the Dysfunctional Family.** (Videotape)

Kellogg, T. **Compulsive Addictive and Self-Destructive Behaviors.** (Videotape)

Kellogg, T. **Feelings/Learning to Live, Learning to Love.** (Videotape)

Kellogg, T. **Co-dependency.** (Videotape)

* Kellogg, T. **Sexuality, Spirituality and Sexual Addictions.** (2 Videotape Set)

Kellogg, T. (1990) **Interview on Co-dependency and Addictions.** (Videotape)

Kellogg, T. & Harrison, M. (1990). **Interview on Intimacy.** (Videotape)

Middelton-Moz, J. and Dwinell, L. (1986). **After the Tears.** Pompano Beach, FL: Health Communications.

*Miller, J.B. (1986). **Toward a New Psychology of Women.** Boston: Beacon Press.

Peck, M.S. (1978). **The Road Less Traveled.** New York: Simon & Schuster.

*Reed, P.B. (1980). **Nutrition: An Applied Science.** St. Paul, MN: West.

*Rogers, C.R. (1961). **On Becoming a Person.** Boston: Houghton Mifflin.

Ryan, W. (1971). **Blaming the Victim.** New York: Random House.

• Staub, E. (1979). **Positive Social Behavior and Morality . . . Vol. 2, Socialization and Development.** New York: Academic Press.

Storm, H. (1972). **Seven Arrows.** New York: Ballantine.

Whitfield, C.L. (1987). **Healing the Child Within.** Pompano Beach, FL: Health Communications.

Will, R., Marlin, A.T., Corson, B. and Schorsch, J. (1989). **Shopping for a Better World: A Quick and Easy Guide to Socially Responsible Supermarket Shopping.** New York: Council on Economic Priorities.

---

*The titles with an asterik (*) may be of special interest but not limited to people in the helping professions.

• The titles with a bullet (•) are specifically targeted for helping professionals.

APPENDIX:
Contacting The Authors

Terry Kellogg and Marvel Harrison offer training seminars, educational programs, lectures and workshops on a wide variety of subjects, including Intimacy, Sexuality and Spirituality, Addictions, Co-dependency, Recovery, Eating Disorders, Body Image and Self-Concept. Terry Kellogg's Lifeworks Clinics are offered in various cities around the United States and Canada. The Lifeworks Clinic is a four-day intensive program designed to help participants work through the family-of-origin roots of their self-defeating patterns of living. A special Lifeworks Leader Training Program for therapists is also available.

For more information, write or call:

BRAT Inc.
6 University Dr., Suite 225
Amherst, MA 01002
1-800-BRAT (2728)

Names and addresses of National Mutual Support Organizations.

For information about most self-help groups in the United States, call Mutual Aid Self Help (MASH), a national clearinghouse for self-help groups: 1-800-FOR-MASH.

ALCOHOLICS ANONYMOUS
For adult alcoholics.
468 Park Avenue South
New York, NY 10016

AMERICAN SCHIZOPHRENIA ASSOCIATION
For people with schizophrenia.
1114 First Avenue
New York, NY 10021

ASSOCIATION FOR CHILDREN WITH LEARNING DISABILITIES
For children with learning disabilities and their parents to share information, obtain referrals, and advocate for changes in educational methods and opportunities.
4156 Library Road
Pittsburgh, PA 15234

CANDLELIGHTERS
For parents of young children with cancer for peer support.
123 C Street SE
Washington, DC 20003

THE COMPASSIONATE FRIENDS
For bereaved parents: peer support
P.O. Box 1347
Oak Brook, IL 60521

EMOTIONS ANONYMOUS
For people with emotional problems; a 12-Step Program, adapted from the Alcoholics Anonymous Program.
P.O. Box 4245
St. Paul, MN 55104

EPILEPSY FOUNDATION
For people with epilepsy and their families.
4351 Garden City Drive
Landover, MD 20785

FAMILIES ANONYMOUS
For concerned relatives and friends of youth with a wide variety of behavior problems.
P.O. Box 344
Torrance, CA 90501

GAMBLERS ANONYMOUS
For compulsive gamblers.
P.O. Box 17173
Los Angeles, CA 90017

GRAY PANTHERS
An intergenerational movement.
3635 Chestnut Street
Philadelphia, PA 19104

HEART TO HEART
A one-to-one visitation program coordinated by local American Heart Association groups of those who have had coronary problems to those facing them.
7320 Greenville Avenue
Dallas, TX 75231

JUVENILE DIABETES FOUNDATION
For children with diabetes and their parents.
23 East 26th Street
New York, NY 10010

LA LECHE LEAGUE
For nursing mothers.
9616 Minneapolis Avenue
Franklin Park, IL 60131

MAKE TODAY COUNT
For people with cancer and their families.
P.O. Box 303
Burlington, LA 52601

MENSA
For people with high IQs.
1701 West 3rd Street, Suite IR
Brooklyn, NY 11223

MUSCULAR DYSTROPHY ASSOCIATION
For muscular dystrophy patients and their families; peer support and advocates for increased research.
810 Seventh Avenue
New York, NY 10019

NARCOTICS ANONYMOUS
For narcotics addicts: peer support for recovering addicts.
P.O. Box 622
Sun Valley, CA 91352

NATIONAL ALLIANCE FOR THE MENTALLY ILL
For families and friends of mentally ill individuals; peer support and advocacy.
1234 Massachusetts Avenue, NW
Washington, DC 20005

NATIONAL FEDERATION OF THE BLIND
For blind people and their families; peer support and advocacy.
1346 Connecticut Avenue, NW
Washington, DC 20036

NATIONAL GAY TASK FORCE
For gay people.
80 Fifth Avenue, Room 1601
New York, NY 10011

NATIONAL SOCIETY FOR AUTISTIC CHILDREN
For autistic children and their families; peer support, advocacy for research and treatment.
1234 Massachusetts Avenue, NW
Washington, DC 20005

NEUROTICS ANONYMOUS
For people with neurosis.
1341 G Street, NW
Washington, DC 20005

OVEREATERS ANONYMOUS
  For people who struggle with eating disorder problems; peer support and programs.
2190 West 190th Street
Torrance, CA 90504

PARENTS ANONYMOUS
  For parents of abused children; peer support, information, crisis intervention.
22330 Hawthorne
Torrance, CA 90505

PARENTS WITHOUT PARTNERS
  For single parents and their children; peer support.
7910 Woodmont Avenue
Washington, DC 20014

REACH TO RECOVERY
  For women who have had mastectomies; visitation by peers, peer support, through local cancer societies.
777 Third Avenue
New York, NY 10017

RECOVERY, INC.
  For former mental health patients; peer support.
116 South Michigan Avenue
Chicago, IL 60603

SURVIVORS OF INCEST ANONYMOUS
  For incest survivors.
P.O. Box 21817
Baltimore, MD 21222-6817

THEOS FOUNDATION
  For the widowed and their families.
The Penn Hills Mall Office Bldg., Room 306
Pittsburgh, PA 15235

UNITED CEREBRAL PALSY
  For people with cerebral palsy.
66 East 34th Street
New York, NY 10016

WIDOWED PERSONS
  For widows and widowers; peer support.
1909 K Street, NW
Washington, DC 20049

WORKAHOLICS ANONYMOUS
  For work addicts.
Westchester Self-Help Clearinghouse
75 Grasslands Road
Valhalla, NY 10595

Ajzen, I., and Fishbein, M. (1982). **Understanding Attitudes and Predicting Social Behavior.** Englewood Cliffs, NJ: Prentice-Hall, 4-9, 40-77.

Averill, J.R. (1990). "Emotions As Episodic Dispositions, Cognitive Schemas, And Transitory Social Roles. Steps Toward An Integrated Theory Of Emotion." In D. Ozer, J.M. Healy and A.J. Stewart (Eds.), **Perspectives In Personality.** Vol. 3. Greenwich, CT: JAI Press, 137-65.

Bass, E. and Davis, L. (1988). **The Courage To Heal: A Guide For Women Survivors Of Child Sexual Abuse.** New York: Harper & Row.

Belenky, M. (1986). **Women's Way Of Knowing.** New York: Basic Books.

Bem, D.J. Self-perception theory. In L. Berkowitz (Ed.), **Advances In Experimental Social Psychology.** 6. New York: Academic Press, 1-33.

Blatner, A. and Blatner, A. (1988). **The Art Of Play: An Adult's Guide To Reclaiming Imagination And Spontaneity.** New York: Human Sciences Press.

Brown, D., Brooks, L. & Associates (1984). **Career Choice And Development.** San Francisco: Jossey-Bass.

Brownell, K.D., & Foreyt, J.P. (1986). **Handbook Of Eating Disorders.** New York: Basic Books.

Cassell, C. (1984). **Swept Away: Why Women Fear Their Own Sexuality.** New York: Simon & Shuster.

Chaplin, J. (1988). **Feminist Counseling In Action.** London: Sage.

Chernin, K. (1986). **The Hungry Self: Women, Eating And Identity.** New York: Harper & Row.

Dweck, C.S. (1975). "The Role Of Expectations And Attributions In The Alleviation Of Learned Helplessness." *Journal of Personality and Social Pyschology.* 31:674-85.

Festinger, L. (1957). "An Introduction To A Theory Of Dissonance" in **A Theory Of Cognitive Dissonance.** Evanston, IL: Row, Peterson, 1-15.

Fiske, S.T. and Neuberg, S.L. (1990). "A Continuum Of Impression Formation, From Category-Based To Individuating Processes: Influences Formation And Motivation On Attention And Interpretation. In M.P. Zanna (Ed.), **Advances In Experimental Social Psychology.** 23. New York: Academic Press.

Fredrickson, R.H. (1982). **Career Information.** Englewood Cliffs, NJ: Prentice-Hall.

Freeman, S A (1986) **Women And Men Conversing. A Task Of Cross Cultural Communication.** Paper presented at the Third Annual Conference on Gender and Communication, University Park, Pennsylvania.

George, D. (1974). **My Heart Soars.** Saanichton, British Columbia, Canada: Hancock House.

Gilligan C. (1982). **In A Different Voice.** Cambridge: Harvard Univerisity Press.

Goldberg, N. (1986). **Writing Down The Bones.** Boston: Shambhala.

Goolishian, H. and Anderson, H. (1989). Understanding The Therapeutic Process. From Individuals And Families To Systems In Language. In Kaslow, F. (Ed.), **Voices In Family Psychology.** Newburg Park: Sage Publications.

Gordon, S. and Brecher, H. (1990). **Life Is Uncertain . . . Eat Dessert First.** New York: Delacorte Press.

Gordon, S. (1988). **Why Love Is Not Enough.** Holbrook, MA: Bob Adams, Inc.

Green, R.J. and Framo, J. (1981). **Family Therapy: Major Contributions.** New York: International Universities Press, Inc.

Harrison, M., Kellogg, T. and Michaels, G. (1990). **Butterfly Kisses: Little Intimacies For Sharing!** Amherst, MA: BRAT Publishing.

Harrison, M., Kellogg, T. and Michaels, G. (in press). **Hummingbird Words: Self Affirmations And Notes To Nurture By.** Amherst, MA: BRAT Publishing.

Harrison, M., Kellogg, T. and Michaels, G. (in press). **Roots And Wings: Words For Growing A Family.** Amherst, MA: BRAT Publishing.

Harrison, M. and Stewart-Roache, C. (1989). **AttraACTIVE Woman: A Physical Fitness Approach To Emotional And Spiritual Well-Being.** Park Ridge, IL: Parkside Publishing.

Harrison-Davis, M. and Swarth, J. (1989). **The Wellness Workbook For Correctional Officers: A Step-By-Step Guide To Reaching Your Health Potential.** New Mexico: Corrections Academy.

Hazen, C. & Shaver, P. (1987). "Romantic Love Conceptualized As An Attachment Process." *Journal of Personality and Social Psychology.* 52: 511-24.

Ivey, A.E., Ivey, M.B. and Simek-Downing, L. (1990). **Counseling And Psychotherapy: Integrating Skills, Theory And Practice.** Englewood Cliffs, NJ: Prentice-Hall.

Ivey, A.E. (1990). **Development Strategies For Helpers: Individual, Family And Network Interventions.** Pacific Grove, CA: Brooks/Cole.

Izard, C. (1990). "Facial Expressions And The Regulation Of Emotions." *Journal of Personality and Social Psychology.* 58: 487-98.

Janoff-Bulman, R. (1989). Assumptive Worlds And The Stress Of Traumatic Events. Applications Of The Schema Construct. Special Issue On Social Cognition And Stress. **Social Cognition.** 7: 113-36.

Jervis, T. (1986). "Deterence, The Spiral Model And Intentions Of The Adversary. In R.K. White (Ed.), **Psychology And The Prevention Of Nuclear War.** New York: New York University Press, 107-30.

Kegan, R. (1982). **The Evolving Self.** Cambridge: Harvard University Press.

Keith-Spiegel and Koocher, J. (1985). **Ethics In Psychology: Professional Standards And Cases.** Hillsdale, NJ: Erlbaum.

Kellogg, T. (1990). **Broken Toys, Broken Dreams: Understanding And Healing Co-dependency, Compulsive Behaviors And Family.** Amherst, MA: BRAT Publishing.

Lankton, S. and Lankton, C. (1983). **The Answer Within: A Clinical Framework Of Ericksonian Hypnotherapy.** New York: Bruner/Mazel.

Lankton, S. and Lankton, C. (1989). **Tales Of Enchantment: Metaphors For Adults And Children In Therapy.** New York: Bruner/Mazel.

Larkin, D.M. and Zahourek, R.P. (1989). "Therapeutic Storytelling And Metaphors." **Holistic Nursing Practice.** 2 (3): 45-53.

Matthews, W.J. (1984). "Dating Violence In College Couples." **College Student Journal.** 2: 150-59.

Maturana, H. and Varla, F. (1987). **The Tree Of Knowledge: The Biological Roots Of Human Understanding.** Boston: Shambhala.

McGoldrick, M., Pearce, J. and Giordano, J. (1982). **Ethnicity And Family Therapy.** New York: Guilford.

Middelton-Moz, J. & Dwinell, L. (1986). **After The Tears.** Pompano Beach, FL: Health Communications.

Miller, A. (1981). **The Drama Of The Gifted Child.** New York: Basic Books.

Miller, J.B. (1986). **Toward A New Psychology Of Women.** Boston: Beacon Press.

Mineka, S. (1987). "A Primate Model Of Phobic Fears." In H.J. Eysenck and I. Martin (Eds.), **Theoretical Foundations Of Behavior Therapy.** New York: Plenum, 81-111.

Minuchin, S. (1974). **Families And Family Therapy.** Cambridge, MA: Harvard University Press.

Minuchin, S. (1984). **Family Kaleidoscope.** Cambridge, MA: Harvard University Press.

Ortony, A. and Turner, T.J. (1990). "What's Basic About Basic Emotions?" *Psychological Review.* 97: 315-31.

Passons, W.R. (1975). Gestalt Approaches In Counseling. New York: Holt, Rinehart & Winston.

Peck, M.S. (1978). **The Road Less Traveled.** New York: Simon & Schuster.

Petty, R.E. and Caccioppo, J.T. (1984). "The Effects Of Involvement On Responses To Argument Quantity And Quality: Central And Peripheral Routes To Persuasion." *Journal Of Personality And Social Psychology.* 46: 69-81.

Porter, L. & Mohr, B. (1987). **Reading Books For Human Relations Training.** Arlington, VA: NTL Institute.

Reed, P.B. (1980). **Nutrition: An Applied Science.** St. Paul, MN: West.

Rogers, C.R. (1965). **Client-Centered Therapy.** Atlanta: Houghton Mifflin.

Rogers, C.R. (1961). **On Becoming A Person.** Boston. Houghton Mifflin.

Rogoff, B. & Morelli, G. (1989). "Perspectives On Children's Development From Cultural Psychology." *American Psychologist.* 44: 343-48.

Rothbart, M. & Oliver, J. (1985). "Social Categorization And Behavioral Episodes: A Cognitive Analysis Of The Effects Of Intergroup Contact." *Journal Of Social Issues.* 41: 81-104.

Ryan, W. (1971). **Blaming The Victim.** New York: Random House.

Simon, S. (1973, May). "Values Clarification — A Tool For Counselors." *Personnel And Guidance Journal.* 51 (9): 614-18.

Sternberg, R.J. (1987). "Liking Versus Loving: A Comparative Evaluation Of Theories." *Psychological Bulletin.* 102: 331-45.

Storm, C. & Storm, T. (1987). "A Taxonomic Study Of The Vocabulary Of Emotions." *Journal Of Personality And Social Psychology.* 53: 805-16.

Storm, H. (1972). **Seven Arrows.** New York: Ballantine.

Taylor, S.E., Wood, J.V. and Lichtman, R. (1983). "It Could Be Worse: Selective Evaluation As A Response To Victimization." *Journal Of Social Issues.* 39: 19-40.

Tronick, E.Z. (1989). "Emotions And Emotional Communication In Infants." *American Psychologist.* 44: 112-19.

Weiner, B. (1982). "An Attributionally Based Theory Of Motivation And Emotion: Focus, Range, And Issues. In N.T. Feather (Ed.), **Expectations And Actions.** Hillsdale, NJ: Lawrence Erlbaum.

Weinstein, G. & Alschuler, A. (1985). "Educating And Counseling For Self-Knowledge Development." *Journal Of Counseling And Development.* 4: 19-25.

White, R.K. (1986). Motivated Misperceptions. In R.K. White (Ed.). **Psychology And The Prevention Of Nuclear War.** New York: New York University Press 279-92.

Whitfield, C.L. (1987). **Healing The Child Within.** Pompano Beach, FL: Health Communications.

Wilson, J.P. (1989). **Trauma — Transforming And Healing: An Integrative Approach To Theory, Research, And Post-Traumatic Therapy.** New York: Brunner/Mazel.

Will, R., Marlin, A.T., Corson, B. and Schorsch, J. (1989). **Shopping For A Better World: A Quick And Easy Guide To Socially Responsible Supermarket Shopping.** New York: Council on Economic Priorities.

Other Books By . . .
Health Communications

ADULT CHILDREN OF ALCOHOLICS (Expanded)
Janet Woititz

Over a year on *The New York Times* Best-Seller list, this book is the primer on Adult Children of Alcoholics.

ISBN 1-55874-112-7   **$8.95**

STRUGGLE FOR INTIMACY
Janet Woititz

Another best-seller, this book gives insightful advice on learning to love more fully.

ISBN 0-932194-25-7   **$6.95**

BRADSHAW ON: THE FAMILY: *A Revolutionary Way of Self-Discovery*
John Bradshaw

The host of the nationally televised series of the same name shows us how families can be healed and individuals can realize full potential.

ISBN 0-932194-54-0   **$9.95**

HEALING THE SHAME THAT BINDS YOU
John Bradshaw

This important book shows how toxic shame is the core problem in our compulsions and offers new techniques of recovery vital to all of us.

ISBN 0-932194-86-9   **$9.95**

**HEALING THE CHILD WITHIN: *Discovery and Recovery for
Adult Children of Dysfunctional Families*** — Charles Whitfield, M.D.

Dr. Whitfield defines, describes and discovers how we can reach our Child Within to heal and nurture our woundedness.

ISBN 0-932194-40-0   **$8.95**

A GIFT TO MYSELF: *A Personal Guide To Healing My Child Within*
Charles L. Whitfield, M.D.

Dr. Whitfield provides practical guidelines and methods to work through the pain and confusion of being an Adult Child of a dysfunctional family.

ISBN 1-55874-042-2   **$11.95**

**HEALING TOGETHER: *A Guide To Intimacy And Recovery For
Co-dependent Couples*** — Wayne Kritsberg, M.A.

This is a practical book that tells the reader why he or she gets into dysfunctional and painful relationships, and then gives a concrete course of action on how to move the relationship toward health.

ISBN 1-55784-053-8   **$8.95**

3201 S.W. 15th Street,
Deerfield Beach, FL 33442-8190
1-800-851-9100

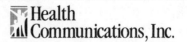
Health
Communications, Inc.

New Books . . .
from Health Communications

ALTERNATIVE PATHWAYS TO HEALING: The Recovery Medicine Wheel
Kip Coggins, MSW
This book with its unique approach to recovery explains the concept of the
medicine wheel — and how you can learn to live in harmony with yourself,
with others and with the earth.
ISBN 1-55874-089-9   **$7.95**

UNDERSTANDING CO-DEPENDENCY
Sharon Wegscheider-Cruse, M.A., and Joseph R. Cruse, M.D.
The authors give us a basic understanding of co-dependency that everyone
can use — what it is, how it happens, who is affected by it and what can
be done for them.
ISBN 1-55874-077-5   **$7.95**

THE OTHER SIDE OF THE FAMILY:
A Book For Recovery From Abuse, Incest And Neglect
Ellen Ratner, Ed.M.
This workbook addresses the issues of the survivor — self-esteem, feelings,
defenses, grieving, relationships and sexuality — and goes beyond to help
them through the healing process.
ISBN 1-55874-110-0   **$13.95**

OVERCOMING PERFECTIONISM:
The Key To A Balanced Recovery
Ann W. Smith, M.S.
This book offers practical hints, together with a few lighthearted ones, as a
guide toward learning to "live in the middle." It invites you to let go of your
superhuman syndrome and find a balanced recovery.
ISBN 1-55874-111-9   **$8.95**

LEARNING TO SAY NO:
Establishing Healthy Boundaries
Carla Wills-Brandon, M.A.
If you grew up in a dysfunctional family, establishing boundaries is a
difficult and risky decision. Where do you draw the line? Learn to recognize
yourself as an individual who has the power to say no.
ISBN 1-55874-087-2   **$8.95**

3201 S.W. 15th Street,
Deerfield Beach, FL 33442
1-800-851-9100

Health Communications, Inc.

Helpful 12-Step Books from . . .
Health Communications

12 STEPS TO SELF-PARENTING For Adult Children
Philip Oliver-Diaz, M.S.W., and Patricia A. O'Gorman, Ph.D.

This gentle 12-Step guide takes the reader from pain to healing and self-parenting, from anger to forgiveness, and from fear and despair to recovery.

ISBN 0-932194-68-0   **$7.95**

SELF-PARENTING 12-STEP WORKBOOK: Windows To Your Inner Child
Patricia O'Gorman, Ph.D., and Philip Oliver-Diaz, M.S.W.

This workbook invites you to become the complete individual you were born to be by using visualizations, exercises and experiences designed to reconnect you to your inner child.

ISBN 1-55874-052-X   **$9.95**

THE 12-STEP STORY BOOKLETS
Mary M. McKee

Each beautifully illustrated booklet deals with a step, using a story from nature in parable form. The 12 booklets (one for each step) lead us to a better understanding of ourselves and our recovery.

ISBN 1-55874-002-3   **$8.95**

VIOLENT VOICES:
12 Steps To Freedom From Emotional And Verbal Abuse
Kay Porterfield, M.A.

By using the healing model of the 12 Steps emotionally abused women are shown how to deal effectively with verbal and psychological abuse and to begin living as healed and whole people.

ISBN 1-55874-028-7   **$9.95**

GIFTS FOR PERSONAL GROWTH & RECOVERY
Wayne Kritsberg

A goldmine of positive techniques for recovery (affirmations, journal writing, visualizations, guided meditations, etc.), this book is indispensable for those seeking personal growth.

ISBN 0-932194-60-5   **$6.95**

3201 S.W. 15th Street,
Deerfield Beach, FL 33442-8190
1-800-851-9100

Health
Communications, Inc.